Caveats and Critiques

Caveats and Critiques

PHILOSOPHICAL ESSAYS IN LANGUAGE, LOGIC, AND ART

MAX BLACK

Susan Linn Sage Professor of
Philosophy and Humane Letters
Cornell University

Cornell University Press

ITHACA AND LONDON

First published 1975 by Cornell University Press.
Published in the United Kingdom by Cornell University Press Ltd., 2-4 Brook Street, London W1Y 1AA.

International Standard Book Number 0-8014-0958-6
Library of Congress Catalog Card Number 74-25365

Printed in the United States of America by Kingsport Press, Inc.

To Michal

Mann muss zuweilen wieder die Wörter untersuchen, denn die Welt kann wegrücken und die Wörter bleiben stehen.

Die gefährlichsten Unwahrheiten sind Wahrheiten mässig entstellt.

—Lichtenberg

Preface

The following essays take up where my last collection, *Margins of Precision,* of 1970, left off. As usual I have written for the "general reader" as well as for professional philosophers. The nonprofessional could start with the first three and the last three essays.

The first three deal once again with nonformal modes of reasoning; the next two discuss relatively technical and still controversial logical issues; four more deal with language and symbolic representation. Of the last three, two—my polemical encounters with Noam Chomsky and B. F. Skinner—attempt to assess different but widely influential contemporary views. The last essay begins what I hope will be a series on the methodology of the humanities.

Permission to reprint by editors and publishers is hereby gratefully acknowledged (for full details see "Additional Notes and References" at the end of the book). As always, I am much indebted to the authors whom I have criticized, and to the students and colleagues who have read and discussed several of these pieces. I must thank Mr. Lee Cannan and Mr. John Simmons for compiling the index and reading proofs.

MAX BLACK

Ithaca, New York
May 1975

Contents

Caveats and Critiques

I

Reasonableness

Preliminaries

Many say and some believe that it is a good thing to be reasonable. Yet it would be heroic folly to aspire to be reasonable in all situations: those who wish to be as reasonable as it is reasonable to be may well feel uncomfortable with Reason's traditional status as a supreme value.

How far reasonableness is praiseworthy, and on what grounds, and what limitations there are upon its scope, are questions that cannot fail to engage our interest. But lurking behind them is another question, still more fundamental and at least as difficult: *What is it to be reasonable?* It is to this mind-twister that I shall address myself.

Let us remind ourselves of the kind of answer that has traditionally been offered. Two examples will suffice.

The distinguished sociologist Morris Ginsberg once explained that "a rational person is one . . . who is able to bring to bear on a particular situation a knowledge of general rules which he has laid down for himself on the basis of his experience and insight."[1] We are entitled, I think, to treat "rational" in this passage as a mere stylistic variant upon "reasonable." Now Ginsberg's criterion, if taken strictly, has the depressing consequence that hardly anybody is ever in a position to be "rational." Let the reader ask himself how often he can apply to a particular situation rules that he has *"laid down for him-*

---

[1] "The Function of Reason in Morals," *Proceedings of the Aristotelian Society*, 39 (1938–39), 251.

self" on the basis of "experience and insight." (And is it to matter whether the rules are correct?) Independent discovery of applicable rules is so rare that to insist upon it would make rationality as scarce as handcraft. With rules as with instruments, we must usually employ those that others have made. The best we can hope for, nearly always, is to choose wisely, not to create.

Another distinguished thinker, the late Karl Mannheim, once defined "substantial rationality" as "intelligent conduct based upon one's own insight into the connections between events."[2] Here we have the same emphasis upon the agent's originality ("one's *own* insight") already criticized above, with the extra complication of an invocation of intelligence (*"intelligent* conduct") , an idea no less obscure than the notion of rationality it is supposed to clarify.

Such statements as those quoted illustrate the common fault of inflated definition. Fired by enthusiasm for an ideal of "Reason" or "Rationality," a thousand writers have offered persuasive definitions of what they think *ought to be valued.* In this way zeal breeds distortion and sober analysis is supplanted by high-minded rhetoric. Too often also, the path to these inflated answers is what C. S. Peirce called the "high priori" way: we are invited to treat as self-evident what badly needs argumentative support.

I shall undertake here the more modest task of beginning to explore *what we actually mean* by "reasonable." I start with the adjective rather than the noun, because it resists the reification that "Reason" positively invites. Our topic is the reasonable, with a small "r," not Reason with a capital "R."

My replacement of the original question "What is reasonableness?" by its linguistic correlate "What do we mean by 'reasonable'?" is deliberate. For an answer to the latter will necessarily be an answer to the former: I know no better way of clarifying what philosophers have called the "concept" of

[2] *Man and Society* (London, 1940) , p. 53.

something than by exploring the ways in which mastery of the concept is manifested in uses of the words expressing that concept. To render explicit how "reasonable" and related words are used is *ipso facto* to anatomize reasonableness: there are not two tasks, but one. This sober linguistic approach to our problem has the advantage also of providing specific tasks, and difficult ones at that.

The full program, then, would be to render explicit some of the rules governing the uses of "reasonable" and such closely related words as "reason" and "justification." Some such rules will look somewhat superficial, in their concern with grammatical categories, or with what linguists call "constraints upon co-occurrence" (rules determining the linguistic associates of "reasonable") ; other rules, specifying conditions in which "reasonable" may be properly applied, may seem more probingly related to the meanings of "reasonable." But both types of rule, "syntactic" and "semantic," in showing how we use "reasonable," help to clarify its meanings.

As to evidence, I can rely only upon the reader's knowledge of what can properly be said in English or in any language into which English can be translated. That the reader possesses the requisite knowledge, in common with the writer and other competent English speakers, is certain. That still leaves plenty of room for disagreement about details, since it is so much easier to use a word than to explain *how* one uses it. But let us begin.

What Kind of Thing Can Be Called "Reasonable"?

Since "reasonable" and "unreasonable" are adjectives, they come attached to nouns that they "qualify." But which nouns? In a phrase of the form "a reasonable (unreasonable) *N*," which nouns, when substituted for *"N,"* will make sense? Some will not do so: it is nonsensical, in a primary context, to speak of "a reasonable wart," or "an unreasonable star," although we might succeed in attaching some metaphorical sense to each of these remarkable expressions.

By a "primary context" I mean a situation in which a speaker seriously, literally, and prosaically uses the expression in question, but without talking *about* it. If there were no primary contexts for a word's use, there could be no secondary uses either: jokes and lies, tropes and word-play, are parasitical upon the plain speech of primary contexts. But the "secondary" resources of speech are inexhaustible: any string of words could, with sufficient ingenuity, be used in an intelligible utterance. A cat might jokingly be called unreasonable; "a reasonable *if*" probably occurs in some poem of e e cummings; the sentence "a reasonable footprint makes no sense" makes good sense. In such cases, the context is "secondary" or abnormal: the hearer needs special information about the speaker's intentions in order to make sense of what he hears.

Among the admissible substitutions for *"N"* in "a reasonable *N*" are the following: "man," "woman," "child," "parent," "husband," "chairman"—but not "horse," "fish," "table," or "lake"; also "demand," "question," "objection," "offer," "compromise," "explanation," "expectation," "prediction," "claim" —but not "change in weather," "rise in cost of living," "memory," or "knowledge." "Plan," "proposal," "strategy," "design" will fit—but not "shape," "consequence," "configuration," "constellation"; "belief," "hope," "fear," "resentment," "disappointment" will do—but hardly "joy" or "pain." (Some of the nouns cited will couple more readily with "unreasonable" than with "reasonable.")

Such preliminary and unsystematic samplings might usefully be supplemented by seeking admissible substitutions in the expression-forms "It is (would be) reasonable (unreasonable) to X." In this way we would get specific instances of the general categories elicited by the first test. (Cf. "a reasonable demand" with "it is reasonable to demand an explanation for an overcharge.")

These simple exercises soon reveal a great variety of nouns or nominal expressions to which "reasonable" and "unreasonable" can be sensibly attached: they include references to persons, sometimes specialized with regard to sex ("man," "woman"), age ("child"), status ("husband") or function ("chairman"); references to some but not all actions—including those of demanding, questioning, objecting, etc.; or, by a natural extension, to what the content of such actions might be—the demand *made,* the question *asked,* etc.; also various attitudes and feelings. This catalogue is of course incomplete.

Yet if "reasonable" and its opposite seem uncommonly hospitable in their linguistic alliances, they are not wholly promiscuous. A common thread unites this miscellany of instances: all have to do, more or less directly, with human beings, and more specifically with what human beings can *do* (actions) or with what they can *have* (feelings, attitudes). I shall ignore here anthropomorphic extensions to higher animals—or, in another direction, to spirits, angels, and deities. This observation serves to explain why such things as tables, oceans, or stars are ineligible for appraisal as "reasonable" or the reverse.

Further discriminations are needed, since some things that human beings do, such as breathing or stumbling, cannot be called "reasonable"; and the same holds for some but not all feelings and attitudes. Let us begin with actions, as being more easily discussed than features of "inner life." We may usefully employ two techniques in searching for what makes actions reasonable: the examination of linguistic affiliations and repugnancies—and the construction of "paradigm cases."

Affiliations and Repugnancies

Actions amenable to appraisal as reasonable or the reverse can also be characterized by a large variety of other adjectives: "rash," "well-considered," "impulsive," "far-sighted," "intelligent," "sensible," "foolish," "prudent," "wise," "dangerous," "futile," "successful," "pointless," "inconsiderate," "clumsy," "clever," "imaginative," "willful," "irresponsible," "wicked," "vicious," "irrational" and many many more. Most, if not all, of these imply approval, like "reasonable," or disapproval, like "unreasonable": they may be called "appraisal-adjectives."

I propose now to find a way of testing how these appraisal-adjectives harmonize or clash with "reasonable" and "unreasonable" themselves.

Consider an expression of the form *A but not B*, where *A* and *B* are adjectives or adjectival expressions. One of the obvious uses of the ". . . but not . . ." locution is to defeat an otherwise warranted presumption. For example, on learning that something is made of wood, we are entitled in the absence of further information to presume that the object can float in water; however, the form of words, "made of wood *but not* able to float," defeats that presumption, while acknowledging its presence. It has the approximate force of "Since the object is made of wood you might expect it to float, but for all that it doesn't!"; similarly for "well-designed but unsuitable" and any number of other admissible instances of the "but not" form. This explains why "made of wood but able to float" sounds absurd. Incidentally, the admissibility of an instance of *A but not B* shows that being not-*B* is logically compatible with being *A*, since otherwise *A but not B* would be a flat contradiction like "husband but not married"; the presumption of being *B* when *A* comes only to this: knowing that something is *A*, we are entitled, other things being equal and in the absence of special information, to think that it will be *B*. Alternatively: knowing that an object is *A* is some reason to think that it is also *B*.

Let us now apply these ideas to the formula "reasonable but not *X*" where *X* may be any "appraisal-adjective." We obtain the following selection of admissible values of *X:* "successful," "prudent," "wise." And if we apply the same test to the positive variant "reasonable *but X*," we get, among others: "dangerous," "futile," "short-sighted." It is significant, however, that the following seem to be inadmissible values for either formula: "rash," "foolish," "futile," "stupid," "inconsiderate"—and, on the other hand, "well-considered," "intelligent," "sensible," "far-sighted," etc. We could obtain further insight on the logical connections between these adjectives and "reasonable" by considering which of them could be admissible values in "reasonable *and X*," "reasonable *and hence X*," or their negative variants. The reader may be able to satisfy himself that the connections between the meanings of the nine appraisal-adjectives last mentioned and the presence or absence of reasonableness are tighter than those of mere presumption.

Further work of this sort might lead us to some such summarizing formula as the following:

> In order for an action to be reasonable it must be well-considered, intelligent, sensible, far-sighted, etc. and may be presumed to be prudent, wise, etc.; while its being rash, foolish, futile, stupid, or inconsiderate will normally disqualify it for praise as "reasonable."

This is all very rough as yet, and inaccurate without some rather obvious qualifications. But my aim is to illustrate a potentially useful technique, rather than to apply it in boring detail. In support of the recommended procedure of searching for "affiliations and repugnancies" we can adduce the well-known and somewhat obvious semantical principle that the meaning conveyed by a word is a function of its admissible contrasts: when a speaker calls something "reasonable" the information he conveys depends upon how many other things he might have chosen to call that action instead. (Thus, if the only contrast intended were with "unreasonable," the information conveyed would be minimal.) A detailed exploration of what I have called the "affiliations and repugnancies" of "reasonable" would help us, perhaps better than a formal definition, to understand its role in our language. If such an undertaking also aroused interest in such linguistic cognates as "prudent," "sensible," and "intelligent," so much the better. For "reasonable" is a nodal word—a place at which many semantic threads are knotted together. Like other words, it has a trailing set of friendly and hostile cognates. More generally, our utterances always imply *this but not that* and *this, so* (necessarily, presumably) *that*. And the consequent incompleteness of all explicit formulations—as shown by the possibility of unending elaboration of the tacit implications, presumptions, and suggestions—is inescapable.

Reasonable and rational; unreasonable and irrational. To use "rational" and "irrational" as pretentious variants for "reasonable" and "unreasonable" is to blur some important differences of meaning. The tests we have just used can help to highlight these. I hope the reader will agree that "unreasonable but irrational" makes no sense, and that there is something wrong about "unreasonable and irrational" and about "unreasonable, and hence irrational." Similar dissonances arise from trying to combine "rational" with "reasonable," although it is somewhat easier to treat these positives as straightforwardly synonymous.

One has the impression that in stigmatizing something as irrational—and the censure is part of the meaning—we are going beyond dianoetic[3] appraisal and are moving, as it were, on a different plane. This impression is confirmed by the discrepancies in the ranges of co-occurrence of the two words: we talk about an "irrational impulse," but surely not—or not so freely —about an "unreasonable impulse"?

The explanation seems to be that in calling an action unreasonable we are implying that the agent's reasons are unsatisfactory. So we are at least implying that he *has* reasons to be criticized: the reproach pays him the compliment of supposing him able, as we say, to "listen to reason." But to call him irrational is to imply a more severe disorder: we diagnose his action, rather than take issue with it. (Yet, interestingly enough, we still reprehend it.) An irrational act calls for therapy or restraint rather than for argument, and this may be why we are willing to call irrational what is beyond the agent's control. I can say no more here about this interesting topic.

---

[3] I use "dianoetic appraisal" as shorthand for "appraisal as reasonable or unreasonable."

The Method of "Paradigm Cases"

A more direct attack upon the meaning of "reasonable" and its opposite can be made by trying to describe what philosophers call "paradigm cases"[4]—examples of the use of a word, so clear and unproblematic that they exhibit part of that word's meaning. A paradigm case of the use of "reasonable action" would be a real or imaginary action of which we could properly say *"That* is a reasonable action, if anything is!" Such an exemplary instance could be used as a standard—to remind ourselves of what we mean by "reasonable," to test another's understanding of the word, or to teach its meaning to a child. For to refuse to apply "reasonable" to such a paradigm, when fully acquainted with its character, would be to fail to understand how we use the word and so to betray partial ignorance of the English language or to manifest some eccentricity of usage.

But if we now try to produce some paradigmatic cases of reasonable action, we find an unexpected hitch. It is relatively easy to describe paradigmatic—clear, unproblematic, exemplary—instances of *un*reasonable action, but surprisingly hard to find equally uncontroversial instances of the reasonable. One may suspect that "unreasonable" is the word that "wears the trousers," to use a phrase of J. L. Austin's, and that the root idea of "reasonable" is no more than "not unreasonable."[5] At any rate,

---

[4] This term is further explained in my book *Models and Metaphors* (Ithaca, N.Y., 1962), pp. 156–159, where there is a detailed application to the analysis of causation. See also the article "Paradigm-Case Argument" by Keith S. Donnellan in *The Encyclopedia of Philosophy*, Paul Edwards, ed. (New York, 1967), VI, 39–44. Philosophers sometimes appeal to paradigm cases of the use of some word *"W"* to show that there can be no doubt that instances of *W* exist. I do not need this type of argument in the present essay, since I take it as obvious that some actions are reasonable and some are not.

[5] This conjecture is supported by the familiar sense of "reasonable," otherwise ignored in this essay, to mean "moderate, not excessive" (cf. "a reasonable price"). This may derive from Aristotle's influential doctrine of right action as a "mean" between extremes. Even if the "extremes" of excess are well defined, there is usually plenty of room for argument about what would be neither "too much" nor "too little." On this view,

it may do no harm to begin with clear cases of unreasonable actions in the hope of capturing the notion of reasonableness by indirection.

I accordingly propose the following as clear, paradigmatic cases of *un*reasonable actions:

   (a) to look for somebody's telephone number in the directory, when you know that he has no telephone;[6]

   (b) to buy a dog if you don't like dogs and have no use for one (say as a watchdog) ;

   (c) to look for pound-notes on the pavement;

   (d) to guess the date of the siege of Vienna when a reference book with the information is at your elbow;

   (e) to assert before you have looked into a bag that it will contain black marbles (assuming that you have no special knowledge about the bag) ;

   (f) having drawn ten white marbles from the bag, to claim that the next to be drawn will not be white;

   (g) to complain that a man is ungrateful for an injury you have done him; and so on.

In each case,[7] we can explain why the verdict of unreasonableness is in order, though the fault varies from case to case: futility (case (a)), pointlessness (b), action on infinitesimal probability of success (c), choice of defective means to the end in view (d), absence of sufficient reason (e), action in conflict with evidence (f), action based upon assumptions plainly false (g).

---

the reasonable might well have a partially indeterminate nature. See also the remarks in note 8 about combining probabilities with utilities.

   [6] Is this irrational, rather than unreasonable? I think not. If I badly wanted to speak to the man whose number I was looking up, I might justify myself by saying that he might have a telephone after all—even if I "knew" that he hadn't! But perhaps this kind of case does verge upon the irrational.

   [7] Ideally, several people who understand the paradigm case procedure should be asked to construct large and varied lists for comparison and discussion. One man's choices may show unconscious bias or inattention to potential diversity. My examples have, in fact, not been chosen altogether at random.

The Analysis of Reasonable Action

Reflection upon the failures of reasonableness in the examples listed above and upon similar examples which I omit suggests the following budget of necessary conditions for the reasonableness of actions.

1. *Only actions under actual or potential control by the agent are suitable for dianoetic appraisal.* Behavior that may be thought undesirable, such as irrepressible grimaces or clumsy and uncoordinated gestures, can be called reasonable or unreasonable only if the person in question can be held *responsible* and so able, at least in principle, to exercise choice, decision, and restraint. Such actions may be called voluntary, with a side-glance at the slipperiness of that word: they may, however, be performed without conscious intention or calculation. Here we may recall that we do not speak of reasonable sensations or of unreasonable physical pains, and it would make sense to speak of a reasonable dream only if the dreamer had the extraordinary power to choose what he dreamed.

2. *Only actions directed toward some end-in-view can be reasonable or unreasonable.* Where nothing is hoped of an action, nothing intended, it is absurd to praise it as reasonable or to denigrate it as unreasonable. This is perhaps why it sounds so strange to speak of "reasonable walking" or "reasonable eating," *simpliciter,* although both activities are voluntary; and "reasonable painting" is just as odd, because there is no definite end-in-view. But it is quite natural to say "It is reasonable to eat more in order to reduce your indigestion" or "It would be reasonable to walk in order to have a better chance to catch a bus." Reference to an end-in-view at once reinstates the propriety of dianoetic appraisal.

3. *Dianoetic appraisal is relative to the agent and to his choice of end-in-view.* It may be reasonable for you to buy a bicycle if you can afford one and enjoy cycling, and unreasonable for me to do the same if I am crippled. And the very same action, say answering a question about the time by saying

"Buddha is a dung-heap," may be reasonable or not under different aspects. It makes a difference whether you want the interlocutor to know the time—or whether you hope to prod him into satori. The Zen masters are not necessarily unreasonable, however absurd their actions may seem.

Here is a convenient point at which to distinguish between reasonableness (or the reverse) *from the agent's standpoint*— and the dianoetic judgment of a competent observer. What may be thought reasonable, given the agent's limited knowledge, may still be judged unreasonable from a more comprehensive perspective. But we shall soon see that the agent's subjective judgment of the reasonableness of what he is doing cannot be insulated from—indeed, positively invites—the more objective verdict of a disinterested and better-informed spectator.

4. *Judgments of reasonableness are appropriate only where there is partial knowledge about the availability and efficacy of the means.* When we are quite ignorant of what to do (which we almost never are) any action is as reasonable as any other— that is to say, in one sense not reasonable at all.

When we know the sole means to achieve our end, there is a weak irony or facetiousness about calling the obligatory action "reasonable." There is nothing reasonable about dowsing a fire—though it would be highly unreasonable not to do so. Nor is there anything merely reasonable about accepting the answer of a correct addition sum. Here, "reasonable" is an implausible meiosis.

Dianoetic appraisal, to make the point in another way, is characteristically appropriate when we have to act in conditions of uncertainty (as we do most of the time). This may be why "reasonable" will not combine with such "achievement words" as "know," "remember," "see," "recognize," etc. The natural habitat of "reasonable" is a situation in which a task is to be performed, with the outcome still in doubt.

Among the obviously relevant criteria for reasonable action in uncertainty are the likelihood of success and the cost of the available means in relation to their probable efficacy and the value of the outcome. It is unreasonable to try slicing meat with a very blunt knife, when a sharper one is at hand; and it is unreasonable in another way to pay an expert £10 to help you save £5 on your income tax.[8]

It follows that dianoetic judgments are—or perhaps ought to be—typically *comparative:* if we can sometimes say that one action is more reasonable than another, we are very seldom able to choose a single action as uniquely reasonable.

5. *Dianoetic appraisal can always be supported by reasons.* In the jargon of philosophers, "reasonable" and "unreasonable" always refer to "supervenient" characters of a situation: the question "What is reasonable (unreasonable) about that?" must always admit of an answer. If what has been said under the previous heading is right, a defense of a judgment recommending one action rather than another will typically invoke relative probabilities and relative utilities, in some plausible combination. "It's reasonable to do *A* rather than *B,* because it's more likely *to achieve what you want*—and, besides, it costs no more."[9] Now the moment we begin to argue, in some such way, we produce reasons, and reasons are no respecters of persons. Where we have taken account of the agent's own choice of ends (point 3 above) and his own scale of relative values ("utilities" and "disutilities"—rewards and hurts), we leave no room for further subjectivity. An acceptable answer about

---

[8] There is an extensive technical literature about alternative ways of combining probabilities and "utilities" to calculate most-preferred actions under uncertainty. A disconcerting outcome is the wide range of choice of plausible solutions. It looks as if even in theory and in highly simplified situations, there can be no *determinate* answer to "What is the most reasonable way to act?" Here we have perhaps another illustration of the indefiniteness of the notion of reasonableness, already hinted at earlier.

[9] But what if *A* does cost more than *B?* Here we encounter the type of difficulty mentioned in the last note. Is it reasonable to pay one surgeon ten times as much as another in order to raise your chance of surviving an operation from 5/6 to 7/8? It is too facile to reply that it depends on how much you value your life. I believe that the question has no determinate answer.

reasonableness, relative to a given end and a given set of preferences, must be as impersonal, as "objective," *if it exists,* as a question about the right conclusion to a logical argument. Thus, all attributions of reasonableness, however casually or privately made, have a built-in thrust toward objective justifiability. Whatever is reasonable must also be justifiable, that is to say supportable by reasons that *any* unbiased impartial judge would have to accept. Unfortunately, this doesn't give us much practical help in deciding what is reasonable, or relatively more reasonable, in problematic cases; for the notion of "a reason" is at least as controversial as the topic of this essay.

6. *To call an action reasonable is to approve it, and to call it unreasonable is to censure it.* This point has been implicit throughout this discussion in my frequent reference to "reasonable" as a term of *appraisal.* It is worth making explicit, however, that the praise is part of the standard meaning of the word (as also in the cases of "fine," "good," "splendid," and the like) and can be overridden in speech only by using irony, paradox, or some other *ad hoc* rhetorical device.

Some philosophers say that the method of paradigm cases fails for "evaluative expressions," at least in establishing uncontroversial cases of the required evaluation: they grant that factual or "descriptive" conditions for application are determined by linguistic convention, but hold it essential to evaluation that the agent be left free to *make* his own evaluations. Thus J. O. Urmson, in his influential paper, says: "There is thus a close logical connexion between an evaluative expression and the accepted standards for its appropriate use; but this cannot be identity of meaning, *for no evaluation can be identical in meaning with a description*" (my italics) .[10]

This is, however, to take an indefensibly narrow view of meaning and of the purpose of appeal to paradigms. To the extent that approval is built into the proper use of "good" in

[10] "Some Questions Concerning Validity," in *Essays in Conceptual Analysis,* A. Flew, ed. (London, 1956) , p. 128.

certain situations, such approval is part of its meaning; and the same is true of "reasonable." In finding paradigm cases of the use of "reasonable," we are therefore producing cases where by linguistic conventions a speaker counts as approving of what he labels "reasonable." If we don't like the implied set of standards, we can try to change the language, avoid using the word in question, or override the *prima facie* connotation of approval by using appropriate devices. But that is another story.

I once heard some students condemn a talk about student grievances as "too reasonable." Intelligible as this comment was, it depended upon the general understanding that to call something reasonable is, *so far,* to praise it. Saying of somebody that he is "too virtuous" is an instance of the same device.

Yet if to dub something as reasonable is, at least provisionally, to praise it, the praise is faint and has in most contexts something depreciatory about it. A reasonable action, as we have seen, may turn out to be unsuccessful—or even *wrong,* however justified: a reasonable move in a game of chess might be just the one to permit a crushing yet unforeseeable combination. There are often better things for an action to be than merely reasonable, even if reasonableness is the best we can aim at. "Intelligent" and "imaginative" are rather warmer, while "reasonable" has something of the tepidity of "sensible," "defensible," and "respectable." In moral contexts, and some others, "right" is a good deal stronger than "reasonable."

It begins to look as if reasonableness is a somewhat humdrum, pedestrian virtue, involving as it does a problematic calculation of probabilities and expected values in situations of inescapable fallibility. This is why "reasonable" with a small "r" smacks too much of the prudential for some tastes.

The Reasonableness of Feelings and Emotive Attitudes

Our preliminary investigation into the reasonableness of actions could be summarized by some such formula as the following:

In a situation in which it is uncertain which action to take, an action is reasonable if there is some sufficient reason to take it, and no better reason to choose one of the alternatives.

Here the reference to "reasons" points implicitly to the complex tangle of factors—conduciveness to the end-in-view, probable efficiency, cost (in the wide sense), and the like— which I have mentioned.

If we try to apply some such formula as this to the case of feelings, in the belief that use of the same label of approbation is no accident, we shall encounter certain difficulties. For one thing, the notion of conduciveness to an end-in-view will have to be replaced by something like appropriateness, although the root idea of justifiable reason will still survive. We call a fear unreasonable, for instance, if the object feared is not really dangerous enough to justify the degree of fear evoked. Here, perhaps, it is not difficult to see a connection with the pattern of reasonableness in actions proper.

A more serious difficulty is that it is commonly agreed that feelings and emotive attitudes are not so plainly under control as actions. It is hardly fair, one might object, to call a fear unreasonable, and so to condemn it, if there really is no way to repress that fear. Well, its manifestation at least is more or less under control: a man beset by cowardly fears may still be able to act bravely. And an appraisal of the feeling itself may appeal from the unbridled immediacy of momentary feeling to a cooler verdict in the future—from Richard drunk with emotion to Richard soberly recollecting his feelings. The long-term influence of such appraisal should not be underrated. David Hume said that reason was the slave of the passions, but the desire to be reasonable may itself be a "passion," able to contend with other passions and sometimes to curb them.

Being Reasonable

We have proceeded far enough to see, at least in outline, how reasonable behavior looks. A man will be acting reasonably to the extent that he tries to form a clear view of the end to be achieved and its probable value to him, assembles the best information about available means, their probable efficacy, and the price of failure, and in the light of all this chooses the course of action most strongly recommended by good reasons. (A similar account, suitably modified, will apply to the choice of attitudes and ends, to the extent that choice of these is possible.) Such a posture has quasi-moral implications, since the requisite calculation demands a sustained effort to supress bias and, in striving for impartiality and objectivity, to pay a decent respect to the opinions of others. To act reasonably is to be willing to reason and thereby to submit to impersonal judgment. But a morality entirely based upon reasonableness would be at best anemic and frigid: a man can reason and reason and still be a villain.

To many, and perhaps especially to the young, there will be something unattractive about the character of dispassionate deliberation here evoked: the reasonable man will smack too much of the conscientious judge. But consideration, respect, kindness, mercy, and love are not really competitors for justice —except for the muddled: if perfect love casteth out reasonableness, that is no reason for being unreasonable. The case for being reasonable—when the question properly arises—is that there is nothing better to do. That, of course, is a consideration that will appeal only to those who are already at least potentially reasonable.

II

Induction and Experience

> I think that it is not only legitimate to appeal to inductive
> reasoning in defending inductive reasoning, but that it is in-
> dispensable. This is a rather audacious statement to make, be-
> cause it looks like defending a vicious circle. But I believe all
> procedures of self-clarification, of making clear to ourselves what
> it is we have in mind, are in a way circular. We clarify *B* through
> *A*, and then we turn around and explain *A* with the help of *B*.
> If a person were unable to distinguish valid from invalid steps
> in inductive reasoning, even in the simplest cases, in other words,
> if he were inductively blind, then it would be hopeless to try to
> convince him of anything in inductive logic.
>
> —Rudolf Carnap[1]

Samuel Butler once said that thinking about thinking was
like having an itch—the more you scratch the more you want
to scratch. The same could be said of theorizing about theorizing, especially when the theories investigated are the most
basic of all—the very procedures of inference that we employ
in providing rational justification, explanation, and clarification for anything. But there is no remedy for philosopher's
itch. Even at the risk of lapsing into incoherence and nonsense,
a philosopher feels the urge to thrust against the limits of
justification and clarification and to view as problematic the
very principles that normally define what counts as rational.

I shall undertake one such exercise in radical clarification, by
considering certain selected aspects of the relations of inductive
rules to their success in practice. The sorts of questions I want
to raise include the following: Can and should accumulated

---

[1] "Inductive Logic and Inductive Intuition," in *The Problem of Inductive Logic,* I. Lakatos, ed. (Amsterdam, 1968), p. 264.

experience about the use of inductive rules modify our trust in them? In favorable cases, can the successful employment of inductive rules provide rational grounds for increased confidence in the rules? Are we enmeshed in hopeless circularity if we try, in this way, to draw inductive lessons about induction? If not, why not?

Before I plunge into the main discussion, it may be helpful to state informally some of the preconceptions or prejudices with which I approach the subject. I find it natural to think of induction as an institution and, indeed, as a rule-governed one. That is to say, as a system of human activities, involving appropriate concepts, expressed in a distinctive terminology and also involving distinctive rules for the derivation of judgments. The inductive institution commits its participants to labeling certain situations in prescribed ways, to drawing inferences in prescribed fashions, and, notably, to adopting certain cognitive attitudes preparatory to taking appropriate actions. Thus the "institution" has nonlinguistic as well as linguistic aspects. Roughly speaking: inductive rules tell us what to say, how to think, and, within limits, how to act. All of which is inter-meshed with higher-level critical activities of appraisal and evaluation.

As to the controversial issue of the inductive institution's overall purpose, it may suffice for now to think of it as intended to generate rational judgment, that is to say, justifiable cognitive commitments concerning the as-yet-not-so-well-known on the basis of the relatively-better-known. In short, to facilitate and legitimize the notorious "inductive leap."

I shall not pause to argue with those who derogate this goal as a self-defeating effort to achieve the impossible. Although the inductive institution plays only a limited part in the vaster enterprise of science, recourse to induction at certain crucial junctures is indispensable, in science as in everyday life. Those who hope to avoid appeal to inductive inference by relying upon the deductive "corroboration" of daring conjectures still let induction in through the back door. If we are to avoid a debilitating skepticism concerning the possibility of any empirical knowledge whatever, we shall have to find a place, however modest, for justifiable inductive inference.

Anyone who thinks of induction as a social instrument designed to further certain enduring human interests in rational conjecture cannot conceive it to be immaculately generated or immutably constituted. To be sure, from within any rule-governed institution, the imperatives of the practice have the force of unquestionable demands. "That is the way the game has to be played!" But a philosopher will always itch to take a look "from the outside," as it were. It would be remarkable indeed if the inductive institution, unlike all others, were in principle immune from external criticism: one would expect it to be responsive to the lessons of practice—knowledge about its degree of success or failure in achieving its proper goals ought surely to be relevant, to make some difference. I believe this to be true, and if true, it must be possible. But showing *how* it is possible is no easy matter.

If you ask a man in the street why we should continue to trust some particular principle of inductive inference, he will almost certainly invoke its past successes. Of course, such a question will seem to the innocent layman odd in the extreme. He will have taken it for granted, for as far back as he can remember, that drawing a sample of black balls from a bag provides *some* good reason for expecting that most of the balls in the bag are black, and the suggestion that there might be some doubt about the soundness of this kind of reasoning will be disconcerting. But inside every "ordinary man" there is a philosopher waiting to emerge: the question about justification, once raised, will seem relevant and in need of a reasoned reply. Once the question is seriously entertained, what could be more natural than to point to past successes, that is, to treat the relevant rule of inference as an instrument that has, on the whole, worked well in the past and therefore deserves our confidence in the future? The only alternative is the unpalatable one of treating the outcome of the employment of inductive rules of inference, both in the past and in the future, as irrelevant. Some philosophers have taken this position, to be sure, but even they, I would suppose, would sooner or later be required to explain how and why inductive procedures can be useful.

An appeal to past successes in defense of an inductive principle, however plausible it may seem, is open, however, to a familiar objection of circularity. In order to fix our ideas, let us consider the following principle:

"When a large sample, drawn at random from some collection of things, shows all the members of the sample to share a certain common property, then other things drawn at random from the same collection will (probably) also have the property in question." Let us call this principle E (for eduction). The deliberate imprecision of the formulation of E need not bother us at this stage of our discussion.

The layman's argument for trusting E can be put in the following form: "E has worked in the past (that is, has usually generated true conclusions from true premises); hence we may expect it to work in the future." To which philosophers, almost unanimously, object by pointing out that there is a missing premise, to the effect that what has worked in the past will continue to work. Now this is itself an inductive principle, or a special case of an inductive principle—roughly speaking, a license to infer from the character of a sample to a corresponding character of the population from which the sample was drawn. Indeed, it looks very much like a special case of E itself, applied to a random sample of inductive inferences. Hence the man in the street is *assuming* that induction "works," when he appeals to past successes: worse still, he seems to be assuming something like the very thing that he is trying to prove, namely that E is trustworthy. So the argument "begs the question," is viciously circular, and the same must be true of every attempt to support induction by appeal to its successes in the past. In Hume's words: "It is impossible, therefore, that any arguments from experience can prove this resemblance of the past to the future; since all these arguments are founded on the supposition of that resemblance."[2] Let us call this "the circularity objection."

A principle of inference that generates true conclusions from true premises, in most instances of its use, might be called *reliable*. Now if the circularity objection is well founded, it would seem impossible for us to have any good reasons for thinking any contingent proposition about the external world to be true or even to be more likely true than false. For the proposition that a given rule of inductive inference is reliable, that is that it yields true conclusions from true premises most of the time, is itself a contingent one, expressing some very general truth about the world, about how things behave. If induction "works" on the whole, that is if the principles of inference that we actually use are in the main reliable, that is a matter of fact, not of logic. And the same can be said of those very broad principles, such as J. M. Keynes's Principle of Limited Variety, or substitutes for it, whose truth is needed in order for any known system of inductive logic to succeed in conferring nonzero probability upon any contingent proposition.

I am assuming that in the inductive inferences under consideration the conclusion is not entailed by the conjunction of the premises; that is to say, I am assuming that inductive inference is not a species of demonstrative or deductive inference. On this assumption, it seems obvious, at first sight at least, that any claim about the reliability of some principle of inductive inference must be an assertion about matters of fact that might be falsified in some possible world.

Suppose I am playing a game against you in which I present a coin showing heads or tails at my pleasure, while you guess aloud each time what my choice will be: it is clear that I could defeat your prediction each time, no matter how sophisticated

[2] David Hume, *An Enquiry Concerning Human Understanding*, L. A. Selby-Bigge, ed. (Oxford, 1902), Sec. 4, p. 38.

your inductive procedures, provided that you announced each prediction in advance of my choice. It is plausible to extend this model to the entire universe and to suppose that a malicious demon, with boundless powers, subject to the constraints only of logical possibility, but not bound by what we call "laws of nature," could similarly arrange to defeat our best inductive efforts. And if being thus constantly frustrated, we began to draw morals from our repeated failures and to modify our procedures accordingly, perhaps by adopting a "counterinductive" policy, the demon could respond to such adjustments, just as successfully as before, provided he still knew our predictions in advance. It seems, therefore, that the world might (in the sense of logical possibility) be so disorderly as to defeat all attempts at inductive inference.

I fear, however, that even this line of argument is not as secure as it might at first appear. It could be argued that, in a world as thoroughly disorderly as the one envisaged, language and thought would be impossible. For built into the vocabulary we use are references to other persons, to material objects, and so on, that have implications of inductive regularity and would become unintelligible otherwise. Imagine, if you can, sentient beings attempting to communicate in a situation in which all experience was in Heraclitean flux, and nothing stayed put long enough to be recognized. Clearly enough, in a condition of such chaos and disorder—if indeed the very possibility is conceivable—language and much else would be impossible. It might therefore be argued that the fact that we do have a language and are able to think implies some degree of world order.

Attractive as such a "transcendental" argument may be, it is insufficiently precise for my purpose. I shall therefore adopt the somewhat simple-minded view that assertions about the reliability of inductive principles are straightforwardly contingent assertions of fact.

In any case, I think that a resolute skeptic would not be disarmed by such an argument: might he not retort that we know at best that we have been able to think and speak *in the past,* and that it remains an open question whether we shall be able to do so in the future? And so we are brought back, again, to the argument from past successes.

Now it would be very remarkable if some contingent propositions, like Keynes's principle, differed from all other contingent propositions in being utterly beyond the reach of empirical support. The truth seems rather to be that if experience does not and cannot support the reliability of any inductive principles, experience cannot provide a basis for rational belief in any contingent empirical principles. The rejection of empirical support for induction leads, as Hume clearly saw, directly to unqualified skepticism about the possibility of knowledge or rational belief about the truth of all empirical propositions. The issue to be discussed is, therefore, of quite fundamental importance.

Hume said, as my earlier quotation illustrates, that no argument from experience could prove the "resemblance of the past to the future," since any such argument must be "founded on the supposition of that resemblance." Let us apply this objection to the layman's argument in defense of the future reliability of the principle I called *E*. (*E* was the principle purporting to justify inference from the sharing of a common property by the members of a randomly drawn sample to the probable possession of that property by further, randomly drawn, members of the population.) The layman's argument runs as follows:

(a) *E* has been reliable in a random sample of inferences in the past. *Therefore,*

(b) *E* will be reliable in further randomly selected inferences in the future.

Hume's objection, I take it, is that the argument, if this is all there is to it, is a blatant *non sequitur:* the conclusion simply does not follow from the single premise. We ought therefore to treat the layman's argument as an enthymeme, with the missing premise, say:

(c) If *E* has been reliable in the past, then it will be reliable in the future.

Now, with the addition of (c), the argument becomes valid, being an obvious instance of *modus ponens*. If you do not care for the specific form of the unstated additional premise, I can imagine Hume saying, you will have to choose another one at least as strong, that is to say, another premise which, in conjunction with the original premise (a), will entail (b). For anything weaker than this will leave the reconstructed argument invalid.

But (c), the weakest premise that will serve, claims that reliability of *E* in the past is sufficient to ensure reliability in the future. And how could we know this to be true—or, for that matter, know it to be even probable? Either you have no reason to assert it, except the desire to present a valid rather than an invalid argument—or else you must take it as a special case of the correctness of arguing from a shared character of the members of a sample to the presence of that character in further members drawn at random. In other words, your only good reason for asserting the extra conditional premise must be your commitment to the principle *E,* which is just what was in dispute. It sounds like a knock-down objection.

I have taken Hume to be treating the "layman's argument" as intended to be demonstrative, so that in questioning the possibility of a "proof," he was attacking the possibility of offering an argument in support of *E*'s reliability that would employ premises known to be true, or at least probably true, and would also be valid.

The first answer to this attack is that the layman's argument is—or, at least, ought to be taken as being—nondemonstrative. But in nondemonstrative or inductive inference, as I conceive it, we have to be clear from the outset that the canons of demonstrative inference are inapplicable. By definition, a nondemonstrative inference, whether correct or not, is one whose conclusion is not a demonstrative consequence of the premises. Thus, the accusation of lack of validity or, failing that, of "circularity" is, strictly speaking, beside the point. To reject such arguments on the score of vicious circularity and to complain that an inductive inference is not "valid" is like complaining that a hammer is not much use as a walking stick or that butter is not a good glue: it is to fall into the old trap of confusing nondemonstrative inference with demonstrative inference, and so into illicitly judging the correctness of inductive inference by canons appropriate only to deductive inference. (Incidentally, if the argument from experience were circular, as alleged, it would certainly be valid in the deductive sense, no matter what other faults it had. But a nondemonstrative inference does not aspire to be valid.)

I fear that this first retort to Hume, however, though important and sound, may seem unsatisfactory, and for good reason. A sympathetic critic might grant, at least proleptically, that inductive inference, if there is such a thing, is entitled to have its own standards of correctness, distinct from demonstrative validity, and yet remain dissatisfied with the "layman's argument." Even if it is clear that we are not seeking a proof of the conclusion, by means of a valid argument, is there not a gap between the single premise and its conclusion? Should it not, perhaps, be treated as an inductive enthymeme, lacking a further premise, logically weaker than the one previously supplied, but still lacking it, for all that?

In order to answer this, we must distinguish between inductive arguments that are genuinely incomplete, and others that only seem so, in virtue of the attraction of the deductive model of inference. If I argue: "That man has turned pale, so he is probably angry," I might, reasonably enough, be challenged to explain why I treat the premise as a reason for the truth of the conclusion, even though I am understood to be arguing nondemonstratively. I might then offer the extra premise, "Men who turn pale in that way are usually angry," which fleshes out the original argument, by offering further relevant information, while still leaving it nondemonstrative. But if I am asked, with regard to the expanded argument, why I treat the conjunction of the two premises as a reason for the conclusion, it would be inappropriate to look for a further substantive premise. The conclusion already follows, with probability; the expanded version is already an inductive, nondemonstrative, argument of the correct form, whose premises support the conclusion in accordance with a correct rule of inference. Any further objection must be to the type of argument used, rather than to the completeness of the argument itself—and that is a different matter. To counter such radical criticism by offering further premises would be to behave as foolishly as Achilles in his celebrated encounter with the tortoise. Once Achilles had provided an argument having the form of *modus ponens,* or some other valid form of deductive argument, Achilles ought to have stopped adding premises and should have refused to go on. Once we have elaborated a nondemonstrative argument, originally using some unstated premise, into a form in which it has become an instance of a correct form of inductive argument, we too are entitled to stop. The chain of reasons, as we have been reminded, must end somewhere.

The situation with regard to the layman's argument is that no further premises are needed: the argument *as it stands,* and without benefit of additional premises, exemplifies a correct form of inductive argument. Only the form of argument used is either the same as that of the principle *E* that is in question, or is suspiciously like it. One might therefore justifiably look upon the whole argument as a sort of hocus-pocus. To be sure, it may be innocent of invalidity, given that we are aiming at something other than validity. The conclusion is no part of the argument's premises, so the accusation of formal circularity is out of place. But is there not a more subtle circularity involved in *using* the very principle whose credentials are in question to establish its own credentials? Is this not dangerously like taking a man's own word for his credibility?

Let me state in a summary way what I take Hume's attack to have established. I think he showed, at the very least, that the notion of a demonstrative *proof* of the reliability of induction is a chimera. And I think we can go further than this. The idea that the layman's argument, or anything resembling it in relying upon past successes with inductive methods, could refute wholesale skepticism about inductive inference seems equally chimerical. You cannot persuade anybody by argument who distrusts and rejects all argument; and you cannot persuade somebody who distrusts and rejects all inductive argument by means of an inductive argument. But in this respect inductive argument is in no case worse than deductive argument. There are limits to what can be shown by means of deductive argument concerning the validity of deductive argument; and it would be unreasonable to demand more of inductive argument.

There remains, however, more to be said about the layman's argument, if it is treated, not as a wholesale attempt to refute skeptical objections about induction but rather as an attempt to show that past experience is relevant to the assessment and, sometimes, to the refinement and the improvement of inductive procedures. I shall try to show in what follows that this kind of appeal to experience is possible, and that the progressive character of inductive procedures depends upon it.

Inductive inferences, like deductive ones, can be subject to certain kinds of paralyzing weaknesses, having some analogy at least to deductive "circularity." I shall try to show that some appeals to experience in support of the reliability of inductive rules are free from such defects and really do succeed in raising the antecedent credibility of their conclusions.

For the sake of having a definite and relatively precise illustration, I shall use an old and much-discussed illustration.

Consider the following rule of inductive inference:

R: To argue from *Most instances of A's examined under a wide variety of conditions have been* B to (probably) *The next* A *to be encountered will be* B.

And also consider the following "self-supporting argument" in its defense:

A: In most instances of the use of *R* with true premises, examined in a wide variety of conditions, R has been successful.

Hence (probably)

In the next instance to be encountered of the use of R in an argument with a true premise, R will be successful.

Here, it looks as if the rule governing the argument A is the very same rule that is to be supported by the conclusion. The danger of some kind of circularity, perhaps not that of explicitly assuming the conclusion, seems patent.

In order to forestall possible misunderstanding, I shall now interpolate some explanations about how the illustrative argument A is to be understood.

(a) By "success," I mean the generation of a true conclusion from true premises; a rule that is successful most of the time I call "reliable." Clearly, there can be degrees of reliability, ranging from 0 to 1.

(b) By "the next instance" of the rule's application, I mean much the same as "another instance selected at random." The difference in meaning between these two expressions is unimportant for what follows.

(c) I find it appropriate to require that the conclusion of A (and of other nondemonstrative arguments) be taken to be "detached." This is to say, I am treating the illustrative argument A as offered in support of the unqualified assertion of R's success in another instance; the argument in question does not terminate in a conclusion *about* the probability of further success of the rule. (The function of the word "probably" in the illative link—"Hence [probably]"—is explained below.)

Is it proper to conceive of the conclusions of inductive inferences as "detached," in the way I have proposed? This issue remains controversial. In favor of this view, it can be urged that only in this way can we regard inductive inferences as providing conclusions that make testable assertions about the world. By contrast, the canonical form of an inductive conclusion in Carnap's reconstruction of inductive logic is $c\,(h, e) = n$, whose analyticity is a consequence of the choice of a particular confirmation function, *c,* for a given language. Now, if the only acceptable conclusions of inductive inference had to be conceived as analytic, it would be hard to see how they could constitute genuine information about the world. Of course, Carnap and his followers rely upon a rather elaborate account of how analytical inductive conclusions can be connected, via personal utilities, with bets and perhaps other actions under uncertainty. In company with other critics, I find this way of connecting up confirmations or—what comes to the same thing, probability-assertions—with actions unsatisfactory. It is, for instance, very hard to make sense of rational bets on the truth of generalizations or abstract scientific theories.

Even if one rejects Carnap's view of the matter, but still insists that a proper conclusion should contain a reference to probability in the form, say, of *prob* $(h/e) = n,$ one is still faced with the awkward problem of verification and applicability to test-situations. For the probability assertion is compatible with the falsity of *h,* no less than with its truth. What, then, is being said about the world?

The strongest objection to the detachment view that I know is the contention, forcibly argued by C. G. Hempel and others, that it leads to so-called "inductive inconsistencies." On certain evidence, E_1, I might be led to "detach" the conclusion *h;* but, given certain other evidence, E_2, I might also have to "detach" the contradictory conclusion, *not-h.* Thus, it is said, I might well find myself in the embarrassing position of having to assert on good grounds both *h* and its contradictory.

One answer to this might take the form of a *tu quoque.* For somebody like Hempel, who hopes to establish the connection between probability assertions and rational actions via bets based upon calculations of expected utilities, the situation envisaged, in which different bodies of evidence point in opposite directions, might well be held to lead to "inductively inconsistent" *actions.* If E_1 provides me with good reasons, given my scale of utilities, for betting on the truth of *h,* while E_2 provides

me with equally good reasons for betting on *not-h,* what am I
to do? Thus the problem of "inductive inconsistencies" might
be viewed as a special case of the important but unsolved problem of "total evidence." This reply, however, does not go to
the heart of the matter.

Lurking behind Hempel's bogy of "inductive inconsistencies"
there may be an unacceptably rigid conception of the nature of
rational assertion. He seems to suppose that if, on evidence E_1,
I am justified in asserting h, then I am committed to reiterating
that same assertion—standing by it, as it were—no matter what
other facts come to light. But if I subsequently come into possession of evidence E_2, that, taken alone, would have led me to
assert the contrary conclusion, *not-h,* I am certainly entitled to
review the situation. The rational decision would be to strike h
from my stock of accepted assertions (though without im-
pugning the correctness of the previous judgment made on the
partial evidence E_1) and to suspend judgment as between h
and *not-h,* pending some way to amalgamate all the evidence
now at hand. As another writer has well said: "It seems plain
that a man can be completely certain of some proposition, yet,
later, as he learns new evidence, come to doubt it. This is a
veritable mark of rationality."[3]

I would add that the whole issue becomes clearer if we take
account, in a way now to be explained, of the "index of credibility" which, in sophisticated formulations, should be taken
as attached to the conclusions of inductive inference.

(d) In presenting the illustrative argument A above, I attached the qualifying word *"probably"* to the sign of illation,
"Hence," in order to emphasize, as already explained, that I
wished no reference to probability to be part of the content of
the argument's conclusion. Of course, the qualification, *"probably,"* might also have been attached to the conclusion. But then
it ought to be regarded, as already suggested, as a parenthetical
modifier, attached to the whole embedded sentence to which it

[3] Ian Hacking, *The Logic of Statistical Inference* (Cambridge, 1965),
p. 223.

is attached. Its role, in such parenthetical use, I take to be that of facilitating the expression of what might be called a *qualified assertion.*

It is common, in ordinary speech, to qualify an assertion by inserting some parenthetical expression that warns the hearer, in a fashion whose utility is obvious, about the speaker's degree of confidence in making the assertion in question. Consider such assertions as *"With some hesitation,* I say the fine weather *will* continue" or *"To the best of my knowledge,* his name is Smith" or *"I have good reason to believe that* opium is beneficial to the nerves." Each of these remarks, if made with appropriate intonation and in an appropriate setting, commits the speaker to a categorical assertion: he claims, as the case may be, that the fine weather will continue, that the name of the person in question *is* Smith, that opium *is* beneficial to the nerves. Yet at the same time the speaker supplies his hearer with a useful signal concerning his own confidence in the strength of his reasons for making the assertion in question. (I neglect any more specific information that may be transmitted concerning the nature of the backing evidence.) I construe the parenthetic clause as a side remark, not part of the main assertion but a cautionary comment about it. (Similarly, a scientific instrument may have attached to it a cautionary statement about its reliability that is no part of the instrument's readings but usefully warns the user as to the degree of confidence he should attach to any such readings.)

I wish to interpret the occurrence of "probably" in my illustrative case of a self-supporting argument in just this way. The presence of the word "probably," whether attached to the sign of illation or to the conclusion, warns the reader that a nondemonstrative argument is in question. It alerts him therefore to the absence of entailment between the premise and the conclusion; and prepares him to treat the assertion actually made in the conclusion as provisional and therefore modifiable in the light of further evidence, as previously explained. But although this *index of credibility,* as I propose to call it, does "qualify" the assertion, in the fashion outlined, it leaves the assertion as a straightforward truth-claim: you cannot more or less assert something—assertion is a hit-or-miss affair. And however much the speaker qualifies his assertion, he is still *making* the assertion and will be shown to have been in error if it proves to be false. Consider a limiting case such as the remark "I just have a hunch, nothing more (and my hunches are notoriously unreliable), that inflation *will* cease this year." If this weak-kneed remark is made with a characteristically assertive intonation for the embedded sentence "Inflation *will* cease this year," the speaker is committed to the truth of that assertion and will have to admit that he was wrong if the facts fail to support him. (Of course, his having indicated the weakness of his grounds for making the assertion functions retroactively as an excuse for his mistake. To qualify an assertion is, as it were, to take the sting out of possible defeat by conceding fallibility in advance.)

"Probably" is, of course, a very crude index of credibility. In ordinary life we distinguish between "barely probable," "more probable than not," "very probable," "almost certain," and so on. It is therefore natural to envisage sophisticated ways of presenting inductive arguments in which the simple qualification "probably" might be replaced, at least in special contexts, by a graded index of credibility. In favorable cases, indeed, it seems plausible to locate the appropriate index of credibility within a numerical interval or even to estimate its numerical value. When a standard symbolism is used, such a quantified index of credibility might be imagined preceding an assertion, within a square bracket. In such a formulation, the premises of an inductive inference would have their own indices of credibility and the canonical form of our original argument would look like this:

$$A': [n_1] P$$
$$Hence\ (probably)$$
$$[n_2] K$$

where "*P*" is supposed to be replaced by the original premise supplied in *A*, "*K*" is supposed to be replaced by the original conclusion, and "n_1" and "n_2" are supposed to be replaced by definite numbers marking the respective indices of credibility of the premise and the conclusion.

From here on, I shall assume that the argument before us is expressed in this sophisticated and more precise form. Thus, the argument form *A*, or its more precise variant *A'*, should be conceived as a schema. A "self-supporting" defense of an inductive rule should be regarded as an argument intended to raise the antecedent credibility of its conclusion.

Let us turn now to a detailed examination of the reasons that can be urged for or against the supposed circularity of the argument *A'*. It would be helpful if we could begin with some explicit understanding of what is intended by the imputation, always pejorative, that a given argument is "circular." But it is surprisingly difficult to produce a suitable definition. The most blatant case of "vicious circularity," in which the conclusion appears explicitly as a premise, offers no trouble—though even here it is worth making once again the obvious point that such an argument is at least valid. We need a more general formula to cover not only such cases of unabashed circularity, but also others not of this type, that are equally objectionable. For instance: any argument to the conclusion *K*, having as one of its premises the conjunction $K \cdot L$, obviously needs to be rejected as having no probative force, although the conclusion is not identical with any of the premises. But what would be a general formula to cover all the intended cases?

I have been unable to find a satisfactory answer to this question in the literature. Indeed, the only serious discussion of the point that I know is in W. E. Johnson's unsatisfactory distinction between what he calls "epistemic" and "constitutive" conditions of inference.

The task of finding a satisfactory analysis of the notion of "vicious circularity" is perhaps not insoluble. I propose, however, to bypass it here. What matters for our present inquiry is whether a particular form of inductive argument, looking suspiciously "circular," whatever that may mean, can serve the proper ends of induction. This approach has the advantage of highlighting the reasons for regarding "circularity" as reprehensible. (The label we apply to this, or to an allied defect, is unimportant; what we need to know is the character of the imputed fault and the reasons why it is objectionable.) Let us call an inference, whether deductive or inductive in character, *effective* when it fulfills the purpose for which such an inference is designed: I propose now to examine the conditions of effectiveness for both types of inference.

Let us begin with the conditions for effectiveness of deductive inference. The purpose of a deductive inference may usually be regarded as that of raising the antecedent credibility of the conclusion: in the most favorable case, a proposition whose truth was antecedently doubtful is rendered certain by being deduced from premises all of which are certain; in the more general case, a proposition whose initial credibility was, say, p has its credibility raised to q, where q is greater than p, by being deduced from premises whose joint credibility is q. (I must ignore in this essay some relevant and pressing questions about what "credibility" means and how it is to be established. I am, at any rate, thinking of "credibility" as relative to available evidence, but not otherwise "subjective.")

Given this conception, we can now state the *objective conditions* for a deductive inference having the amalgamated premise, P, and the conclusion K, as follows:

(i) K must follow from P by means of a *valid* rule of inference (that is $P \cdot \sim K$ must be a contradiction).

(ii) The credibility of P must be higher than the antecedent credibility of K. (From which it follows that if condition (i) is fulfilled, the credibility of K will be raised by the inference in question.)

These conditions, I may add, seem to me both necessary and sufficient. But these objective conditions must now be supplemented by some *subjective conditions* for effectiveness. That these are relevant can easily be seen by considering that a deductive inference might satisfy both the foregoing conditions and so be in some sense an acceptable inference, without yet providing a thinker with any good reasons for increased confidence in the conclusion. Suppose the reasoner does not think the rule of inference he is using to be valid; then the inference in question cannot be made in good faith and does not provide him with acceptable reasons for increased confidence in the conclusion—even if the principle of inference is in fact valid.

As a first try, I suggest the following conditions for subjective effectiveness:

(iii) The reasoner must *think* that the rule of inference he employs is valid.

(iv) The reasoner must *think* that the credibility of the amalgamated premise is higher than the antecedent credibility of the conclusion.

Roughly speaking, then, the reasoner must believe that the objective conditions obtain.

It might perhaps be objected that the last two conditions are necessary but not sufficient. For it may be that the reasoner, though believing the argument to be objectively effective, has no good reasons for his belief. We might therefore try to strengthen our schedule of conditions for subjective effectiveness by demanding that the reasoner's beliefs shall themselves be thought by him to have sufficient grounds (where grounds are appropriate), and this enlarged set of conditions might in turn be strengthened by insisting that those grounds (the reasoner's reasons for holding the inference to be objectively effective) shall themselves be good grounds. And so on. Clearly we have here a gamut of sets of conditions of variable severity, ranging from simple belief in objective effectiveness, through grounded belief, to relatively well-grounded belief, with possible complications introduced by considerations concerning the strength and quality of the reasons in question.

I shall ignore these complications here and will satisfy myself with the formula: A deductive inference is *fully effective* if it is objectively effective (raises the antecedent credibility of the conclusion by the use of a valid rule of inference) and is held to be so, on sufficient grounds (a deliberately vague phrase), by somebody presenting or accepting the inference.

If we now try to apply a similar analysis to the case of inductive inference, the only change needed is the substitution of reliability for validity in our conditions. For what makes an inductive rule of inference good, I suggest, is its capacity to generate true conclusions from true premises most of the time —that is what I have been calling its reliability. This being granted, the effectiveness of the inductive inference, in its "subjective" aspects, will depend upon whether the reasoner is entitled, as before, to think, and with good reason, that he is using a reliable rule to raise antecedent credibility. I shall therefore say that an inductive inference is fully effective if (1) the rule of inference used does yield true conclusions most of the time and does raise the antecedent credibility of the conclusion, and if (2) a given reasoner thinks and has sufficient grounds for thinking that it does both of these things. It looks sufficiently obvious that no fully effective argument can be objectionably "circular."

Let us now see whether an argument of the form *A'* is "fully effective" in the sense explained. I will take the relevant conditions seriatim.

(a) *Does A' use a reliable rule of inference?* This, as I have said before, is a question of fact, as to whether a certain procedure does in practice yield a certain desired result most of the time; it is, therefore, in principle, no different from a question such as: Does boiling eggs usually result in making them hard? I believe there can be no serious doubt about the answer: I take it to be *true* (and I hope none of my readers will think otherwise) that we do get better results by using inductive rules than we would by using so-called "counterinductive" rules. I mean, of course, that the relevant inductive rule not only has worked in the past, but also will work in the future. Here, a skeptic's qualms are irrelevant, since the reliability of the inferential rule is not a premise of the argument. In any case, as I have already explained, the argument is not directed against wholesale inductive skepticism. The only question, for the moment, is whether the rule R is in fact reliable, and to this the answer seems to me plainly, yes.

(b) *Does A' confer a higher credibility upon its conclusion than it antecedently had?* In other words, once we have the evidence stated in the amalgamated premise of A', do we have more reason to expect that R will be successful upon a new occasion than we had before considering the argument? Here again, I cannot see how one can possibly deny it. The evidence is certainly relevant, if we are interested in R's further application: it would be contrary to everything we know to insist that the status of the conclusion (its credibility) is unaffected by the new evidence.

(c) *Do we have sufficient reason to think* R *antecedently reliable?* This can hardly be answered offhand, given the vagueness of the expression "sufficient reason," and the doubts that may perhaps be raised as to when we are entitled to say we have good or sufficient reasons. An opponent might say that if the question were pressed, objectionable circularity would reappear upon considering the alleged reasons at our disposal. I wish only to insist—and this is really my main point—that there is nothing about the form of inference A' to make it impossible, for logical reasons, for us not only to think R reliable, but even to have good reasons, of varying degrees of force, for so thinking. Nor does such well-grounded belief, if it should be at our disposal, render the inference superfluous because "ineffective." For what such well-grounded belief assures us, and all that it needs to assure us, is that R works more often than not. The point of the given inference, however, is to *increase* the credibility of R's successful application in a new instance. Now even if our confidence in R is justified, it is not superfluous to strengthen that confidence for its application in a given instance.

(d) *Do we have sufficient reason to think that argument* A'

will raise the credibility of its conclusion? That is to say, if
the rule R is indeed reliable, are we justified in *thinking* that
its application to the presented evidence would make the conclusion more credible than it was before? I am inclined to say
that we know this on *a priori* grounds, and that the granted
reliability of the rule will guarantee (deductively!) that the
presence of the new evidence will increase the credibility of
the conclusion. For consider what is really at stake. We are supposed to think that we have a rule R of such a character that
it usually associates a true conclusion with true premises; we
are also supposed to think that we have premises that are true,
leading by an application of the rule to the conclusion K; given
all this, the question is whether we are justified in attributing
to K a higher credibility than it would otherwise have had,
that is, in claiming that we have *better reason* for asserting K
than would otherwise have been the case. The affirmative
answer seems to me to be required by our conception of "good
reason" (and the associated notions that figure in this line of
thought). That anybody fully understanding what is meant by
credibility, reliability, good reason, and so forth should refuse
to count such a derivation of K as strengthening the grounds
in its favor would seem to me to show an insufficient grasp of
the relevant concepts. Not to treat K as having its credibility
strengthened would be like seeming to reject the application
of *modus ponens*. That is a sign, not of inductive blindness,
as Carnap implies in the epigraph of this essay, but rather of
a more fundamental failure to have mastered the use of certain
procedures of reasoning to which we are committed by our
language. (Could this have been what Carnap meant?)

On the whole, then, I conclude that there is nothing about
the form of argument A, its critics notwithstanding, to impugn
its effectiveness. Indeed, I hope to have made it at least plausible that argument A could be fully effective. *A fortiori*, then,
it cannot suffer from any kind of objectionable circularity that
would render its use pointless.

There may be something radically wrong with the line of

thought I have been presenting; if so, I shall be glad to be corrected. My experience with critics of the "self-supporting" position has been that it leaves even the most sympathetic uncomfortable: even if no specific flaw can be found, they can't help thinking that something must be wrong—the ghost of vicious circularity still haunts the topic. It may therefore be helpful if I refer briefly in conclusion to the objections raised by the most formidable of my critics.

Peter Achinstein, in two powerful and illuminating papers, agrees that the "self-supporting" argument I have been considering is innocent of deductive circularity, and he agrees that, taken as an inductive argument, it contains no reprehensible overt circularity.[4] It does, however, embody a more subtle yet fatal circularity. For in order to have a right to use the rule R in the second-order argument, we have to "assume" that R is reliable. But "R is reliable" logically implies "R is successful most of the time" (that is, usually leads from true premises to a true conclusion) which in turn logically implies "R will probably be successful in the next (or in a random) instance of its use"—which was the very thing that the second-order argument was supposed to establish. Thus in order to argue to that conclusion, we must "assume" something that entails it, namely that the rule is reliable.

If Achinstein were right, let us notice, the contingent evidence about past successes adduced in the first premise of the "self-supporting" argument would be quite irrelevant, because in trying to argue from such evidence we are already committed to more than we are trying to prove. By the same token, no amount of discouraging report about past failures of the rule could have any tendency to impugn that rule's reliability; no amount of unsatisfactory experience with the rule could provide any reason for diminished confidence in the rule. I find this very hard to accept.

Achinstein's objection suffers from an "all or nothing" at-

---

[4] "The Circularity of a Self-Supporting Inductive Argument," *Analysis*, 22 (1961–62), 138–141, and "Circularity and Induction," *Analysis*, 23 (1962–63), 123–127.

titude to the self-supporting argument, and from failure to consider whether the argument might not have the differential function of strengthening the rule's credibility, rather than "establishing" it. He is right in urging that if we had *no* antecedent reason to use R and to trust it, no inductive argument from past successes could give us a reason to regard R as reliable and hence likely to work in another instance. So used, the argument would indeed be defective. But if we already have some reason to trust R, appeal to past successes may give us better reason to trust it, and evidence of past failures ought to weaken our confidence in the rule. The situation seems to me basically no different from the use of any self-applicable instrument as a check upon its own reliability. If I consult the *Encyclopaedia Britannica* to see what it says about itself, I am, no doubt, "assuming" in something like Achinstein's sense, that the *Encyclopaedia* is generally accurate. Were I to find some article in the *Encyclopaedia* itself accusing the *Encyclopaedia* of gross unreliability, that would be evidence that I could not afford to neglect. By the same token, the absence of such self-depreciating comment is some evidence, however slender, in favor of the assumption of general reliability. Our confidence in inductive rules admits of gradation and can be adjusted in the light of experience. Nothing that Achinstein has urged leads me to believe that there is some fallacy behind this contention.

I will end with a more striking type of objection, presented by Achinstein and others. It takes the form of arguing that my "defense" would "prove" too much: we are offered allegedly "counterinductive" self-supporting arguments which might, it is urged, be used with just as much plausibility (that is to say, quite wrongly!) to support themselves. For instance, the "counterinductive rule" that authorizes a transition from the presence of a character in the members of a sample to the *absence* of that character in another member drawn at random could, it is urged, be used to argue from the failure of this rule in the past to its success in the next instance of its use.

I have replied, in the past, that such a "counterinductive"

rule would be incoherent in the sense of leading to contradictory conclusions when the "second-order" argument in its defense is invoked. We therefore have a reason for rejecting it which does not arise in the case of the conventional "inductive" rules.

There seems to me, however, a more fundamental reason for being suspicious about referring to such allegedly "counterinductive" rules. If we try to imagine a set of people using the term "probably" (and other words belonging to the practice of nondemonstrative inference) in a way which would be consonant with adherence to "counterinductive" rules, we should have to imagine them, also, rejecting the very paradigms that control our own uses of "probably." For example: if a handful of marbles drawn from a bag were all black, the counterinductionists would have to regard that as a clear case of the probability of another ball's being black being diminished. In short they would have built into their practice a convention that distrusted experience.

Now it seems to be very doubtful whether we should be justified in saying that such people would be using "probably" in the same sense that we do. It will hardly do to say that they are inveterate addicts of the gambler's fallacy who simply persist in making mistakes: that would be like saying that people who got addition sums wrong all the time and *were quite satisfied* to do so really meant just what we do by addition— but suffered, merely, from inveterate inability to apply the term correctly. If the wrong sum satisfies them, they cannot mean what we mean by addition—chess played for the sake of losing is not chess but some other game. For such reasons as these, I do not think that the counterexamples of self-supporting arguments for "counterinductive" rules are much to the point.

My contention could be put in this way: there is an *a priori* aspect to the rules governing inductive inference and the practices that are demanded of those properly using those rules: given our present language and the system of concepts that it embodies, we are logically unable to imagine wholesale deviations from them. (We are unable to imagine in full detail what a "counterinductive" world would be like.) But this does not mean that we have to be dogmatic: the constitutive rules of the inductive institution allow for considerable play in the differential judgments we make concerning inductive conclusions, the reliability of rules, and so on. Now it is the purpose of appeal to past experience to supply just such a basis of rational grounds for reinforcing or, within modest limits, for modifying the inductive institution and its components. Appeal to past experience can, however, be only gradualist and revisionist (to use political language): for revolutions in our modes of thought we must look elsewhere.

III

Some Questions about Practical Reasoning

1. Beliefs about matters-of-fact or about actions appropriate to them can bear upon conduct in obvious ways: even Diogenes might have been moved to action by the thought that his barrel was on fire. In such situations, and in others less dramatic, reasoning can have an intelligible bearing upon rational conduct and should in this way count as "practical." It is not clear, however, why intelligent response to situations of danger or advantage demands any more recondite modes of reasoning than the familiar ones of deductive or inductive logic.

2. Yet some philosophers have maintained that certain types of reasoning deserve to be recognized as "practical" in a more striking sense, as supporting conclusions having some more or less direct *logical* connection with appropriate actions. Thus G. E. M. Anscombe calls Aristotle's "practical syllogism" a "completely different form of reasoning from theoretical reasoning or proof-syllogism" (and chides Aristotle for "giving cases of it which made it as parallel as possible to the theoretical syllogism") .[1] In the same vein, she says that "practical reasoning," as she conceives it, "is another type of reasoning than reasoning from premises to a conclusion which they prove."[2] G. H. von Wright, in a recent paper, regards the topic as important, partly because practical reasoning has a

[1] G. E. M. Anscombe, *Intention* (Oxford, 1957) , p. 59.
[2] *Ibid.*, p. 61.

special role to play in modes of explanation of action appropriate to the "human sciences."[3]

I shall try to determine how strong the case is for recognizing a special kind of reasoning deserving to be called "practical."

3. I assume that there is no philosophical advantage in distinguishing traditional modes of reasoning (Anscombe's "proof-syllogisms," to which we may add the argument-forms of inductive reasoning) that are merely *about* actions. The case for doing so would be no stronger than for recognizing "culinary reasoning" or "athletic reasoning" on the ground of mere difference in subject matter. I therefore propose to render our topic more determinate by examining the following three contentions:

(A) There are certain types of reasoning whose conclusions and doubtless some of their premises are nonpropositional, i.e., lack truth-values.

(B) Some such conclusions have a logical relation of implication, or some weaker logical relation, with certain related actions.

(C) Reasonings conforming to these specifications have distinctive forms, i.e., are subject to principles of derivation that are not of the familiar deductive or inductive sort.

These three contentions, taken together, might be called the *thesis of the autonomy of practical reasoning.*

I propose now to render these vague formulations more definite and to evaluate the considerations that might be brought in their defense.

4. What form are the conclusions of practical reasoning supposed to take? We may get a hint from the following

---

[3] Georg Henrik von Wright, "On So-Called Practical Inference," *Acta Sociologica*, vol. 15 (1972). He says, "Practical inference as a schema of explanation plays a comparable role in the human sciences to that of nomological deductive explanation in the natural sciences" (p. 39). This claim is defended more elaborately in his *Explanation and Understanding* (Ithaca, N.Y., 1971).

remarks with which A. J. Kenny prefaces an essay containing a vigorous plea for the autonomy thesis: "It is beyond doubt that in addition to theoretical reasoning there is also practical reasoning. We work out, with the aid of logic, not only what is the case but also what we are to do. In practical reasoning as in theoretical we pass from premises to conclusion. The premises, however, set out our desires or our duties; they set out also the facts of the case and the possibilities open; the conclusions are actions or plans for action."[4]

Let us fasten upon Kenny's contention that in practical reasoning "we work out . . . *what we are to do.*" A clear case of this sort, though not the only kind to be considered, might be one in which the reasoner asks himself the question "Given such-and-such—the starting-point and the constraining conditions of his problem—*what shall I do?*" But then an appropriate answer, reached at the end of a process of reasoning, should plausibly have the form "I *will* do such-and-such." The speech-act consisting of uttering such a sentence with conviction is an act of resolving, and the content of the act— what *is* resolved—is a resolution, and not a proposition. Other examples might be conclusions that are intentions or promises. These kinds of cases demonstrate the *prima facie* truth of thesis (A): there do seem to be correct types of reasoning terminating in nonpropositional conclusions.

Such examples incidentally highlight a weakness of the traditional, but in some ways misleading contrast between the "theoretical" and the "practical." Reasonings terminating with logical force in some action would indeed be in sharp contrast with reasoning terminating in assertions of what is the case (propositional conclusions). But what are we to do with conclusions that express intention, or determination to act, or something of the sort? I suggest that we need to consider classes of statements that might be called "praxigenic," bearing a particularly close relation, though not one of logical implica-

⁴ A. J. Kenny, "Practical Inference," *Analysis,* 26 (1966), 65.

tion, with the relevant action. (How to specify the class of "praxigenic" statements is a problem that I shall not pursue here.)

5. I shall find it convenient to have an umbrella term to refer to whatever can be affirmed, whether propositional or not. Let us call the content of such an affirmation a *dictum*,[5] i.e., roughly speaking, what a man says when he says something sincerely or what he thinks when he performs the corresponding act of thought. Thus a man who says "I will answer that letter" will normally be affirming a dictum which might, according to circumstances, be identified as the resolution to answer the letter in question, or the corresponding intention, or the corresponding promise, and so on. Propositions, then, will be a special kind of dicta, viz., those that can be either true or false. Reasoning terminating in propositional dicta might be called *propositional reasoning* (a label that I prefer to "theoretical reasoning").

6. It may have been noticed that, in the later part of the remarks that I have quoted from Kenny's paper, he suggests that the conclusions of a piece of practical reasoning may be *"actions* or plans for actions." I cannot, however, see that an act—or, for that matter a plan for action—could properly be viewed as a dictum, something that might be affirmed in speech or thought. If there are, as Kenny implies, correct modes of reasoning whose conclusions are actions, i.e., things done and not dicta merely affirmed, we should indeed have a fundamental contrast with propositional reasoning. Anscombe says, approvingly, that in Aristotle's examples of practical syllogisms he "appears to envisage an action as following" (i.e., as being logically connected with the premises)[6] and Von

[5] An alternative label might be *affirmable,* since a dictum, as here conceived, is essentially something that can be affirmed, whether in speech or in thought. So far as I know, there is no generally acceptable term available. *Judgment,* which some writers use, is too suggestive of idealistic conceptions of logic to be satisfactory.

[6] Anscocmbe, *op. cit.,* p. 59.

Wright says, of what is admittedly a special case, "the conclusion *is an action*" and adds, "This is exactly what Aristotle says it should be."[7] Can we adopt this suggestion?

7. There seems, at first sight, something absurd about the notion that a nonverbal action, such as swimming, could stand in a *logical* relation of entailment, or some weaker logical relation, to given premises. The suggestion sounds as preposterous as that of a monkey being suspended from propositions. It may be that a notion of premises as abstract entities is partly responsible for the initial revulsion. If so, the initial impression of confusion of categories can be somewhat mitigated by taking the conclusion to be a dictum, i.e., something whose affirmation constitutes a *speech-act*. Since a fully verbalized train of reasoning does consist of a sequence of speech-acts, there is nothing intrinsically absurd about the notion of a set of such speech-acts implying another speech-act. Commitment to some speech-acts can imply commitment to others. But this is still a long way from the suggestion that a train of reasoning might terminate, with logical necessity, in something as sheerly nonverbal as eating or opening a door.

Perhaps the most sympathetic rendering that can be supplied of the notion of actions as conclusions might run somewhat as follows: Let the acts consisting of affirming the premises of a certain argument be $A_1, A_2, \ldots, A_n$. Suppose it now is logically impossible that anybody should be doing A_1–A_n, without thereby doing something else, $B;$ then the action B might perhaps, without undue strain, be said to be entailed by the corresponding premises. On the plausible assumption that speech-acts can entail only speech-acts, the class of actions thus logically derivable from dicta-premises would

---

[7] Von Wright, "Practical Inference," p. 47. Von Wright's case is that of the reasoning, "X intends (now) to make it true that E; he thinks that unless he does A now, he will not achieve this; therefore he does A now." It is hard to see how in this case an intention is "transmitted" to the conclusion, as Von Wright claims for the more general case. His example looks at best like a degenerate case of "inference."

be severely circumscribed, and would certainly not answer to the ambitious intentions of those who wish to make a place in the logical sun for "practical reasoning."

8. Fortunately, we need not pursue this topic any further. I have previously said that a natural answer to a question of the form "What shall I do, in such-and-such a given situation?" would be the expression of a resolution, "I shall do *A*," where *A* is a place-holder for the specification of an action or a course of action. I wish to contend that a reasoner would not affirm such a resolution unless he had actually affirmed a dictum of the form "I *should* do *A*," or would be willing to do so. We can ignore a case in which a man does what he thinks he should not, since neither the reasoner himself nor a critic would then regard the action in question as justified by the antecedent reasoning.

The 'should'-dictum "I *should* do *A*," which might be called a *deontic* conclusion, is logically weaker than the corresponding resolution-dictum "I *will* do *A*," inasmuch as a man could not be committed to, could not affirm, the second unless he was willing to be committed, would be willing to affirm, the first. But the converse is untrue. A man might conclude that he should do something and yet not do it, through "weakness of the will," indolence, or for some other reason. In such cases, we need not brand the reasoning as incorrect if we approve the derivation of the deontic conclusion from its premise-dicta; the matter of ultimate performance seems to raise questions that do not involve logical calculation.

I therefore imagine interposed between the final action, if it occurs, and the premises of the practical reasoning leading up to and supposedly justifying action, two intermediate conclusions, "I will do *A*" and "I should do *A*," where the weaker 'should'-dictum can at most be regarded as a kind of minimal explanation of the resolution. ("Why did you resolve to do *A*?" "Because I thought I *should* do *A*." That goes without saying! That looks more like "immediate inference" than genuine support by a reason.)

This series of interposed conclusions can be prolonged. Between the 'should'-conclusion and its supporting premises we can insert the further intermediate conclusion "*A* is the right thing to do, given my situation"—or, colloquially, "*A* is the thing to do." (I use the phrase "given my situation" as shorthand for a specification of the aim to be achieved and the conditions to be satisfied by any acceptable fulfillment of that aim.)

More realistically in many cases, the intermediate conclusion might rather take the form "*A* is a satisfactory (or sufficiently satisfactory) thing to do, considering my situation."

Let us call a dictum attesting to the rightness or satisfactoriness of the proposed action, the *verdictive* conclusion, or simply the *verdict*. Then I would argue, as before, that the verdict is logically weaker than the corresponding 'should'-conclusion, in the same sense of "weaker," and for a similar reason, viz., that somebody might think action *A* was the right thing to do, given his situation, and yet be unwilling or unable to commit himself to saying or even thinking that he should do it. But with this relatively noncommittal verdictive conclusion, we have reached a propositional dictum. That *A* is the right thing, or a satisfactory thing, to do in a given situation is either true or false, and, if true, susceptible of demonstration from true premises. (Those who might wish to contest this might be invited to reconsider how we do in fact reach "verdicts" in determinate problems of action.) I shall now argue that we can "normalize" every plausible candidate for the title of a piece of practical reasoning in such a way that at its core or center there appears a wholly propositional argument of a certain sort. The "want"-, "intend"-, or "will"-dicta that lend the whole train of thought or speech its "motive power" can then be considered as "latched on" to this central propositional core.

9. Prime examples of allegedly "practical" reasoning, as supplied by those who accept the autonomy thesis, usually commence with some statement of the reasoner's "want,"

"desire," or "intention" and end with what I have called a "praxigenic statement" (or, as I should now prefer to say, a praxigenic dictum). For present purposes, a praxigenic dictum may be taken to be a first-person affirmation,[8] whose sincere utterance provides a reasonable presumption, *ceteris paribus,* of ultimate performance. I have already proposed that we consider as an intermediate conclusion a "verdictive" dictum having the form "Such-and-such is the right or a satisfactory thing to do," leaving the connection between such a conclusion and the subsequent praxigenic conclusion for later examination. A similar procedure of "normalization" can now be applied to the start of the supposedly practical reasoning. In place of an initial affirmation of want, desire, or the like, we imagine instead the *specification of a task or problem.* (I shall use "task" and "problem" interchangeably in what follows.)

This leads us to recognize, at the heart, as it were, of a train of practical reasoning, the solution of a given task, regarded "objectively," no longer tied to the particular commitment of somebody who wishes or is obliged in some way to solve the problem.

Imitating the form traditionally used for geometrical problems, we might formulate such an objective task-kernel as follows:

(a) *Given:* Such-and-such a starting situation, S.

(b) *Required:* To describe a sequential procedure, P (course-of-action), that will bring about a given state, E.

(c) *Subject to:* Such-and-such conditions, C, that any acceptable solution must satisfy (the possible courses of action that the reasoner for mathematical, logical, prudential, moral, or other reasons, is allowed to entertain).

In short, a task or problem, thus abstractly conceived, may be regarded as the content of a requirement to transform a

---

[8] I reserve for discussion elsewhere the important relations between first-person praxigenic reasonings and their second- and third-person variants.

given *S*, sequentially,[9] into a given *E*, using transformations satisfying given conditions *C*. Thus full specification of *S*, *C*, and *E* fully determine a particular problem. For instance, a "two-move chess problem" provides an initial chess configuration, with the requirement that a mating position be derived, in no more than two moves both of which are "legal" according to the rules of chess. Similar analyses will apply to the less structured situations considered by such thinkers as Von Wright, where, for instance, a man is considering the necessary conditions for the attainment of some given goal. (Consider, say, the "task" of finding a word in a large dictionary as "quickly as possible"—or of learning to use a new kind of razor. The conditions of satisfactory solution can, up to a point, be rendered explicit.) The scheme is basically the same as that applied in "programming" a computer for the solution of a given problem or task. (It is worth remembering that computers can now be programmed to produce "good" moves and to play something like intelligent chess. Principles of strategy are not exempt from codification.)

A satisfactory verbal solution to such a problem-formulation will consist, first, of finding some description satisfying clauses (b) and (c) above, i.e., describing some *P* leading from *S* to *E* and satisfying *C*; and second, of demonstrating that the proposed solution does in fact conform to the specification of the problem. *This* type of reasoning is certainly no different from those codified in deductive or inductive logic. Indeed, our proposed formalization of a "problem" applies just as well to cases where the task is to demonstrate that something *is* the case as to cases where the task has the character of finding out what to do, under given constraints of performance. That *S* satisfies the defining conditions of a given problem is, in either type of case, a "theoretical" truth.

---

[9] I wish to stress this point, since it is characteristic of acceptable solutions of tasks that they prescribe trains of actions, some conditional upon the performance of antecedent ones, that are to be performed *in a given temporal order*.

10. At all events, a theory of problem solution is a much neglected undertaking, whose elaboration might reveal some points of more than routine interest.[10] I conceive of such a theory as confined, in the first instance, to such conceptual tasks as the clarification of the basic notions of task or problem, solution, compounding and reduction of solutions, the relations of partial to total solutions, and so on. Such a theory might, I believe, throw some light upon certain notorious paradoxes of imperative or deontic logic.[11]

[10] A pioneering work in this field is the remarkable and unjustly forgotten essay of A. Kolmogoroff, "Zur Deutung der intuitionistischen Logik," *Mathematische Zeitschrift*, 35 (1932), 58–65. It is of interest in the present connection to recall that by construing the connectives of the intuitionistic logic of Brouwer and Heyting as applying to problems (*Aufgaben*) rather than propositions, Kolmogoroff is able to show that we can dispense with a deviant "intuitionist" logic. This is consonant with the main suggestion of the present essay.

[11] For example, much has been written upon the supposed "paradox of addition" in imperative logic. It is natural to think of an imperative demanding an action, say d (A), as calling for the production of a state of affairs, A, and, consequently, to suppose that if A's obtaining entails the obtaining of B, then d (A) logically implies d (B). But then let C be any situation whatever: it would seem that d (A) should logically imply d $(A$ or $C)$, which can be "obeyed" or "satisfied" by producing C. For instance, if I am required to shut the door, I could shut the window, pleading that I had at least done part of the task, by obeying the implied order to shut the door or the window! (For discussion of related issues, see, for instance, Alf Ross, *Directives and Norms* (London, 1968), p. 167.) The task conception throws some light on this: not everything entailed by the desired end-state, E, can count as a partial means to achieving E—notably if the entailed state is also entailed by not-E, as in the example just considered. Only an entailed condition whose satisfaction reduces the original task to something less than it was should count as a means. (This line of thought is also applicable to the notorious "paradoxes of confirmation." Indeed, confirming or verifying an assertion is a special case of a task, in our sense.)

Thus, by an analysis of the notion of means, which has its proper *locus* in a theory of tasks and their solutions, we can dodge the alleged paradox and need not here concern ourselves with the question, which might be important in another context, whether an imperative of the form d (A) can be regarded as logically implying an imperative of the form d $(A$ or $C)$. Whether it does or not, the requisite task-analysis is unaffected.

It might be urged in favor of this way of viewing and analyzing "practical reasoning" that it allows for the impartial and impersonal criticism and evaluation of at least the "objective kernel" of any such train of reasoning. More importantly, it lends itself to the consideration of problems and their solutions, in abstraction from commitments to the premises or to action in line with the task solution—a process essential for all complex deliberation. Also, if I am not mistaken, it obviates multiplication of distinct and unrelated kinds of new logics.

11. It might be objected that by the use of such expressions as "required" I am assuming the application of principles of deontic logic,[12] which, in formalization of a task pattern, would be shown by the presence of a deontic operator. My reply would be that the deontic aspect of the specification of a problem, as I conceive it, seems to be, quite literally negligible. The entire problem or task of passing from starting point to goal by means of a permitted route is in some sense understood to be "demanded" or "required"; but that overall demand does not require insertion of deontic operators, or their ordinary-language equivalents, into the *interior* of a problem-solution or into the interior of a proof of such a solution's acceptability. It is worth noting, especially, that there is no need to take formal account in such a solution of "possibilities" as opposed to "necessities," since this is already taken care of by the specification of the constraining conditions *C*. (Thus, *some* chess moves are obligatory, others merely "permitted" at the player's discretion, yet the logical relation between the obligatory and the merely permitted, which is of central interest to deontic logic, is of no importance for the solution of a chess problem, being eliminated once and for all by a specification of *admissible* transformations.) Of course, a problem *about* deontic logic, say that of deriving a given deontic theorem from given

[12] For a useful exposition of which see, for instance, D. Føllesdal and R. Hilpinen, "Deontic Logic: An Introduction," in Risto Hilpinen, ed., *Deontic Logic: Introductory and Systematic Readings* (Dordrecht, Holland, 1971).

deontic premises, would be another story. Should we call *such* a problem "practical"?

12. The scheme here proposed for a task solution does not presuppose a unique solution for a given problem. There may be a task T, say, such that both P_1 and P_2 will indifferently transform S into E under conditions C, and either of the P's would qualify as a "satisfactory" rather than the "right" solution. The proposed scheme for task specification can accommodate this kind of case by rewording, the goal now being specified, say, as that of producing *any* P satisfying certain supplementary conditions (e.g., of not being rated lower than another P satisfying C, according to some provided or understood scale of preferences). More interesting is the type of case encountered when the problem's specifications, even with plausible supplements, are insufficient to determine a satisfactory solution—the case of a radically incompletely defined or partially indeterminate problem.

13. It is worth dwelling a while on this case because the presence of indeterminate problems, in situations calling for ultimate action, seems to be one of the main reasons why Anscombe, and perhaps others, have urged recognition of a radical difference between practical and theoretical reasoning.

One of Anscombe's characteristic examples of a piece of practical reasoning is "They have Jersey cows in the Hereford market, so I'll go there":[13] it is of such examples of reasoning that she says they exemplify "another type of reasoning from premises to a conclusion *which they prove*."[14] She also points out that the additional premises needed to make such reasonings deductively valid would be "insane."[15] It may be granted that to import a premise of the form, say, "Anybody who wants a Jersey cow ought to go to any market where they are to be found" would be absurd.

From the standpoint I am recommending, the reasoning about Jersey cows has behind it a certain task, if we want to

---

[13] Anscombe, *op. cit.*, p. 65.   [14] *Ibid.*, p. 61.   [15] *Ibid.*, p. 60.

call it anything so pretentious, say that of getting a Jersey cow, using such-and-such means—this task, however, having no determinate solution. Suppose the reasoner were to know that there were also cows at Peterborough and had no reason to favor going to the one market rather than the other: it would be preposterous for him to imitate Buridan's ass by going nowhere. Here there is room and need for arbitrary but not irrational *decision*. In other cases, we typically *judge* one solution to be "better" than another, on grounds that we cannot formalize.

Practical decisions do indeed often demand such an element of judgment and stipulation. But as much can be said of realistic episodes of "theoretical" reasoning. In cases of what might be called deliberative theoretical reasoning, we are typically faced with adopting conclusions that are supported or discredited in varying, and perhaps in the end unformalizable, ways by evidential considerations. A scientist making up his mind about which explanatory hypothesis to accept on evidence which points in different directions will, in the end, need to use judgment—and *decide*. But in this familiar fact there is no ground, once more, for making a sharp distinction between "practical" and "theoretical" reasoning.

14. But will this type of analysis do justice to the "motive power" of a practical argument in its full form? Can it be used to explain why somebody expressing some initial intention may be motivated either to adopt a derived intention, based upon the solution of his task, or to modify that first intention?

I believe that a reasonably adequate, if partial, conception of what we mean when we ascribe an intention to an agent, on the basis of his honest and sincere expression of it, will allow us to answer these questions affirmatively.

Expression of an honest intention to achieve *E* can be regarded as providing a *presumption* of performance. That is to say, *ceteris paribus,* if the agent comes to be able to produce *E,* and has not changed his mind, or is not suffering from some neurotic or psychotic weakness of will *(akrasia)*, he can be expected to do *E*. Alternatively: if he does do *E,* we should regard his having previously framed the corresponding intention as at best an unilluminating explanation of his action, just because of the presumptive bond I have already mentioned. (What *might* call for a substantial explanation would be the performance of an apparently purposeful action in the absence of a corresponding intention.)

It might be helpful here to invoke a physical analogue: If a body is under the influence of a certain force, there is a presumption that it will move in a certain direction, with specifiable acceleration. Here, too, there is an associated set of escape clauses: that the force is not counterbalanced by an opposing force, that no obstacles intervene, that the force continues to hold, and so on. And we take it as a very weak though perhaps still barely informative explanation of the body's actual motion, when it occurs, that it was under the influence of a corresponding force.

Here, the "presumption" has a conceptual basis: "force" is introduced as a theoretical term to facilitate a general overview of situations where empirical reasons enable us to predict, with appropriate reservations, the motions of physical bodies; thus it is a conceptual or definitional truth that a body under the influence of an "impressed force" will "tend" to move in a certain direction with a definite acceleration. And we may say, for similar reasons, that it is a conceptual or definitional truth that a person having a certain intention will, with relevant reservations, tend to "move" toward his goal. There is as much, or as little, mystery about this as there is about the motion of physical bodies.

15. One respect in which the "motion" of a conscious agent toward a goal differs from the physical analogue is that he envisages or foresees the goal, together with its temporally preceding conditions and its probable consequences. We might say that an intention spreads over space and time, encompassing within its scope the envisaged events leading up to the goal and the events that may be expected to follow attainment. How

much interest there is in the antecedents and the consequents of the desired terminus, E, partly specifies the intention in question, but there can be no "pure" intention that is wholly indifferent to the means of attainment and its consequences. A man setting out to reach the top of a mountain cannot be indifferent to how he is to get up—and get down again. That, too, is a conceptual truth about intentions—based in the end, like other "conceptual truths," upon facts about human nature and human action.

Thus the function of explicit argument about intentions, whether in the form preferred by friends of practical reasoning, or, in the alternative "objective" form of a task solution here proposed, is to articulate a partially undefined purpose by making the necessary or sufficient conditions for fulfillment and the necessary or likely consequences explicit. Whether the outcome will then be performance of the auxiliary actions (realizing sufficient or necessary means for fulfillment) will, of course, depend upon the strength of the original intention and the acceptability of the implications revealed by the reasoning.

16. There is in all this more analogy with straightforward theoretical reasoning than might at first sight appear. For if we consider episodes of occurrent theoretical reasoning, rather than the abstract arguments derivable from them, we shall be inclined to view them as rational attempts to articulate the implied *beliefs* necessitated by previous belief-commitments. And as in the case of articulated intentions, the outcome of sound argument may either be the further crystallization of a previously held, but only partially explicit, belief or, in other cases, some modification of the original belief.

17. I conclude, therefore, that there is no clear advantage to be gained by marking off so-called "practical reasoning" as a special domain having distinctive constituents and distinctive styles of correct reasoning. The analysis I have proposed isolates a kernel of "problem solution" which constitutes that part of the practical task that involves rational calculation and

where appropriate, the exercise of judgment and decision. I am inclined to think that the formal aspects of such argument are somewhat trivial and not worth a good deal of attention. What renders a substantial practical or praxigenic argument satisfactory (excluding perhaps the over-simple illustrations used above) seems rather to turn upon such questions as whether the reasoner sufficiently heeded relevant information, adequately ordered his relative preferences, properly envisaged the probable consequences of the alternative actions, correctly estimated the "costs" as well as the "benefits" and so on. In short, the kinds of considerations that are pertinent to calculation and reasoning in economics.[16] If so, a formal theory of practical reasoning may have only the modest practical function of warning us against gross blunders arising from inattention. Such a theory would then be overshadowed by a nonformal theory of rational choice and decision. Such reasoning, so far as I can see, requires neither nonpropositional elements, nor esoteric principles of reasoning. Its "motive power," which accounts for the interest it has aroused in philosophers, is intelligible once a problem analysis is attached to intentions or given some other "praxigenic" setting. That correct calculations of the solution of problems posed by given intentions or desires should influence the nature of such intentions, whether by further specification or modification, should not be a cause for wonder. Nor is there any point in wondering why an intention should result in action, when it does. That puzzles about intentions remain I would not deny. Only it seems unhelpful to confuse them with the pseudo-problem of delineating an allegedly peculiar sort of logic or reasoning. Logics are not to be multiplied beyond necessity. I have argued that in the cases considered the necessity remains to be shown.

[16] For further elaboration of such an approach, see David A. J. Richards, *A Theory of Reasons for Action* (Oxford, 1971), especially chapter 3, "The Principles of Rational Choice."

IV

The Logical Paradoxes

The following paradox was suggested by a paper by Peter Geach entitled "On Insolubilia," which in turn appears to have arisen from a paper by Haskell B. Curry, "The Inconsistencies of Certain Formal Logics."[1] It would be no surprise to learn that the paradox was already known to Buridan or to some other medieval logician.

The paradox has some interest as a puzzle on its own account. It has still more interest, however, for the light it sheds upon the familiar logical and semantical paradoxes, which have been intensively but inconclusively discussed for well over half a century.

Imagine somebody to utter the following words: "What I am now saying is not so unless God exists." (Alternatively, the speaker might be taken to say instead: "Nothing that I now say is so unless God exists." This would generate much the same puzzles.) To make the truth of a single utterance depend, in this way, upon God's existence, seems harmless enough at first sight, if somewhat surprising. Yet extraordinary consequences follow, as will soon become clear.

"What I am now saying is not so unless God exists." I shall suppose that the speaker is using the expression, "is not so," merely as a device for negation, and not as a way of making an assertion about an assertion. I shall also assume—and this is the crucial point—that the expression, "What I am *now* say-

---

[1] Geach, in *Analysis*, 15 (1954–55), 70–71; Curry, in *Journal of Symbolic Logic*, 7 (1942), 115–117.

ing," is intended to apply to the whole of what is being said. So we have the self-reflexiveness that typically characterizes the classical paradoxes.

Not P unless Q is logically equivalent to *P only if Q*, and this in turn is logically equivalent of *If P then Q*. If we represent the whole of the proposition that the speaker presents himself as affirming by *S*, and the proposition that God exists by *E*, we obtain the equation

$$S = (S \supset E).$$

Here *E* may be regarded as given, and *S* as unknown, so that the speaker is making a cryptic remark whose content has to be unraveled by solving the equation.

Now there may be all sorts of reasons why our imagined speaker might wish to make a cryptic statement in this way: he might be a spy, or a true believer forced to say *something* in the torture chamber. Or he might believe, like the members of certain religious sects, that the truth of *all* utterances depends upon God's existence.

My use of the horseshoe in the above formula is intended to mark the occurrence of material implication, and not some stronger logical relation. I assume that this answers to the speaker's intention, so that he is saying, in effect, "It is not the case, *as a matter of fact,* that what I am now saying is the case, while God does not exist."

The chief questions I wish to raise are: Is the equation legitimate? and if it is legitimate, does it have any solution?

There is a familiar and plausible way of arguing that the equation is insoluble, and hence illegitimate, because it involves a circular definition of the unknown, *S*.

The equation purports to specify *S* by means of the expression on the right-hand side. But the unknown *S* also appears in the *explicans*. If we try to remove the right-hand occurrence of *S* by substitution, we get

$$S = ((S \supset E) \supset E)$$

which still contains S on the right-hand side and is a more complex equation than we started with. And if we repeat this attempt to eliminate S from the explicans, we get

$$S = (((S \supset E) \supset E)) \supset E),$$

which is still more complicated, and is marred by the same defect. This procedure gets us nowhere. As a student once said to me: each time we peel the onion, we find another skin underneath and never succeed in getting to a core. I think this is substantially the point of Gilbert Ryle's argument about the impossibility of removing the "namely-clause" in the heterological paradox.[2]

This attack against the equation is unsound. We have not yet shown the equation to be insoluble. Consider for a moment the following arithmetical equation:

$$x = (2x + 4).$$

If we applied the same procedure as before, we should obtain, successively:

$$x = (2(2x + 4) + 4)$$

and then:

$$x = (2(2(2x + 4) + 4) + 4)$$

and so on. But the moral of this is only that *this* way of proceeding is misguided. Our failure to solve the arithmetical equation in this way does not foreclose the existence of other methods of solution. Indeed, we all know a simple and direct way of determining the value of x. All we need do is to shift the $2x$ term to the left, getting

$$x - 2x = 4$$

and

$$-x = 4$$

[2] "Heterologicality," *Analysis*, 11 (1950–51), 61–69.

and

$$x = -4.$$

It is a pity that we can do nothing as straightforward with our original equation in S.

The analogy, however, encourages us to try some elementary manipulation. We can rewrite the first equation as

$$S = (\sim S \vee E)$$

Conjoining S to both sides yields:

$$S \cdot S = S(\sim S \vee E) = S \cdot \sim S \vee S \cdot E = S \cdot E,$$

or

$$S = SE.$$

Again, multiplying both sides of the original equation, this time by E, instead of by S, provides:

$$S \cdot E = (\sim S \vee E) E = \sim S \cdot E \vee E \cdot E = E,$$

or

$$SE = E.$$

So we have obtained $S = SE = E$, and hence $S = E$.

The reader may have some qualms about the use of identity between propositions in the foregoing derivation. Nothing that is crucial, however, turns upon this. The only properties of propositional identity needed are: (i) $A = B$ logically implies that $AC = BC$, (ii) If $A = B \vee K$, where K is a contradiction, then $A = B$, (iii) $A \supset B = \sim A \vee B$, (iv) $A(B \vee C) = AB \vee AC$, (v) $A = B$ and $B = C$ logically implies $A = C$. All of these are at least plausible, where contingent propositions are in question. In any case, parodoxical consequences would also follow if the speaker's original utterance were to be weakened by having material equivalence replacing identity, with the starting formula now:

$$S \equiv (S \supset E).$$

An even shorter derivation would be:

$$S \supset (S \supset E) \quad \text{(from the starting formula)}$$
$$\therefore S \supset E \quad \text{(absorption)}$$
$$\therefore S \quad \text{(from the starting formula)}$$
$$\therefore E \quad (\textit{modus ponens}).$$

We now seem to have found a definite solution to the original equation. It looks as if the original speaker might be taken to have chosen a roundabout way of affirming *E*, i.e., of saying that God exists. And why not?

Well, if $S = E$, we ought to be able to substitute one of these propositions for the other in the original equation. But if we do so, we obtain:

$$S = (E \supset E),$$

and also

$$E = (E \supset E).$$

From the first of these results it follows that what the speaker said is not only true, but necessarily true. And from the second it appears that the existence of God is a tautology!

Since these outcomes are so extraordinary, it is worth checking the whole analysis by truth-tables. We get the following pattern:

S	=	(S	⊃	E)
T	T	T	T	T
T	F	T	F	F
F	F	F	T	T
F	F	F	T	F

The only line in the truth-table that allows the equation to hold is the first. Hence, we get, as before, that both *S* and *E* must be true in all possible worlds.

In our original equation, *E* might have been any proposition whatever. So we cannot treat this as a veridical paradox, whose conclusion, however startling, we are forced to accept. It is preposterous to suppose that by saying something of the form $S \supset E$, where E is arbitrary, a speaker could guarantee, not only the truth of E, but even its necessary truth. What has gone wrong?

One thing seems certain: we cannot blame the self-reflexiveness of S. In order to enforce this point, I shall now consider the following equation:

$$S = (S \equiv (S \equiv E)).$$

This would correspond to a case in which the speaker said: "What I am now saying is the case if and only if what I am now saying is the case if and only if God exists." The self-reflexiveness is patent. Yet the right-hand side is logically equivalent to E, so that the whole equation reduces simply to:

$$S = E.$$

This time the speaker really can be taken to be covertly asserting, but unparadoxically, that God exists.

It is worth checking this result, as before, by truth-table analysis. We get:

S	$=$	$(S$	$\equiv$	$(S$	$\equiv$	$E))$
T	T	T	T	T	T	T
T	F	T	F	T	F	F
F	F	F	T	F	F	T
F	T	F	F	F	T	F

We see that in order for the equation to hold (lines one and four), S must have just the same truth-values as E, but E may be either true or false. And if we substitute E for S in the original equation, we get

$$S = (E \equiv (E \equiv E))$$

which in turn reduces to

$$S = E$$

without paradox. Here, in spite of self-reflexiveness, we have the speaker cryptically asserting that God exists. This may be eccentric, but it is not logically reprehensible.

It is instructive to see what happens if, in the original equation we considered, the right-hand formula is replaced by its converse. We then have:

$$S = (E \supset S).$$

An easy way of seeing what this implies is to convert it into:

$$S = (\sim E \lor S)$$

and then to construct a Venn diagram (Figure 1), from which

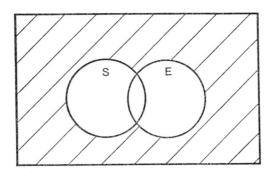

Figure 1

it can be easily seen that the general solution is:

$$S = \sim E \lor KE,$$

where K is anything we please. Or, to put the solution in another way, we can write:

$$S = \sim E \lor L,$$

where L is arbitrary.

We could therefore choose to suppose that a speaker who makes an utterance represented by S in the present case is saying something arbitrarily weaker than not-E. He might be taken to be saying, implicitly, "Either God does not exist, or something or other is the case." Alternatively, "If God exists, then something or other is the case." This could be criticized as indefinite and pointless, but not as paradoxical. There is an analogy here with an arithmetical equation allowing infinitely many solutions. (The reader might also wish to examine, as an exercise, what happens when a speaker says *"Everything* I say is the case only if God exists.")

What then is really responsible for the paradoxes we uncovered in our first example? We shall get a clue if we reconsider the truth-table analysis. It will be remembered that we rejected every line except the first because, in all the other lines, an F appeared under the sign of equality. But that means we assumed that the original equation *could* be legitimately satisfied. This led us to conclude, from the first line, that S was identical with E and also with $E \supset E$. By assuming that the speaker was not contradicting himself—but *only* in that way— we got the paradoxical result.

But this is really no more defensible than starting with the equation

$$x + 3 = x + 5$$

and hence "proving" that $3 = 5$. Here, too, if we assume that the equation *can* be solved, we generate absurdity.

The mistake committed consisted in implicitly defining S as being at one and the same time identical with E and also identical with a tautology. We tacitly assumed that there *was* a solution (encouraged by the fact that not all lines of the truth-table were assigned an F). But this is as indefensible as assuming that the arithmetical equation above must have a solution. Now, we are never entitled to smuggle dubious assertions in this way into a definition or into a specification of what we claim to be saying.

Were there no such restrictions upon correct definition, we could specify S, more directly, by using the following clauses:

$$S = E \text{ and } S \vee F = S \vee \sim F,$$

where F is anything we please. Now, the second clause, *if we
assume that it can be satisfied,* makes S necessarily true; and
then the first clause yields E also as a necessary truth. But nobody is entitled to suppose that, by merely formulating a definition, he can show some independently chosen proposition to be
necessarily true. If this seems to follow from his definition,
then so much the worse for his definition.

These remarks about definition may have some bearing upon
certain forms of the ontological argument. It is possible to
define God in such a way that any proposition whatever about
God entails God's necessary existence. So that a would-be
agnostic could say nothing about the Necessary Being without
committing himself to that Being's necessary existence. But
such a definition must be rejected as illegitimate, because it
smuggles in, without justification, a debatable assumption. If
the procedure were acceptable, we could just as easily establish
the necessary existence of a new planet called Minerva, by
simply defining Minerva in such a way that its necessary existence followed from any proposition about it. One cannot conjure things into existence by definition.

We have seen that an implicit definition of something said,
having the form:

$$S = f(S, E),$$

where f is some function of S and another proposition, E, is
sometimes legitimate, in the sense of having a definite solution,
and sometimes not. Can we lay down any general conditions for
the legitimacy of such implicit definitions? The following considerations will show, if I am not mistaken, that the answer
must be No.

Consider, once again, the arithmetical analogue. An implicit
definition of an unknown number, x, will have the form:

$$x = f(x),$$

where f is an arbitrary function. The question becomes: Can
we say in general when an equation of this form admits of a

determinate solution for *x?* One way of seeing the correct answer is to replace the above equation by the following two equations:

$$y = f(x)$$

and

$$y = x.$$

In graphical representation (Figure 2), the first of these equations corresponds to an arbitrary curve, and the second to

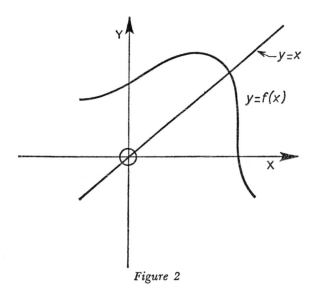

Figure 2

a line through the origin inclined at 45 degrees to the *x*-axis. Thus the equation, $x = f(x)$, will have a solution if and only if the curve and the straight line intersect.

Now there can be no completely general conditions for this to happen. It all depends upon the nature of the function *f*. According to circumstances, the two curves may fail to intersect, may intersect in one point or many, and so on.

The same conclusion can be reached by the following line of reasoning. Our equation can be put in the form:

$$f(x) - x = 0,$$

where f is an arbitrary function. Now it is easy to see that the set of functions, $f(x) - x$, thus specified is simply the set of functions in general. Hence our question becomes: Does the equation,

$$g(x) = 0,$$

where g is an arbitrary function, have any real roots? (Alternatively, does the corresponding curve intersect the x-axis?) Now we know that it is hard enough to give an answer in very special cases (e.g., when g is a quadratic function) ; there is no prospect at all of finding any completely general condition for the roots of an equation whose character is not further specified.

The moral for cases of the form $S = f(S, E)$ is obvious. It would be too much to expect some general condition of legitimacy. Of course, the situation here is somewhat simpler than in the mathematical analogue. Since there are just sixteen essentially distinct truth-functions of S and E, we could sift out those that allowed S to have a determinate value (which must be E or $\sim E$). But this hardly seems worth the trouble, especially in view of the fact that reflexive paradoxes may well involve nonextensional functions of propositions.

When Bertrand Russell tried to supply a rationale for the Theory of Types, he said: "The principle which enables us to avoid illegitimate totalities may be stated as follows: 'Whatever involves *all* of a collection must not be one of the collection'; or, conversely: 'If, provided a certain collection had a total, it would have members only definable in terms of that total, then the said collection has no total.' We shall call this the 'vicious-circle principle,' because it enables us to avoid the vicious circles involved in the assumption of illegitimate totalities."[3] The difficulty in applying this "vicious-circle principle" arises from the presence of the words, *"only* definable in terms of that total," in the definition of an "illegitimate totality." How are we to tell whether a given totality is illegitimate? There will normally be many ways of identifying members introduced in terms of a class to which they belong; and there will be no obvious way of deciding whether they can be identified *only* by reference to all members of that class.

Consider the following examples. A class K_1 is defined as consisting of three members (a, b, c), where $a = 3$, $b = 5$, and $c =$ the sum of all the members of K_1. Here, we cannot determine the value of c independently, if only because its definition leads to a contradiction. But now consider a three-membered class, K_2, where $a = 3$, $b = 5$, and $c =$ the average of all the numbers that are members of K_2. Here, there is no difficulty in determining the value of c as 4, even though its definition refers to all the members of K_2.

Now take the following variant upon the well-known Heterological paradox. Call an adjective "mesological" if and only if the property expressed by the adjective is a property of *at least one* adjective. Now ask whether "mesological" itself is mesological. This means, does at least one adjective apply to at least one adjective? And the answer is clearly Yes—since "polysyllabic" is such an adjective. Here, then, no paradox emerges, even though the definition of "mesological," like the definition of "heterological," involves quantification over *all* adjectives.

Russell's "vicious-circle principle," and the theory of types suggested by it, has the effect of forbidding all implicit definitions. I think I have shown that this is too severe a restriction, since such implicit definition is sometimes harmless.

As to the proper approach to the paradoxes, I think the best suggestion so far made has been that of Kurt Gödel, when he

[3] *Principia Mathematica,* 2d ed. (Cambridge, 1925), I, 37.

said: "It might even turn out that it is possible to assume every concept to be significant everywhere except for certain 'singular points' or 'limiting points,' so that the paradoxes would appear as something analogous to dividing by zero."[4] I cannot see that there could be any completely general method for detecting such "singularities." Each paradox, as it emerges, needs individual attention.

[4] *The Philosophy of Bertrand Russell,* P. A. Schilpp, ed. (Evanston and Chicago, 1944), p. 150.

V

The Elusiveness of Sets

If we remove the veil and look underneath, if, laying aside the expressions, we set ourselves attentively to consider the things themselves which are supposed to be expressed or marked thereby, we shall discover much emptiness, darkness and confusion; nay, if I mistake not, direct impossibilities and contradictions.

—Berkeley, *The Analyst*, sec. 8

Whether there can be science of the conclusion where there is not science of the principles? And whether a man can have science of the principles without understanding them? And, therefore, whether the mathematicians of the present age act like men of science, in taking so much more pains to apply their principles than to understand them?

—Berkeley, *The Analyst*, sec. 50, query 36

The most important and most basic term to be found in modern mathematics and logic is that of *set* or class. . . . The modern mathematical theory of sets is one of the most remarkable creations of the human mind. Because of the unusual boldness of some of the ideas found in its study, and because of some of the singular methods of proof to which it has given rise, the theory of sets is indescribably fascinating. But above this, the theory has assumed tremendous importance for almost the whole of mathematics. It has enormously enriched, clarified, extended and generalized many domains of mathematics, and its influence on the study of the foundations of mathematics has been profound.

—H. Eves and C. V. Newsom[1]

To bring clearly before the mind what is meant by *class*, and to distinguish this notion from all the notions to which it is allied,

---

[1] *An Introduction to the Foundations and Fundamental Concepts of Mathematics* (New York, 1958), p. 226. I owe this reference, and some others, to the kindness of J. R. Trotter of the Australian National University.

is one of the most difficult and important problems of mathematical philosophy.

—Russell, *Principles of Mathematics*, p. 66

Nowadays, even schoolchildren babble about "null sets" and "singletons" and "one-one correspondences," as if they knew what they were talking about. But if they understand even less than their teachers, which seems likely, they must be using the technical jargon with only an illusion of understanding. Beginners are taught that a set having three members is a single thing, wholly constituted by its members but distinct from them. After this, the theological doctrine of the Trinity as "three in one" should be child's play.

Bourbaki once said, "As every one knows, all mathematical theories can be considered as extensions of the general theory of sets." Paul Cohen said, "By analyzing mathematical arguments, logicians became convinced that the notion of 'set' is the most fundamental concept of mathematics."[2] One might therefore expect mathematicians and logicians to possess a firm concept of "set." But then they owe laymen and beginners— and philosophers, too—full explanation of a concept so fundamental and so important.

Can the notion of "set" be too basic to permit elucidation and too familiar to need it? So some pundits claim. A report on the teaching of mathematics, commissioned by the Office for European Economic Coordination, urges that "from the very beginning . . . the teacher should see to it that students acquire, by their own effort, an understanding of the concept of 'set,' building largely upon *examples that they have encountered in their social life, their experiences at school and in the world about them.*" And it adds, "In this manner, students will be taken into the confidence of the teacher."[3] It is reassuring to know that the meaning of "set" is not to be kept confidential.

---

[2] *Set Theory and the Continuum Hypothesis* (New York, 1966), p. 50.
[3] *Synopses for Modern Secondary School Mathematics* (Paris, 1961), p. 15, emphasis added.

We can learn what familiar examples to expect from the opening of Paul R. Halmos' book, *Naive Set Theory:* "A pack of wolves, a bunch of grapes, or a flock of pigeons are all examples of sets of things."[4] It ought then to make sense, at least sometimes, to speak of being pursued by a set, or eating a set, or putting a set to flight. But perhaps such ways of speaking reflect what Halmos calls "erroneous understanding." For, on the same page, he says that the "point of view adopted assumes that the reader has the ordinary, human, intuitive (and *frequently erroneous*) understanding of what sets are; the purpose of the exposition is to delineate some of the many things that one can correctly do with them."

How erroneous is the "intuitive" notion? Frege once took Ernst Schroeder to task, with characteristic vehemence, for regarding sets as "collections of individuals." Frege said, "I regard as futile the attempt to make it [a set] rest, not on the concept, but on single things. . . . The extension of a concept does not consist of objects falling under the concept, in the way, e.g., that a wood consists of trees."[5] Frege thought that logic and mathematics have nothing to do with packs and bunches and flocks. And many other experts, from Hermann Weyl to Adolf Fraenkel and Willard Quine, agree in insisting that sets are "abstract objects" (about which more later). But no abstract object ever ran across the steppes, or hung from a bush; so perhaps the "intuitive" notion is *radically* wrong? As wrong, perhaps, as the idea that numbers are made of chalk and ink—which some advanced thinkers are still ready to maintain.

The confusions and evasions that disfigure contemporary textbooks on set theory can be attributed to two main reasons. One is a persistent and unresolved dispute between theorists who profess a highbrow view of sets as "abstract entities" and others who endorse some refinement of the lowbrow view of sets as collections (aggregates, groups, multitudes). It would

[4] New York, 1960, p. 1.
[5] P. Geach and M. Black, eds., *Translations from the Philosophical Writings of Gottlob Frege,* 2d ed. (Oxford, 1960), p. 106.

be optimistic to expect any definitive resolution of this conceptual hassle. A more tractable source of expository muddle is an outmoded and inadequate conception of the purposes of definition.

Writers on set theory often seem to assume that the only admissible form of definition is *per genus et differentiam*. Where that is inapplicable, as must often be the case, they seem to think an author is excused from explaining how he uses his basic ("undefined") terms. Now the only available synonyms for "set"—and approximate ones at that—may well be such equally problematic words as "class," or "group," or "collection." But this by no means exempts a writer from explaining how he uses "set," especially if he intends to deviate from lay senses of the word.

A word is, among other things, an instrument for expression, communication, and reference, and synonymous words can be viewed as verbal instruments having the same specific uses. But the use of a tool is not usually explained by producing an equivalent tool: nobody would be foolish enough to insist on having the use of a hammer explained by some hammer-substitute; then why not be as liberal in our demands on explanations of meaning? Perhaps "set" cannot be defined, upon some restrictive interpretation of definition; but its employment can surely be elucidated. The point is not to "define" the word, but to delineate its functions—and that, too, deserves to be called "definition."

Professional mathematicians are often content to treat "set" as primitive or "indefinable," in the sense in which "point," "between," and other primitive terms of an axiomatic geometry are indefinable. Well, we do have elegant axiomatic set theories—but they are used, "applied," outside those theories. Otherwise, "set," for all that mathematicians cared, could mean any objects we pleased—footballs or walking sticks—that satisfied the set-theoretical axioms. (And no axiomatic theory can preclude such deviant interpretations.) But when we have occasion to talk about "the set of integers," we intend to mean something definite. A set must be something better than "the ghost of a departed quantity" (to borrow Berkeley's splendid phrase). So back to the rigors of "honest toil."

If we are to be satisfied with something other than a formal definition of "set," then what are we to demand? What should be our criterion for a sufficiently clear concept? I can conceive of no general answer to this very general demand. But the notion of "(natural) number" provides a satisfactory exemplar: any reasonable man should be content, for a start, to understand "set" as well as he understands "number."

To have mastered the primary uses of "number" means *inter alia:* to know when and how to count and how to get the answer right; and to know how to calculate (to do sums) and how to get the answers right. In short: to use numbers, according to accepted rules and procedures, outside as well as inside arithmetic. The correspondingly modest requirements upon the concept of set are: to know when and how to exhibit specific sets; and to know how to calculate with sets—how to pass from premises about them to warranted conclusions. The first demand might be called *quasi-ostentation;* it is flunked by almost all expositors, however distinguished.

Cantor's Explanation

Georg Cantor's famous formula (1895) does sound like a recipe for quasi-ostentation: "By a 'set' we understand any assembly (*Zusammenfassung*) into a whole *M* of definite and well-distinguished objects *m* of our perception (*Anschauung*) or thought."[6] Later, Cantor remarks: "Every set of well-distinguished things can be regarded *as a unified thing in itself (für sich)*, in which those things are components or constitutive elements."[7]

A hundred textbook writers have thought Cantor's formula sufficiently illuminating to be echoed, sometimes with a side

[6] *Gesammelte Abhandlungen* (Hildesheim, 1962), p. 282, my translation.
[7] Page 379, emphasis in original.

remark about its not counting as a genuine definition. The following version is characteristic: "As a description of the idea [of a set] it is enough to say: A set is a collection of well-defined objects thought of as a whole."[8] Is it enough?

Let us strip Cantor's formula of its inessentials. The reference to "objects of our *perception* or *thought*" is otiose. (To translate *"Anschauung"* as "intuition" rather than as "perception" will not help.) Suppose some "objects" really exist; then that suffices to make them eligible elements of a set. Whether we perceive them, think about them, name them, or describe them, has nothing to do with their capacity to generate authentic sets. Sets are not thought or designated into existence. (Cantor was a "realist," with reservations: he thought that mathematical entities have "transeunt" reality, although they can be introduced into mathematical inquiry only through adequate symbolization.) So we can simply expunge the references to perception and thought in Cantor's formula.

The reference to "definite" and "well-distinguished" objects does have a serious point, however: Cantor wants to recognize as elements of a set only sharply demarcated objects (numbers, but not clouds), subject to sharp criteria of identity and difference (men but not electrons). Allen's epithet "well-defined," in the passage quoted above, sufficiently captures Cantor's intentions.

So Cantor's formula, stripped to essentials, runs quite simply: "A set is an assembly into a whole of (well-defined) objects." Here, the phrase, "assembly into a whole," certainly suggests that something is *to be done* to the elements, in order for the "whole" or "the unified thing" which *is* the set to result. But *what* is to be done, if not merely thinking about, the set? And what difference can thought make to distinct objects?

What kind of unification is in point? Tell a child to take three pennies and make a "whole" out of them; what is he supposed to do, and how shall we tell him what to do?

[8] R. G. D. Allen, *Basic Mathematics* (London, 1962), p. 88.

The supposed assembly or collection prerequisite to the emergence of a set cannot involve any physical manipulation, if only because the elements may be abstract entities, such as numbers. A typical dictionary definition of "collection" is "a group of objects or an amount of material accumulated in one location, especially for some purpose or as a result of some process."[9] Consider, then, the set composed of the Hapsburgs and the resurrection that would be needed to bring *them* into "one location."

Quine (who is far from being a Laputan) says: "Sets are classes. The notion of class is so fundamental to thought that we cannot hope to define it in more fundamental terms. We can say that a class is any aggregate, any collection, any combination of objects of any sort; if this helps, well and good. But even this will be less help than hindrance when we keep clearly in mind that the aggregating or collecting or combining here is to connote no actual displacement of the objects."[10]

That is to say, a set may be regarded, "if this helps," as a collection of things that are not collected—or an aggregate of things that are not aggregated, a combination of things that are not combined. I do not think this "helps." This way of talking is no better, and no more intelligible, than defining a Pickwickian omelet as what results from breaking and cooking eggs, even though no eggs are broken or cooked. In fact, sets are in a worse case, since it would be a conceptual blunder to think that the physical proximity of objects had *anything at all* to do with their constituting a set.

If talk about "assembling" or "unifying" is irredeemably figurative, what literal sense, if any, lurks behind it?

Some philosophers—Husserl, for one—have thought that the problematic assembly and unification of objects into a set could be accomplished by some peculiar act of the mind. And textbook writers, for want of anything better, sometimes yield

---

[9] *Random House Dictionary of the English Language* (New York, 1966).
[10] *Set Theory and Its Logic* (Cambridge, Mass., 1963).

to the same seduction. "A set is the *mental construct* obtained by regarding several discrete things as constituting a single whole. Forming a set is thus a *mental act:* the human mind arbitrarily brings together certain things and regards the collection itself as a new kind of thing. This new thing is an artificial entity, in the sense that the unity lies entirely in the concept and not in the things themselves."[11]

So "the human mind" can annihilate space and time in an extraordinarily productive way. Apparently, it succeeds in "arbitrarily bringing together" entities, such as 7, 11, and 13, say, which remain *three* distinct and separate numbers, in order to produce *one* thing of "a new kind." How is this feat accomplished? We are left wholly in the dark as to what this new thing might be. We could, of course, add the numbers together and get 31, or multiply them and get 1001, but that is certainly not intended. But so long as no sense has been supplied for "assembling" or "collecting," the expression "assembling *in thought*" is a *flatus vocis:* what makes no sense in reality, the mysterious conversion of several things into one, makes no sense "in thought" either.

Given all this, there seems hardly any point in adding that appeal to the generative powers of "thought" would make mathematics a branch of psychology, and would limit the stock of sets to the finite number of "mental acts" exercised in "creating" them. Or can the mind go in for wholesale creation?

Russell, after considering at length the question "Is a class which has many terms to be regarded as itself one or many?" has nothing better to say by way of an answer than: "[there is] an ultimate distinction between a class as many and a class as one, [so that we must] hold that the many are only many, and are not also one. The class as one may be identified with the whole composed of the terms of the class, i.e., in the case of men, the class as one will be the human race."[12] When in per-

---

[11] W. L. Schaaf, *Basic Concepts of Elementary Mathematics* (New York, 1960), p. 11.

[12] *Principles of Mathematics*, 2d ed. (London, 1937), p. 76.

plexity, invoke an "ultimate distinction." Isn't this an example of what Berkeley called the "darkness and confusion of mathematics"?

The truth is that once the elements of a set have been identified, *nothing* need or can be done to produce the corresponding set. (The "numerical conjunction" of which Russell once spoke, the bringing together of objects by means of "and" is a mere chimera.[13]) A quadrilateral is sometimes regarded as a set of four lines; but once I have drawn four mutually intersecting lines in a plane, no more needs to be done in order to produce the quadrilateral. It would be ridiculous to require in addition some—no doubt immaterial—curve encircling the quadrilateral.

Yet the picture behind all this talk about assembling, gathering, and collecting is indeed that of tying things in a bundle—that famous "unity" composed of its "elements." But it is essential for this picture's effect that the string be of that kind—useful for doing in thought what cannot be done in reality—that is invisible and intangible. The "line" around the elements must be as "imaginary" as the equator.

In the thought of those who follow Cantor, the notion of "assembly" or "collection" is treated in a figurative way that voids it of application by stretching it to absurdity. (One is reminded of the celebrated Euclidean "definition" of a point as something having position but no magnitude—a body so small that it doesn't exist at all.) If so, Cantor's formula is useless: it cannot begin to help somebody to understand what a set is. The learner asks for clarification, but receives obfuscation.

If the notion of "collection," as unified assembly without displacement, is mysterious, how much more so are the notions of "collecting" a single thing to produce *another* entity (the corresponding unit-set) and collecting nothing at all to produce a unique object (the "null set"). From the standpoint of Cantor's formula, this is mystification on stilts.

[13] *Ibid.,* pp. 57, 67.

Sets as Abstract Entities

The apparently insuperable difficulties in regarding sets as collections, in Cantor's style, are responsible for such remarks as the following:

A class in an abstract entity, a universal, even if it happens to be a class of concrete things. . . . Indeed, there is no call even to distinguish attributes from classes, unless it is on this one technical score: classes are identified when they coincide in point of members, whereas it may be held that attributes sometimes differ though they are attributes of just the same things.[14]

Sets as ordinarily understood, are what philosophers call universals.[15]

Classes (or sets) may be viewed as properties of a special kind. . . . On this view there corresponds to each property f a special property called the *extension of f* or *the class defined by f*.[16]

Such uses of "universal" and "property" are careless at best: a man is not properly called an *instance* or a *case of* the class of men; and it would be ungrammatical to say that a man had the property of *the class of men*. But the grammatical solecisms can perhaps be patched up: behind them, there is an imposing alternative to the "collection" view which merits close examination.

Frege, to take the ablest of the sets-as-abstract-entities theorists, conceives of what would nowadays be called a set as the "extension" of *a concept* (or, as we might say, of a property or attribute). This approach would make a set a feature of something itself abstract, a property. And the way is then open to recognize that properties having no instances, or only single instances, have extensions *in the same sense* in which all properties do. So now "set" must be taken to be short for "set con-

[14] W. V. Quine, in P. Schilpp, ed., *The Philosophy of Alfred North Whitehead* (Evanston, Ill., 1941), p. 147.

[15] A. A. Fraenkel and Y. Bar-Hillel, *Foundations of Set Theory* (Amsterdam, 1958), p. 333.

[16] R. Feys and F. B. Fitch, *Dictionary of Symbols of Mathematical Logic* (Amsterdam, 1969), p. 13.

nected with a certain property, of which it is the extension";
and where there is no such property there can be no question
of a corresponding set.

The term "extension" suggests something like the reach, or
scope, or incidence of the corresponding property. Which now
makes sense of that perplexing notion of "assembly": what,
figuratively speaking, "assembles" the members of the extension
is just their *having* the associated property. And that is why the
"assembly" is of the peculiar sort that in no way changes the
things "assembled." To locate the members of a set is the very
same thing as giving a necessary and sufficient condition for
membership in the set, i.e., formulating a suitable property
having the extension in question.

Those who invite us to consider a set as a property "of a
special kind" (as in the above quotation from Feys and Fitch,
for example) sometimes have the following conception in mind:
Consider a case where a number of properties, $P_1, P_2, P_3, \ldots$,
are "coextensional," i.e., apply to the very same objects a,
$b, \ldots, k$, so that these objects, and no others, all have each
of the properties P_i. Then, conceive of the same objects as all
having some *more abstract property*, say Q, by virtue of which
they and they alone also have each of the properties P_i. Q is to
be considered as the sophisticated replacement for the crude
notion of the "collection" composed of $a, b, \ldots, k$.

The following might serve as an analogy. A number of material bodies might have in common such properties as *acquiring the same acceleration under equal impressed forces, bal-
ancing the same bodies in scales,* and so on. Now these
observable properties, shared in common by the bodies, are
commonly ascribed to the joint possession of a more abstract,
theoretical property, that of *having a certain mass.* Similarly, in
the more general case, the "more abstract" property, Q (or "the
extension" of any of the P_i), is to be construed as a certain
property, coextensive with each of the P_i, but not identical with
any of them. On this view, a formula of the form $a \, \varepsilon \, Q$ is just another way of writing the more familiar formula $Q(a)$; and "is

a member of" is just a somewhat unhappy way of saying "has" or, "has the property of."

But then, what is Q? One might be tempted to identify it with the disjunction $P_1 \vee P_2 \vee P_3 \vee \ldots$ of all the P's, except that we are not told yet how to complete the disjunction, i.e., how to eliminate the terminal dots.

A more natural answer would run somewhat like: *the property of being just the "members" in question and no others.* In symbols: $Q(x) . = .x = a \vee x = b \vee \ldots$ But this conception will satisfy only those willing to accept identity with a given object $(x = a)$ as an intelligible "property." (And it will break down, of course, for infinite sets.)

Suppose one of the P's is the property of being a prime number $(Px = x$ has no factors except 1 and $x)$. Then the Q-property would presumably have to be identified by some such phrase as: "the property of being just *those things that are prime numbers.*" But here, the italicized phrase is just an example of ordinary language's primitive way of designating a set. This becomes clear if we try to symbolize the supposed definition of Q as:

$$Qx = x \, \varepsilon \, \hat{x} \, (Px)$$

in which the role of Q is that of $\varepsilon \, \hat{x} \, (Px)$. So it looks as if our conception of Q presupposes our prior possession of the concept of a set. In any case, the suggested conception of the Q-property will fail for null-extensions: the form of words "the property of being just those things and no others" reduces to vacuity when "those things" are *no* things at all.

Sets as Arising from Equivalence Relations Between Properties

Frege thought he could by-pass these difficulties by applying a technique for "introducing abstract entities" already familiar in geometry and elsewhere.

Consider the problem of defining a "direction" in geometry.[17]

---

[17] *Foundations of Arithmetic,* tr. by J. L. Austin (New York, 1960), secs. 64–67.

The relation of parallelism between lines (say Pxy), assumed to be given, is plainly reflexive, symmetrical, and transitive. Therefore, the set of all straight lines can be split, by reference to P, into a set of mutually exclusive subsets, each composed of mutually parallel lines. With the idea at the back of our minds of eventually identifying "directions" with the subsets previously mentioned, we can begin to explain the notion of "direction" by introducing Dx (= "x is a direction") by the formula

$$Dx = Dy . \equiv . Pxy \qquad (1)$$

That is to say, we count lines as having the same direction if and only if they are parallel.

Now if this procedure is respectable, as it certainly is, why should we not similarly hope to "introduce" the "abstract property" Q by the analogous formula

$$Q(X) = Q(Y) . \equiv . (u)(Xu \equiv Yu) \qquad (2)$$

where X and Y now stand for properties, whose coextensionality plays a role like that of parallelism between lines in (1)?

But Frege is clear about the limitations of such a formula as (1), which provides a means of translating identities between "directions" into intelligible assertions of parallelisms. For (1) does not yet tell us what a direction *is*, does not say whether a direction is to be regarded as a privileged line, some property of lines or, perhaps, if we want to be fanciful, even some number or other. We know, from (1), the necessary and sufficient conditions for directions to be identical, but everything else about directions is left completely open.

This lack of definition of a notion such as direction is easily overcome in geometry by taking a given direction as the *class* or *set* of all lines parallel with a selected line, *e:*

$$D(e) = \hat{x}(Pxe)$$

But this presupposes that the notion of a class or set is already available, and obviously fails for our attempt to introduce Q

by an abstractive definition. The analogue there would be to say that the extension of a given property, *P*, is the *class* or *set* of all properties coextensional with *P*. As an explanation of "extension" this is clearly circular, since "class," on the view here under discussion, is a mere synonym for "extension."[18]

How did Frege cope with this problem, in his crowning masterpiece, the great *Grundgesetze?* The crucial context is that in which he tries to pass from assertions of coextensionality [in modern notation, $(x)\ (P_1 x = P_2 x)$] to the admission of certain associated *objects*, which we may regard as "extensions." (Frege actually speaks of *"Werthverläufe"* or "courses of values," that is to say, something like a class of pairs of ordered entities corresponding to a given function, the first member of each pair being a value of the independent variable and the second the corresponding value of the function. But this difference between an "extension" and a "course of values" is unimportant for the present discussion.)

Frege's defense of this procedure, which is an essential step in his attempt to reduce arithmetic to logic, consists of the following two assertions: (i) the step from the *equivalence* of a certain sort of a "logical principle" *(ein logisches Grundgesetz)*,[19] indeed one that mathematicians and logicians have in fact universally accepted in talking about "classes," "sets," "multiplicities," and the like (II, 148). For instance, the whole of the Leibniz-Boole calculus of classes depends upon it (I, 14). (ii) This step from properties to certain associated objects, their extensions, is indispensable, in order to define integers in such a way that generalization over integers and so the assertion of arithmetical *laws* is to be possible. (Any attempt to construe extensions as "improper objects" [*uneigentliche Gegenstände*] and their purported names as mere "apparent names" [*Scheineigennamen*], Frege rejects for this reason [II, 255].)

---

[18] Cf. Charles D. Parsons in Max Black, ed., *Philosophy in America* (Ithaca, N.Y.: Cornell University Press, 1965), pp. 184–185.
[19] *Grundgesetze,* 2 vols. (Hildesheim, 1962), II, 147.

What this amounts to is that we need extensions, in order to construe arithmetic as Frege wishes (as a series of analytical principles) ; and that, in any case, their existence is, in fact, generally accepted. So far as I know, this is the only place where Frege ever rests his case upon the authority of established practice. Both of these reasons, as Frege later came to see, are swept aside by Russell's discovery that unrestricted assignment of extensions to predicates results in contradictions.

Of course, Frege had no illusions about what he was doing in introducing extensions as objects. With his unremitting hostility to so-called "creative definitions," he was (unlike Weyl) armored against supposing that the mere introduction of new signs can somehow conjure entities into existence. He is at pains to point this out in connection with his own acceptance of extensions (II, 147) and, indeed, makes it perfectly clear that extensions in his system are *not* defined, since they are introduced only by means of identities in which extension signs stand on both sides. (He tries to remedy the lack of reference thus produced by stipulating the truth-values of certain combinations into which extensions enter, but that is a matter we need not pursue here.)

If we think of the situation quite naively, allowing ourselves to use the term "set" as if we really understood it, we might say that the abstraction procedure that purports to lead us from equivalent properties to certain abstract entities, leaves much that we need to know still unspecified. If P_1 and P_2 are held to have *something* in common by virtue of the fact that they apply to exactly the same objects, we might think of that common feature, indifferently, as the set of all properties equivalent to P_1 (or, of course, to P_2, which would come to the same thing), as the disjunction of P_1 and all properties equivalent to P_1, as some *second-order* property of all the properties equivalent to P_1, and so on indefinitely. Without a supplementary determination of the meaning of "set" or some synonym thereof, we are unable to choose between these alternatives and are left in the dark as to what extensions are really intended to be. Whatever emerges will be so unlike what laymen, and mathematicians too, think of as "sets" that it might be advisable to have some different technical label to mark the difference—say "the theory of extensions" or even "the theory of functional spreads."

The formula "a set is something shared in common by co-extensive properties" is somewhat better than "a set is anything you like." But this formula still leaves the concept of a set much darker than that of a number. If *that* is what a set really is, it would be hard to see how beginners could learn what it is "from their own experience"—or, indeed, learn it at·all. Getting the idea of "coextensive properties" across would be hard enough. But suppose the teacher managed to produce two such properties, P_1 and P_2; consider the difficulty of com-municating the notion of "something that P_1 and P_2 have in common" to which the teacher (no wiser surely than Frege) *can attach no firm sense*. Would it be a *stupid* child who asked, "What do P_1 and P_2 have in common?" (Is it fair to feed caviar to the young—and to pretend that it is breakfast food?)

Sets in Ordinary Language

We are not forced to choose between thinking of sets as mysterious aggregations of distinct things into "unified" wholes and thinking of them as unknown things shared in common by certain coextensive properties. For, in ordinary languages, we do manage to identify sets and reason about them, without the inconveniences of a superfluous mythology. If we can become sufficiently clear about how we *talk* about sets, we shall have all the clarity about "the concept of set" that we need for a start.

It is easy to forget while wrestling with the mystifying ex-planations that master logicians have offered, that the word "set" *does* belong to ordinary language. If the word is used so naturally in such expressions as "my set of chessmen" or "that set of books," the task of exhibiting the underlying rules of use should not be insuperably difficult. Let us then consider how we manage to talk about *several things at once*.

Plural reference. The most obvious ways of referring to a single thing are by using a name or a definite description: "Aristotle" or "the president of the United States." Equally familiar, although strangely overlooked by logicians and philosophers, are devices for referring to several things *together:* "Berkeley and Hume" or "the brothers of Napoleon." Here, *lists* of names (usually, but not necessarily, coupled by occurrences of "and") and what might be called "plural descriptions" (phrases of the form "the-so-and-so's" in certain uses) play something like the same role that names and singular descriptions do. Just as "Nixon" identifies *one* man for attention in the context of some statement, the list "Johnson and Kennedy" identifies two men at once, in a context in which something is considered that involves both of them at once. And just as "the president of the United States" succeeds in identifying one man by description, so the phrase "the American presidents since Lincoln" succeeds in identifying several, in a way that allows something to be said that involves all of them at once.

The notion of "reference" here invoked is only a slight sophistication of an ordinary language concept. In ordinary life, the question "To whom are you referring?" is usually in place only when there is some *prima facie* possibility of doubt as to the person in question. (The question "To whom were you referring when you said 'Aristotle' just now?" would be met with a blank stare.) But suppressing this pragmatic condition gives us just what we need: E is about P if and only if the proposition in which E is being used attributes something to P. We can here ignore the difficulties in making this kind of formula sufficiently accurate to cope with some obvious objections. What we are talking about is sufficiently perspicuous at the level of intelligibility that we are aiming at.

The notion of "plural" or simultaneous reference to several things at once is really not at all mysterious. Just as I can point to a single thing, I can point to two things at once—using two hands, if necessary; pointing to two things at once need be no more perplexing than touching two things at once. Of course, it would be a mistake to think that the rules for "multiple pointing" follow automatically from the rules for pointing proper; but the requisite conventions are almost too obvious to need specification. The rules for "plural reference" are no harder to elaborate.

A rough test of the occurrence of a singular referring expression is provided by considerations of identity. If I say, referentially, "The president of the United States is a Republican" and if the president is Ford, then my assertion is true if and only if Ford is a Republican. (If I *think* that Ford is a Republican, I must consider myself committed to the second statement when I make the first.) A similar test involving identity will certify plural expressions as occurring with genuinely multiple reference. If I say, referentially, "All Napoleon's brothers were Corsicans" and if Napoleon's brothers were Tom, Dick, and Harry, then my original statement is true if and only if Tom, Dick, and Harry were Corsicans. (If I think the multiple identity is true, I must consider myself committed to the second statement if I make the first one.)

The main point of using "plural referring expressions," such as lists and plural descriptions, is obvious enough. It is typically to permit concise statements about several things at once. A further important benefit in using plural descriptive phrases is that of being able to talk about several things at once, in cases where the precise identity of the things in question is unknown or irrelevant. Consider, for instance, the announcement "All arriving passengers proceed to customs." The announcer, in this case, does not know and need not care *who* the arriving passengers are, but his announcement is intended to refer to all of them. This second use, but not the first, parallels an obvious advantage in using singular definite descriptions.

In an elaborated description of the rules governing the uses of plural referring expressions, we might find it convenient to speak about their *identity conditions, membership conditions,* and *retrieval conditions.* The first kind of condition determines when two plural referring expressions count as referring to the same things and are then mutually substitutable *salva veritate;* the second kind of condition (a special case of the first) determines *which* things are referred to by a given plural referring expression. Roughly speaking, both types of condition reduce identities involving plural referring expressions (names or definite descriptions). The detailed specification of conditions of these types (which are within the competence of all users of ordinary language) would be tedious, but not difficult. More interesting are the routes by which we can—at least in principle—eliminate plural referring expressions from certain basic statement-contexts in which they occur. In trivial cases ("perfect distribution"), assertions about plural subjects, identified by lists or plural descriptions, are immediately convertible into conjunctions of separate statements about each of them; in the typical and more interesting cases ("imperfect distribution"), the original predicates also need transformation, in ways not readily reducible to simple formulas. (Cf. "Tom and Harry were young" with "Most of the Beatles were ready to part company.")

Suppose that π is some plural referring expression, occurring in the context $f(\pi)$ and referring there simultaneously to the objects, $a_1, a_2, \ldots, a_n$. Then, in order to understand $f(\pi)$, I must know the *retrieval conditions* for referential descent, for the use of π in this context. That is to say, I must know how to pass from the assertion f to the assertions g_i that are explicitly about the a's. (To take a fairly awkward case: In order to understand "His brothers are two in number" I must be able to pass from that assertion to "Tom (say) is one of his brothers, and Dick is another, and that is all of them.") Anybody who has sufficient mastery of the retrieval conditions for certain plural referring expressions, and of the identity conditions for those expressions already has *some* mastery of the concept of a set. But so far there has been no need to introduce "the general notion of a set." Let us consider how that word is used.

One primitive use of the word "set" is as a stand-in for plural referring expressions of the kinds discussed above. If I say "A certain set of men are running for office" and am asked to be more specific, then I might say "To wit, Tom, Dick, and Harry"—or, in the absence of knowledge of their names, I might abide by my original assertion. One might therefore regard the *word* "set," in its most basic use, as an indefinite surrogate for lists and plural descriptions. To know how to use the word "set" correctly at this level is just to know the linguistic connections between such uses of "set" and the uses of more definite multiply-referring devices.

Ostensibly Singular Plural Referring Expressions

It is a peculiarity of English and many other languages to admit collective expressions such as "the Hungarian Quartet" and "the Cabinet" which are allowed to behave, at least part of the time, as if they were singular names or descriptions. (And this fact is perhaps one of the main sources of the inclination to regard a set as some peculiar entity constituted by, but not identical with, its elements.) This ambivalent role of such expressions is betrayed in the absence of firm rules for their grammatical "number"—thus Fowler says that an expression like "the Cabinet" can be indifferently followed by a verb in the singular or the corresponding plural.

Expressions that look superficially like singular descriptions but really serve to refer to several things at once can fit quite comfortably into our program. The role previously played by "plural identities" (of the form "the P's are $a_1, a_2, a_3, \ldots, a_n$") is now taken over by statements of the form "the G *is composed of $a_1, a_2, \ldots, a_n$*" (where "the G" is now an ostensibly singular referring expression). What was said earlier about the need for "identity conditions" and "retrieval conditions" still applies. We must, for instance, know when we should identify, say, the Cabinet and the Smith brothers; and how, in principle at least, we should proceed from statements about the Cabinet to statements about Tom, Dick, and Harry, if they are, indeed, all the members of the Cabinet.

It is not at all clear that we need "ostensibly singular referring expressions," or that we would be seriously inconvenienced by their absence. (It is worth recalling that we have regular ways for converting them into overtly plural referring expressions, as when we pass from "the Cabinet" to "the members of the Cabinet." The losses of nuances of meaning that result from such transformations are not irreparable.)

Sets of sets in ordinary language. Set talk (the use of plural referring expressions) is especially convenient when we cannot or need not identify the corresponding memberships—as when we are interested only in the number of members and in nothing more. But these and other considerations that give talk about sets its rationale can also lead naturally to forming lists of sets (second-order lists). If a number of committees are to be formed from a certain group of men, and each committee is to have a separate secretary or a separate meeting place, we shall be interested only in the number of the sets or their diverse memberships. And then there will naturally emerge lists in which plural referring expressions follow one another ("the finance committee, the membership committee, and the rules committee"). Hence, also, we might find it useful to introduce second-order expressions such as "the set of committees." (Or we might raise such a question as "How many different committees could we form from this set of men?") I do not think this interesting and undoubtedly useful extension of primitive set talk offers any serious obstacles for our program (although the step is certainly of crucial importance). We need only be sure that we have at our disposal adequate devices for connecting such "second-order" discourse with the lower level discourse already discussed, by means of "retrieval conditions." In short, we need to know how we could, if necessary, convert the more abstract talk about "sets of sets" into assertions about sets *simpliciter* (sets composed of persons or other things that are not sets) .

The way is now open for mathematicians to introduce sets of sets of sets, and so on. The necessary restriction upon this kind of reiteration in order to prevent inconsistency and paradox do not concern us here. Nor are we at present interested in ticklish questions about "existence axioms" for sets or the "richness" of the requisite ontology.

Of course, any transition from colloquial set talk to the idealized and sophisticated notion of making sense of a "null set" and of a "unit set" (regarded as distinct from its sole member) will cause trouble. From the standpoint of ordinary usage, such sets can hardly be regarded as anything else than convenient fictions (like the zero exponent in x^0) useful for rounding off and simplifying a mathematical set theory. But they represent a significant extension of ordinary use; and nothing but muddle will result from ignoring this point.

A Retrospect and Some Objections

The program here recommended, for building the idealized set talk of mathematicians upon the rough but serviceable uses in ordinary language of "plural referring expressions" has the merit of being pedagogically feasible. Beginners, who will be already competent to handle plural referring expressions—though, of course, not under that title—can be readily shown the connections between the uses of such expressions, the uses of "ostensibly singular expressions," and the intended use of the more abstract word, "set." Collective terms such as "herd," or "team," or "orchestra," etc. have the sense of *a number of things* (animals, persons, etc.) *such that so-and-so*. We need only drop the such-that clause, and the specific information it conveys, to get the abstract notion of a set as *a number of things considered together* (Cf. the French name for a set, *ensemble*) or *several things referred to at once*. This is the nearest we need to approach a formal definition and if it helps to elucidate the technical notion—as I think it does—that will suffice. (We shall, of course, eschew mystifying formulas about "assembly" and "unification.") And difficulties presented by the null set and by unit sets will have to be faced head-on, in full recognition of the sophisticated conceptual maneuver involved. (Whether it is wise to introduce mathematical dodges at the very outset of an introduction to mathematics need not be discussed here.)

Now it may be objected that, at best, what is here being advocated is a theory of sets as collections or aggregates and not—as would be desirable—of sets as certain "abstract entities." To which the following replies may be made: (1) Mathematicians do in fact think of sets as collections and the heuristic utility of the notion of a set depends upon their so thinking. (2) There seems no ready way of connecting sets as "abstract entities" with ordinary language or informal thought. If set theory is to be identified with the theory of *such* entities, then beginners will, in fact, be taught something else and there is risk of a fraud being perpetrated upon them. (3) Nobody knows what the supposedly "abstract entities" are intended to be (as I have argued earlier in this essay) so it is not an exaggeration to say that the intended "theory" has no firm or intelligible subject matter.

Escaping from Mythology?

Now the questions that invite a mythology of sets can perhaps be side-stepped.

(1) "Is a set a thing 'in its own right'?" "Well, it is clearly nonsensical to identify "Tom, Dick, and Harry" with either Tom, or Dick, or Harry, or anyone else. And if that is what is meant by saying that a set is a thing in its own right, I can agree."

(2) "But what *kind of a thing* is a set?" "This is a question that deserves another. What sort of answer do you want? I might reply uninformatively that a set—is a set. But that wouldn't satisfy you. But why should there be *any* answer?

(Call a set *sui generis* if that helps—but it really shouldn't) ."

(3) "What is it that 'unites' the elements of a set into the set?" "Nothing at all. Nothing happens to Tom, Dick, and Harry, when you refer to them all at once as 'Tom, Dick, and Harry.' But you *can* refer to them *at the same time,* in the context of a *single* statement."

(4) "But then does the set exist?" "Well, if this is the question whether Tom, Dick, and Harry exist, the answer is, of course, Yes—and similarly for other cases. But what more do you want?"

(5) "But are all the sets waiting to be discovered, like stars before the astronomers see them? Or do they come into existence when one of your 'plural referring expressions' is used? And what about sets that never have been and never will be thus identified? An unseen star is a star for all that—but is an unidentified 'set,' on your conception, *anything* at all?" "You presuppose an obfuscating analogy. Comparing sets with stars is as helpful as comparing mustard with four o'clock. (Constellations would have been another story.) Were the lines of longitude 'waiting to be discovered' before we talked about them? Set talk is a verbal pattern projected on the universe, and set boundaries are as 'real' or 'imaginary' as territorial boundaries. But statements *in* set talk may be as true as those of cartography. And isn't that enough?"

The foregoing sketch, crude as it may be, perhaps sufficiently illustrates how we might envisage the introduction of sets (or rather, the introduction of set talk) without recourse to mystifying explanations that neither explain nor illuminate. Would it not be enough if we could *talk* in full awareness "about sets"? Do we need to know anything more? Is there anything more to be known?[20]

[20] I am indebted to Georg Henrik von Wright for some useful comments on an earlier version of this paper.

VI

Meaning and Intention

> If you think that saying is different from the twitter of fledglings,
> can you prove a distinction, or is there no distinction?
>
> —*Chuang-Tzu*

My object in this essay is to consider the way in which Paul Grice, in an influential paper, has in effect answered Chuang-Tzu's question by an appeal to a speaker's intentions.[1] Grice's paper and his subsequent reply to his critics raise fundamental questions about the analysis of meaning that still await satisfactory resolution.

Like other philosophers of language, Grice is aiming, eventually, at a clarification of the concept of meaning in all its ramifications. By starting with an analysis of what a particular speaker means in a particular situation, he hopes in the sequel to explain what words mean "in general" in a given language

---

[1] H. P. Grice, "Meaning," *Philosophical Review*, 64 (1957), 377–388, and "Utterer's Meaning and Intentions," *Philosophical Review*, 78 (1969), 147–177 (a reply to criticisms). See also his more technical paper, "Utterer's Meaning, Sentence-Meaning and Word-Meaning," *Foundations of Language*, 4 (1968), 225–242.

The following are among the more illuminating discussions of Grice's position: P. F. Strawson, "Intention and Convention in Speech Acts," *Philosophical Review*, 73 (1964), 439–460; John Searle, "What Is a Speech Act?" in Max Black, ed., *Philosophy in America* (Ithaca, N.Y., 1965); Paul Ziff, "On H. P. Grice's Account of Meaning," *Analysis*, 28 (1967), 1–8; T. E. Patton and D. W. Stampe, "The Rudiments of Meaning: On Ziff on Grice," *Foundations of Language*, 5 (1969), 2–16; N. L. Wilson, "Grice on Meaning: The Ultimate Counter-Example," *Nous*, 4 (1970), 295–302.

Many commentators regard Grice as basically correct in his approach, while proposing minor modifications. See, for instance, D. M. Armstrong, "Meaning and Communication," *Philosophical Review*, 80 (1971), 427–447.

or idiolect. At stake, accordingly, is not a mere puzzle about a concept of relatively limited application, but rather the foundations of an ambitious program for clarifying some fundamental features of the manifold phenomena that we subsume, all too summarily, under the rubrics of speech and language.[2]

Emphasis upon intention as an explanatory notion in this type of theory is consonant with some widespread tendencies in recent Anglo-American philosophy, that might be regarded as attempts to recover and refine the insights of continental idealism, by marking a sharp distinction between human *action* and mere animal behavior, and consequently by recognizing a basic opposition in method between the *Geisteswissenschaften* and the natural sciences.[3] The chief enemy of an intentionalist theory of meaning, as it might conveniently be called, is any *causal* theory, such as that of Charles Morris or Charles Stevenson, which typically tries to give a "naturalistic" or behavioristic account of meaning.[4] I shall not be able in this paper to discuss the wider questions behind the controversy over Grice's discussions of "speaker's meaning." My purpose in presenting the largely destructive criticism that follows is not primarily that of convicting Grice of error, which would be easy enough, considering the complexity and difficulties of the topic, but rather to offer some general considerations why any theory of meaning of the intentionalist type must suffer from serious and probably irredeemable embarrassments.

The questions to be discussed may at first seem somewhat

[2] For a statement of Grice's general program, see the 1957 paper, p. 381. A more elaborated account will be found in Grice's 1969 paper, section A.

[3] See, in this connection, the important book by Georg Henrik von Wright, *Explanation and Understanding* (Ithaca, N.Y., 1971), in which this return to the *Geisteswissenschaften* receives sophisticated and precise expression.

[4] Charles Morris, *Signs, Language, and Behavior* (Englewood Cliffs, N.J., 1946), and Charles Stevenson, *Ethics and Language* (New Haven, Conn., 1944). See also Grice's brief rejection of Stevenson's views in the 1957 paper, pp. 379–381.

remote from the concerns of a literary critic or any other interpreter of difficult texts. But even the most "practical" reader relies upon some background theory, however inexplicit or incoherent. It would be optimistic to suppose that lack of clarity about the foundations of philosophical semantics could have no inimical influence upon the interpretation of literature.

Signification and Speaker's Meaning

Let us begin, with Grice, by an attempt to distinguish the interpretation of signs from the grasp of what somebody *says*. (Like Grice, I shall find it convenient throughout to use "say" to cover the utterance of gestures, or other nonverbal symbols, as well as words.) Consider:

(1) The twittering of the fledglings *meant* that they were hungry.

(2) When I said (1), I *meant* that the fledglings were hungry.

It is obvious enough that the verb *to mean* is used in different ways in these two sentences. For one thing, what was asserted as meant by the fledglings' twittering, in (1), was a certain state of affairs, their being hungry, and if that state of affairs did not in fact obtain, the assertion was false; while the assertion expressed by (2) would remain true even if the fledglings were not hungry. The verb "meant" takes different kinds of objects in the two cases.[5]

In order to mark the distinction, let us say that (1) refers to a case of *signification*. The twittering of the fledglings might be called a *sign*, and the fact signified by it, if there is such a fact, its *signification*. On the other hand, I propose to say that (2) refers to a case of *speaker's meaning*,[6] dropping the qualifi-

---

[5] In the 1957 paper (p. 377), Grice offers four additional differentiating features.

[6] In his 1957 paper, Grice dubs the distinction as one between "natural" and "nonnatural" meaning. I find this somewhat misleading, since a sign can be artificial and so, in one familiar sense, "nonnatural." Again, spon-

cation, when no ambiguity results. The (speaker's) meaning of a certain utterance consists in what the speaker meant by the words or gestures that he used on a particular occasion, and must be carefully distinguished from the *lexical meaning,* as I propose to say, that those words have in the language to which they belong.[7] I shall not be dealing with "lexical meaning" in what follows.

The Questions to Be Considered

Given this initial rough contrast between two uses of "mean," Grice proceeds to ask: "What more can be said about the distinction between the cases in which we should say that the word [i.e., "means"] is applied in a natural sense and the cases where we should say that the word is applied in a non-natural sense?"[8] Or, in the terminology I have adopted, "what more" can be said about the distinction between signification and speaker's meaning?

But what does Grice mean by "what more"? He has already supplied a number of criteria for distinguishing signification from speaker's meaning, and it would be easy enough to find further syntactical or semantical differentiae. No doubt, he has his eye on something more interesting, something like the "essential difference" between the two modes of meaning; but "essential difference" is a notoriously confused conception.

We may guess that Grice, like almost all philosophers who have written about meaning, has been provoked by some philosophical perplexity, that might be roughly expressed as "How shall we 'place' meaning, as contrasted with signification?" or, more simply, "What kind of a thing is 'speaker's meaning'?" So conceived, the search is for an illuminating sketch of the "logical grammar" of the two terms, some indications that will help us to understand the philosophically interesting ways in

---

taneous gestures, conforming to no convention, can be "natural" expressions of a speaker's meaning.

[7] For further relevant distinctions, see Grice's 1969 paper.

[8] Grice (1957), p. 379.

which their uses differ. From which it follows that an acceptable answer must employ terms that are less perplexing than "meaning" itself. It would be unhelpful, for instance, to be told, what is no doubt true, that the speaker's meaning is what a suitable hearer would *understand*. For "understand," as thus used, is as much in need of explication as the original explicandum. We shall, therefore, need to consider carefully whether "intention," which is a key term in Grice's analysis, meets this test of relative perspicuity.

A second task, arising naturally from the first, is what Grice calls the "elucid[ation] of the meaning of '*x* meant something on a particular occasion'."[9] Indeed, this is what he addresses himself to in most of his paper. There remains also the interesting question as to *what* a given speaker means by a given utterance. All three questions are to be answered, on Gricean principles, by invoking intentions. That a speaker is saying *something* is to be explained by his having a certain complex intention; *what* he says will be explained by a specific feature of the content of the intention. Grice has so far supplied no more than a sketch of the answer to the third question.[10]

Let us call these three questions, for short, *the distinctiveness question,* the *question of meaningfulness,* and the *question of meaningful content.* They can be roughly expressed as follows:

(i) What distinguishes speaker's meaning from signification?

(ii) What is necessary and sufficient for some sound or gesture produced by a speaker to express something that he means?

(iii) When a speaker *does* mean something on a particular occasion, how is what he means to be identified?

Following Grice's own procedure, I shall, for the present, consider only the second of these, the "question of meaningfulness."

[9] *Ibid.,* p. 381.
[10] See his "first shot" at an answer in paragraph (3) of p. 385 of his 1957 paper, and the further elucidations that he then supplies.

Grice's Theory of Meaningfulness

The basic idea in Grice's approach is that S (a certain speaker) means something by U (a certain utterance) on a particular occasion only if S intends U to produce a certain complex effect upon a given hearer H.[11] A distinctive and stimulating feature of his view is the overall purpose of subsuming under a single analytical formula *all* uses of language, including the utterance of imperatives, interrogatives, optatives, and so on, whose different meanings would be manifested in the different kinds of "effect" intended to be produced in a suitable hearer. Thus, in his first version, where Grice is considering the centrally important case in which the speaker's utterance has a truth-value, the primary intended effect is a belief. The first approximation to an analysis is accordingly:

(3) S means something by U only if he intends thereby to induce H to think that something is the case.[12]

Thus, if I say to you, "It has begun to snow," what I say is meaningful, on this view, because I intend you to treat what you hear as a reason for thinking something, *viz.*, that it *has* begun to snow.

The presence in (3) of "only if," rather than "if and only if" is inescapable, as simple counterexamples will show. Suppose I place some wet galoshes where you can see them later, hoping that you will treat the sight of them as a reason for thinking that it has begun to snow again. One must agree with Grice that in placing the galoshes I was not "telling" you something, not trying to communicate with you—especially so in case I wanted you *not to recognize the intention I had*.[13] So, in

---

[11] Grice prefers to speak of an "audience."

[12] In the 1957 article, Grice used the formula, "was intended by its utterer to induce a *belief* in some 'audience'" (p. 382, italics added). Like Grice, in his later article, I prefer "think" to "believe." Grice makes it plain in both places that the occurrence of U must be treated by H as a *reason* for the induced thought: cases in which U merely causes a thought, without acting as a reason, are to be excluded.

[13] Grice has more striking examples in his 1957 paper.

general: I can produce sign-situations that you will treat as a reason for belief, and intend you to do so, while not wishing you to know what I was up to.

An obvious way out of this difficulty is to modify formula (3) by the additional stipulation that the hearer shall be intended not merely to *recognize* the primary speaker's intention, but also to use such recognition as a reason for thinking what he was intended to think. So we get the following modified analysis:

S means something by U if and only if he intends (i) that H shall think something, (ii) that H shall recognize that first intention, and (iii) that H shall treat such recognition as a reason for conforming to the first intention.

Let us call this, for easy reference, *The Formula.*

It should be noted, for future reference, that *what H* is intended to think, according to clause (i), is taken to be identical with S's meaning.

This ingenious analysis, as Grice shows, is able to handle most examples of communication that come readily to mind. I shall now argue, however, that the conditions expressed in *The Formula* are neither sufficient nor necessary for the presence of a "speaker's meaning." Eventually, I shall also argue that these deficiencies cannot be remedied by *ad hoc* adjustments.

I shall proceed by offering counterexamples (i) of episodes in which an agent is not "saying something" even though he meets Grice's conditions (proof of insufficiency) and (ii) of episodes in which a speaker does say something although he fails to satisfy Grice's conditions (proof of nonnecessity).

Grice's Conditions Insufficient

The case of the handshake.[14] Suppose I offer somebody my hand: then I normally intend the other to think that I am well disposed toward him, or at any rate that I am not hostile.

---

[14] This type of case has not, so far as I can tell, been discussed in the literature, which is otherwise replete with counterexamples.

I plainly have no wish to conceal this intention, nor could I easily do so, in a face-to-face situation. Furthermore, it seems clear that I wish the other person to treat his recognition of my intention as a reason for thinking that I am well disposed. All three conditions of *The Formula* have therefore been met; yet it would seem far-fetched to maintain that in offering to shake somebody's hand, I am *telling* him something or saying something having a truth-value and so, perhaps, even lying. Of course, some information passes with the handshake, but that is another story.

If this case seems unconvincing, consider another in which I offer somebody a gift, perhaps in order to express appreciation. There, too, all three conditions of *The Formula* are satisfied, yet it would be stretching facts to fit a theory to claim that I must be communicating with, saying something to, the recipient.[15] Or consider any case involving cooperation between two or more persons. If I need your help in order to raise a log of wood, then in raising my end without saying anything or even looking at you, I may intend you to think that I want you to raise the other end, intend you to recognize my first intention, and so on. But here, too, it seems far-fetched to hold that my raising the log constitutes a *communication*.

The case of the hoodwinked eavesdropper.[16] *A* is talking to *B* at a cocktail party and knows that *C* can overhear the conversation, while having reason to think that *A* is unaware that his eavesdropping has been detected. So, *A* says to *B:* "I

[15] I have found that social psychologists and sociologists tend to resist this judgment, because they have become increasingly impressed by the "symbolic" aspects of social interaction. It should be noted that I am not denying that offers of a handshake or a gift *signify* something: the point at issue is whether such acts are to count as clear cases of "saying" something. To use "communication," as social scientists like to do nowadays, to cover any case in which actions are significant seems to me to blur an important distinction. Actions may "speak louder than words"—but they do not really *speak* at all.

[16] Suggested by an example used by Strawson, *op. cit.,* p. 447. For Grice's response to this type of case, see his 1969 paper, pp. 154–159.

would like *C* to know that his students detest him and I wish I had the courage to tell him so." Then, *A* wants[17] *C* (i) to think that his students detest him, (ii) to recognize that first intention, and (iii) to treat that recognition as a reason for thinking that he *is* detested by his students. So, all of Grice's conditions are met. Yet it is plain that *A* is not *talking to C*— is not, in Grice's sense, communicating *with him.*

Strawson's proposal for dealing with this type of case is to postulate yet another intention on the hearer's part. For the maneuver that I have described obviously counts upon *C,* the real target of *A*'s performance, remaining ignorant of what *A* was really up to. *C* cannot be hoodwinked unless *A*'s ulterior intention is concealed from him. Now by postulating a further "intention," *viz.,* that *A* should intend *C* to know, roughly speaking, everything that *A* intended to achieve by his remark to *B,* we can avoid the embarrassment of implying that the speaker is really communicating with the hoodwinked eavesdropper.

Grice, like Strawson, accepts this modification but is troubled, like him, by the possibility that more complicated cases might demand the postulation of still more complex intentions on the speaker's part.[18] I shall show (see the *Appendix* to this essay) that Grice's fears are well-founded, because a recursive procedure can be given for producing situations which, on

[17] Here, I have substituted "wants" for "intend," which is desirable on other grounds, and does not materially affect Grice's analysis, except to allow it to deal with some cases which it would otherwise fail to cover.

[18] "[I]t looks as if the definitional expansion of "By uttering *x U* meant something" might have to vary from case to case, depending upon such things as the nature of the intended response, the circumstances in which the attempt to elicit the response is made, and the intelligence of the utterer and of the audience. It is dubious whether such variation can be acceptable" (Grice [1969], p. 159) . It would, indeed, be odd if the correct analysis of a speaker's meaning something required such a range of variation with special circumstances. A recursive definition of meaningfulness would require this range to be captured in a single formula, but it is hard to see how this could be accomplished. (For Grice's way with this difficulty, see below.)

Grice's analysis, would require the transmission of an indefinitely large number of supplementary intentions. Take any number, *n*, however large: then, if I am not mistaken, a situation can be described in which, on Grice's view, *S* would need to frame, and his hearer, *H*, to receive, *n* intentions. (For details, see the *Appendix*.) When a theory implies such complications, its credentials become suspect. It is hard to stomach the idea that speaker's meaning may have so intricate a structure.

Grice's Conditions Not Necessary

The embarrassments of soliloquy.[19] A man may outline a lecture, or write a note to remind himself of an appointment, or simply utter certain words, such as "What a lovely day!" in the absence of an audience. In such cases, it is quite certain that the speaker or writer does mean something by his utterance, yet the absence of a well-defined audience is an embarrassment for Grice's position. I suppose that a defender of the intentionalist type of analysis might accommodate the second of these examples by claiming that the note-maker was trying to communicate with his later self. But this maneuver, whether plausible or not, will not serve in cases of pure soliloquy. It would, for instance, be the height of absurdity to claim that when a man says, "I must go to that meeting," he is intending to provide himself with a reason for keeping the appointment.

The trouble revealed in such simple counterexamples is rooted in the manifold uses of speech.[20] If one insists that *all*

---

[19] For Grice's comments on this type of counterexample, see his 1969 paper, sec. V, pp. 174–177. Grice's idea is that, in the absence of a face-to-face audience, the utterer should intend effects that would be produced if a suitable audience *were* to be or *should* come to be present.

[20] The point has been well made by Noam Chomsky: "Though considerations of intended effects avoids some problems, it will at best provide an analysis of successful communication, but not of meaning or of the use of language, which need not involve communication, or even the attempt to communicate. If I use language to express or clarify my thoughts,

such uses shall be understood on the basis of a model of face-to-face communication, I suppose it would be necessary to think of cases of soliloquy as derivative uses, involving reference to a potential, hypothetical, or fictitious "audience." A man speaking to himself, perhaps in order to express and clarify some thought, would then be behaving *as if* he were talking to another. This kind of account might fit the case of a player playing solitaire chess, *as if* he were seeking to outwit some fictitious opponent, and might well apply to the case of a solitary "dialogue" carried on with an imaginary interlocutor, whether by way of rehearsal or for the sake of developing an idea. But it will not fit all the cases I have cited.

The case of the silenced candidate. A candidate at an oral Ph.D. examination, on being asked for the date of the Battle of Hastings, retorts that he is unable to answer. "In order to tell you, I should have to want you to think that the Battle occurred in 1066. Now, I have too much respect for my examiners to think that they don't already know the answer. It would be absurd for me to *get* you to think what you know already; and hence impossible for me, as a good Gricean, to mean what you would expect me to mean by my answer!"

A way out of this difficulty might be to argue that the examiners do not wish to *know* the date of the battle, but rather wish the candidate to *demonstrate* his own knowledge, so that their "question" is really only a polite way of formulating the request *"Tell* us the date."[21] But in complying with the request, the candidate would still need to mean something by his answer, indeed precisely that the Battle did occur in 1066. And how, on Gricean principles, can he do that?

---

with the intent to deceive, to avoid an embarrassing silence, or in a dozen other ways, my words have a strict meaning and I can very well mean what I say, but the fullest understanding of what I intend my audience (if any) to believe or do might give little or no indication of the meaning of my discourse" (*Problems of Knowledge and Freedom* [New York, 1971], p. 19).

[21] This, roughly speaking, is the line followed by Grice in his discussion of this kind of difficulty, in his 1969 paper, pp. 166–167.

The case of the truthful liar. A man who has a reputation for being an habitual and incorrigible liar is asked, say by a Congressional committee, the question "Are you a communist?" If he lies, according to habit and desire, by saying "Yes," he knows in advance that his audience will take his answer as a reason for thinking that he is *not* a communist, which is indeed the case. Knowing this, the only effect he can intend in the audience is the reverse of what he intends—and hence he will be telling the truth, willy-nilly![22] Another way of looking at the situation is that what the liar must, on Gricean principles, mean by his "Yes" is "No," since this is the inevitable and predictable content of the belief to be induced in the audience.[23]

Grice's Way Out

Grice's way of coping with such counterexamples, and the many others that have been advanced by his critics, is both curious and instructive. The strategy is as follows. Grice is committed to the view that S means something by an utterance, U, if and only if S *intend*s a certain complex effect, say E_1, to be induced in his hearer, H. An ingenious critic now produces an imaginary instance, in which either (i) a *prima facie* act of successful communication occurs, although the effect on H is not E_1, but something else, E_2; or, (ii) the effect E_1 does occur without there being, *prima facie*, a case of successful *communication* between S and H. (Such examples discredit,

---

[22] It reminds one of the old Yiddish joke about a man who, on being asked where he is going, says he is on his way to Minsk. "You say you are going to Minsk because you know that I, knowing what a liar you are, will think that you are going to Pinsk, while all the while you really are going to Minsk. What a liar you are!"

[23] Cf. the counterexample due to Searle (*op. cit.*) and discussed by Grice in his 1969 paper (pp. 160–165) in which a soldier wishes to produce in his Italian captors the belief that he is a German, by reciting a scrap of German verse that he learned in school. Here, the intended effect is that the captors shall believe that the speaker is a German officer, but the prisoner does not use the line of verse to *mean* that he is a German officer.

respectively, claims of necessity and sufficiency for Grice's conditions.) Grice replies in one of three ways. He may deny that the putative case of communication or noncommunication is genuine, so that the alleged counterexample is not really an exception to *The Formula*. Or, in case (i), granting that communication does occur in the absence of the stipulated effect, E_1, he modifies the original analysis by adding, as a further disjunct, the new-found effect, E_2. Thus, the form of the analysis becomes "intends to produce in H either E_1 or E_2, according to circumstances." Finally, in case (ii), Grice seeks some further effect, say F_1, which disqualifies the case in question as one of genuine communication. Thus, the form of the analysis becomes "intends to produce, in H, E_1 but not F_1, or E_2 but not F_2 (and so on), according to circumstances."

Modifications of these types will always be able to dispose of proposed exceptions to the analysis, by adding suitable negative conjuncts, or suitable positive disjuncts, at the cost of progressively increasing the complexity of *The Formula*.[24]

This defensive strategy is both indefinitely pliable and incorrigibly rigid: rigid in its tenacious adherence to the intention-to-produce-in-the-hearer-certain-effects; pliable in its capacity to redescribe no matter whatever happens in consequence of an act of communication as a case of the speaker's *intending* to produce that effect. The choice of "intention" as a central explanatory term serves this defense admirably. For "intend" can be plausibly elaborated as "intend to bring it about that p," where "p" is a place-holder for some desired state-of-affairs. Now a speech-act, like any social intervention, will have *some* consequences, which can always be brought

[24] *The Formula*, in its original form, consisted of a single sentence. Grice's final "redefinition" (pp. 175–176 of the 1969 paper) occupies an entire page, including a good deal of logical machinery and such subsidiary notions as "substituted," "correlation," and "inference-element." It is hard to believe that a notion as familiar as "speaker's meaning" can really call for such Byzantine elaboration. As Einstein is supposed to have said: "Raffiniert is wohl der Herr Gott, aber böse ist er doch nicht" (The Lord God may be subtle, but still he is not malicious).

under the rubric of a certain desired state-of-affairs, p. Thus it will always be possible to attach the intention operator to the p in question and thereby to ascribe to the agent a corresponding intention. But as soon as one perceives how mechanical the adjustment is, one begins to wonder whether anything more is achieved than the invocation of a fictitious intention, that is bound to fit the refractory exceptions.

Consider the following analogue. A philosopher wishes to "explicate" what qualifies a move of chess as a genuine *move,* say that of a pawn, as distinguished from the mere shifting of a piece of wood by somebody ignorant of the game. His first try is to propose that the action counts as a *move,* if and only if intended to prevent the opposing King from moving to a certain square, i.e., intended to produce a certain effect E_1. When it is pointed out that occurrence of the invoked effect is neither necessary nor sufficient, the analyst replies by adding disjuncts or conjuncts in the manner already explained above, thereby accommodating the indefinitely many consequences that a pawn move might have in an actual game. This way of trying to explain *"really* moving" in terms of the *consequences* of a chess move would amount to nothing better than a ritual invocation of the player's "intention." In a particular chess situation, the player who moves may differentially intend one result rather than another, and may or may not succeed in this. In such cases the attribution to him of a specific intention has empirical content, however difficult it may be to confirm its truth. But to say *in general* that a player must intend whatever consequences result, according to the rules of the game and in view of the given situation, amounts to little more than saying that he moves *with intention,* i.e., as a deliberate *player,* and not without knowing what he is doing. But the specification of his intention is not independently possible, without reference to the rules of the game, and the attendant contextual circumstances that constitute his action as a *move.* "He intended, necessarily, the chess consequences" is roughly equivalent to "He *moved"* and has no explanatory power.

It is worth emphasizing that, in this analogue, the specification of the supposed defining effects necessarily uses chess language ("the King," "prevented," and so on). So the overall purpose of the analysis, which is that of explaining chess terms by means of psychological notions, is not achieved. In order to explain that the effects of the move in question concern a *King,* or the opponent's *moves,* we should be required, either to use chess language, or to attempt a further psychological reduction. For how else are we to explain such a phrase as "to prevent the Black King from *moving"?* It is a case of the explanation itself needing explanation. Now it is interesting to observe that Grice gets into just this kind of difficulty. In setting up his defense against counterexamples, he finds it incumbent to pass from what I previously called "the meaningfulness question" to the "question of meaningful content," and then to deal with the latter by a reference to "modes of correlation."

This modification of *The Formula,*[25] which is motivated by an attempt to meet Searle's discussion of the Captured Prisoner case (see note 23), is hard to follow. Searle in effect argues that the captive must intend his "audience" to think that the scrap of German uttered has the standard meaning of "I am a German officer." But since overt reference to meaning would run the risk of generating circularity, Searle's preferred formulation is "the sentence uttered is conventionally used to produce such an effect." That is to say, the hearer is intended, *inter alia,* to think that the utterance type is *conventionally* used to produce the *entire* effect postulated by the Gricean type of analysis. But this still looks potentially circular. Grice accepts Searle's emendation, with the reservation that it excludes cases in which the "correspondence" between the utterance used and its meaning is not conventional but perhaps "iconic, associative" and so on.[26] In the absence of further explanation, I fail to have a

---

[25] For which see the 1969 paper, pp. 160–163.
[26] *Ibid.,* foot of page 163.

clear conception of what Grice means by an associative or iconic correlation between an utterance and its intended meaning or use. But it seems clear enough that, if anything, his extended use of "correlation" does not reduce the chances of circularity. (I shall deal with the circularity of Grice's account in a later section.) It looks as if "correlation" is a thin disguise for signification or meaning. If so, semantical terms creep back into the analysis, after all.

On being faced with such, almost unmanageable, elaborations of the original *Formula,* one is reminded of the man who claimed that he was dead, retorting to his friends' demonstration that he bled on being pricked by saying "That only shows that dead men can bleed." The elaborated version of *The Formula* begins to look like some system of epicycles, infinitely adaptable, but showing less about the ostensible object of analysis than about the ingenuity of its creator.[27]

A defender of Grice might retort that such general objections are inconclusive, since the technique of progressive modification to accommodate apparent exceptions has respectable analogues in the sciences, and that whatever merit there may be in an injunction not to multiply putative intentions beyond necessity, the notion of speaker's meaning may, in spite of initial appearances, really be complicated enough to require nothing simpler than Grice's apparatus. What remains to be done, then, if possible, is to demonstrate the basic error of principle in Grice's approach—or, more generally, in any intentionalist theory.

I shall proceed, accordingly, in the next two sections, to consider the deficiencies of each of the two distinctive features

[27] There is an interesting analogue in the fate of the "Principle of Verifiability," which once raised high hopes of expressing an acceptable and simple criterion of empirical meaning. The staggering number of qualifications and reservations eventually necessitated by counterexamples has for most philosophers rendered the Principle uninteresting. If the Principle has not been formally refuted, which would hardly be feasible, given the revisionary resourcefulness of its defenders, it has at least "faded away."

of Grice's analysis—his appeal to the standard effects produced in a hearer, and his reliance upon the speaker's intention to produce such effects.

The Semantically Relevant Effects of an Utterance

In order for an intentionalist analysis of speaker's meaning to have a definite content, it is essential that the intended effect upon the hearer or audience be specified. Given that any particular utterance will normally induce a variety of effects on a hearer, including comprehension or incomprehension, perception of assumptions and implications, together with emotional or cognitive responses to the speaker's tone, attitude and so on, it is essential to mark off what I propose to call the "semantically relevant effect," i.e., the effect that is, on intentionalist principles, both necessary and sufficient in order for the message in question (what the speaker is primarily *saying*) to be successfully communicated.

In the original version of *The Formula,* Grice stipulated that, when the utterance is informative, the hearer's intended response should consist of a corresponding belief. Thus, if the speaker says and means "It is snowing," his hearer is, in the first instance, intended to *believe* that it is snowing. The reader may be reminded at this point that the hearer is also intended to recognize that first intention, to treat that recognition as a reason for complying with the primary intention and so on. But for present purposes, these further complications can be neglected. My doubts concerning the correctness of this type of analysis already arise in connection with the hearer's supposed response to the basic or primary intention.

In the revised version, "believe" was replaced by "think" or even, in some circumstances, by "be reminded," and so on. To take care of such complications, we might say that the primary intention is that the hearer shall be led to have some *propositional attitude* or other, i.e., that he shall "believe that" such-and-such, or "think that," or "be reminded that," or "be led to wonder whether" such-and-such. If the analysis is to be definite, some designated propositional attitude will, of course, need to be selected. The following criticisms, however, will be independent of any such choice of a propositional attitude.

When the utterance is not indicative but, say, imperative, as when the speaker says "Shut the window," the relevant hearer's response was originally stipulated to be that of performing the action in question and, in the later revision, taken to be the hearer's *intention* to perform. Thus the primary intention of the utterance "Shut the window" would, on this view, be the intention that the hearer shall be led to *intend* to shut the window.

In evaluating these proposals, it will be helpful to use a distinction introduced by the late John Austin between the "illocutionary" and the "perlocutionary" force of a speech act.[28] *In* saying, for instance, "I will be there," the speaker may be making a promise; while, *by* making that promise he may arouse gratitude in the promise's receiver. The illocutionary force of the utterance is what makes it a promise and not some other speech-act; but the consequential effect upon the speaker or another, while it may be the practical point of making the promise, counts only as its "perlocutionary force," and does not belong to what the promise-maker is *primarily* doing.

Let us, accordingly, speak of the (intended) illocutionary effect, upon Gricean principles, of an utterance, in order to contrast it with its (irrelevant) perlocutionary effects. A successful speaker induces in a suitable hearer, on Grice's analysis, an illocutionary effect, the arousal of a certain propositional attitude if the utterance is indicative, or the induction of an intention to perform some designated act, if the utterance is imperative. Unless such an illocutionary effect occurs, the speaker will not have succeeded in communicating his meaning; but whether further, "perlocutionary" effects supervene

[28] See references to "Illocution" and "Perlocution" in the index of J. L. Austin, *How to Do Things with Words,* J. O. Urmson, ed. (Oxford, 1962).

is of no importance for the analysis, whatever practical importance they may have in an actual speech-situation. (The consequent "perlocutionary" effects are, in my terminology, semantically irrelevant.)

Now is it an illocutionary effect, in the case of a successful communication of the thought expressed by "It is snowing now" (to revert to the indicative case, again), that the speaker shall *think* that it is snowing, as Grice proposes? In order to be clear about this, we may as well consider whether the intention that the hearer shall think this (or, for that matter, have any other propositional attitude to the proposition that it is now snowing) can be realized without the realization of some logically prior intention. The answer is clear enough: the hearer cannot think that snow is falling unless he *understands* the speaker to be asserting that fact. Correct understanding, clearly an illocutionary effect in successful communication, has logical priority inasmuch as its absence prevents the generation of an appropriate propositional attitude "on the basis of the utterance," i.e., by using the meaning of the utterance as a partial reason for the belief in question. But suppose the hearer does understand, and fails to believe or think the thought in question, possibly because he distrusts the particular speaker in question, or because he thinks he must be joking, or for some other reason. Should we then say that the speaker's meaning has not been communicated? Surely not. If the speaker's meaning has been understood, communication has occurred, whatever more, by way of a propositional attitude, may or may not be induced in the hearer. A liar or an unreliable informant is understood, no less than somebody whose word the audience trusts. Thus, it looks as if belief on the hearer's part, or, for that matter, the induction in him of any propositional attitude whatever, is "perlocutionary," something of practical importance but irrelevant to a philosophical analysis of the notion of communication, or of the derived notion of speaker's meaning.

Mutatis mutandis, the same can be said about the imperative

case. If I understand a request to shut the door, I have done all
that can be, in the first place, required of me as a competent
partner in the speech-act in question. Whether I am then
obliging enough to perform the requested act, or at least to
form the intention to comply, is semantically irrelevant. When
I have understood the request, my part as a hearer and interpreter is ended. Incidentally, a third party, who has no call to
perform or to form the intention to perform, can, for this
reason, understand the imperative utterance, the request, just
as well as the man to whom it is addressed.

In the light of these considerations, it would seem that *The
Formula* ought to be amended to specify the speaker's primary
intention as that of inducing corresponding *understanding* on
the hearer's part. But this is useless for the purpose of a philosophical analysis. For "understanding," which may be paraphrased as "grasping (or receiving) the speaker's meaning,"
is as much in need of philosophical elucidation as speaker's
meaning itself. Hearer's understanding and speaker's meaning
are two sides of a single speech-transaction: to explain one in
terms of the other would be as futile as to define "husband"
by means of "wife."

This objection, if I am not mistaken, discredits any intentionalist theory committed to explaining speaker's meaning in
terms of some separable and independently identifiable hearer's
response, or the intention to produce such a response. For, in
the sense intended, there is no standard response, no regular
and semantically relevant effect of an utterance, except its
being understood. That, however, is not even a response, in
the sense of a specifiable event or state: there is no distinctive
and unique criterion for understanding a communication.

Puzzles about the Speaker's Intentions

A philosophical analysis or "explication" of meaning has
the ultimate aim of dispelling the initial mysteries and obscuri-
ties that surround the explicandum. This can be achieved only
if the key terms of the analysis are genuinely clearer than the

problematic point of departure. In the case of Grice's analysis, with its crucial reliance upon the speaker's "intention," we can reasonably make the following three demands: (1) that the postulated intentions shall be genuinely discernible in the situations in which they are invoked; (2) that the notion of "intention" shall be less in need of philosophical clarification than the explicandum, "meaning," itself; (3) in order to avoid circularity, that the required sense of "intention" shall not depend upon "meaning" for its analysis. I shall now apply these tests to Grice's position.

Can we literally, and without the introduction of fictions, recognize the presence in standard cases of successful communication of the speaker's "primary intention," and, beyond that, of the second-order and higher-order intentions needed by Grice? Can we, for instance, agree with Grice, that when a speaker, S, seriously says to a hearer, H, "It is snowing now," $(= U)$, he *intends* H to think that it is snowing, and also intends H to recognize that S intends him to think that, and so forth, through the whole set of dependent intentions?

An unwary reader might suppose Grice to be postulating the occurrence in S of some prior and distinguishable act of intending H's response to U. But Grice is careful to disclaim this unplausible contention, saying explicitly that he "disclaim[s] any intention of peopling all our talking life with armies of complicated psychological occurrences."[29] One must agree, of course, that cases of "explicitly formulated linguistic (of quasi-linguistic) intentions are no doubt comparatively rare."[30] So, in the normal case, there can be no question of the speaker himself, or anybody else, discovering, by introspection, or in some other less direct way, the occurrence of some independent act, describable as "S's intending H to think that it is snowing etc." How then are we to know that such an intention is actually present? Grice replies that "An utterer is held to

---

[29] The 1957 paper, p. 386.
[30] *Ibid.*, p. 387.

intend to convey what is normally conveyed (or intended to be conveyed)."[31] This sounds suspiciously circular, since it amounts to saying that S will count as intending to mean what the words he uses would normally mean, a move that is clearly out of order in a theory that ultimately hopes to explicate standard or "timeless" meaning by reference to speakers' meaning in particular speech-acts. Furthermore, Grice's reply will not serve for cases in which the speaker is using some idiosyncratic utterance, with a meaning peculiar to himself, or a case in which he uses some standard form of words in a special sense. Let us therefore try to improve Grice's formulation as follows:

> When S utters U, he knows, or has good reason to think, that H will be led, on the basis of hearing U, to think that it is snowing (and to think that H wanted him to think that, because S uttered U, etc.). Hence, since "we are presumed to intend the normal consequences of our actions,"[32] S does intend the expected responses of H.

Nothing less complex than this will serve, once we have agreed with Grice that reference to a speaker's intentions cannot in general be a reference to some distinctive psychological event, preceding or accompanying the actual utterance. No doubt an ordinary speaker who knows what the expected consequences of his utterance are likely to be will accept responsibility for such consequences; but then such acceptance of responsibility will be the viable content of the attribution to him of a corresponding intention. (An attempt to treat H's response as an *inference* to the best explanation of S's utterance will not do, since it must suppose H to be able to *detect* such an intention in clear cases.) Notice that our specification of the "expected consequence," in H, in the revised formula proposed above, involves a reference to H's intention. The expected response is that H will think that S wanted or intended him to think that it was snowing. So the reference to the speaker's intention has not yet been eliminated, nor is it clear how it could

[31] *Ibid.*
[32] *Ibid.*

be. One can hardly help concluding that the analysis is enmeshed in circularity, by seeking to explicate the speaker's meaning in terms of the speaker's intention and that in turn, as we have now seen, in terms of the hearer's expected detection of that same intention. (It is as if we were to seek to locate a mirror image by reflecting it in another mirror.)

The reason for this predicament is not hard to perceive. A suitably competent hearer detects what S meant by U, by understanding $U;$ only then does he treat his reading of U as, in normal cases, a sufficient condition for ascribing to H the corresponding intention. Cases do occur in which the interpretation proceeds in the opposite direction, as when we encounter, perhaps in some foreign land, a person making apparently meaningful but as yet unintelligible gestures, and are led to wonder what his intention is, and only then use our answer to that question to infer what he means. But such encounters are too atypical to serve as a basis of a general theory of meaning.

I conclude, therefore, that Grice's theory fails all but the second and third of the tests that I formulated at the outset of this section. The relevant sense of "intend" is no more intelligible than the notion of speaker's meaning it is supposed to elucidate, because it includes as a component the original notion of meaning. Given this circularity, the presence of intention in acts of communication is indeed assured, but only tautologically, as following from the definition of speaker's intentions in terms of his meaning and not vice versa.

The Hidden Circularity of Grice's Approach

I shall now try to show that Grice's way of looking at cases of successful communication, through its appeal to intention, involves either circularity or an infinite regress. I shall be concerned here especially with a point that Grice does not discuss, *viz.*, how, on the principles of *The Formula*, the hearer can be expected to *detect* the speaker's meaning.

Let us start with a primitive case in which Grice's account of what transpires in successful communication proves to be adequate. While in India, I am approached by a beggar who opens and shuts his mouth repeatedly, while pointing to what he is doing and looking pleadingly at me. Here, I would correctly infer (i) that the beggar wants me to think that he is hungry, and (ii) wants me to do something about that, no doubt by giving him alms. (I shall ignore the pedantic question as to whether the beggar is to be taken as making an indicative or an imperative utterance.) Here, we might reasonably say that the inference from the "utterance," treated as a sign or indicator of some intention on the part of the "speaker," uses as a true premise the proposition, "He would not do what he is doing unless he wanted me to think that he is hungry," the observed gestures being thereby treated as a sufficient basis for the conclusion. From this inferential basis, I, as hearer, arrive at two related conclusions: that the speaker intends me to think that he is hungry and—what comes in this case, to almost the same thing —that he means by his gesture that he is hungry. There is clearly no need, nor, in general, any possibility, for me *first* to decipher the "message" of the gestures and only subsequently to treat my interpretation as a further basis for ascription of the corresponding speaker's intention. The reason, of course, is that the gestures used are "natural," and not based upon conventions. There is no background rule for translating such gestures. When a foreign interlocutor, however, produces some conventional gesture, as say the Italian one of drawing the hand meaningfully across the throat, understanding the gesture is likely to have logical priority over discovering the intention of which it is the expression.

Now contrast both cases with one in which the speaker uses a conventional form of words. *S* says to *H*, for instance, "Es schneet jetzt," thereby intending, on Grice's principles, that *H* should recognize that he intends him to think that it is now snowing. Let us also assume *H* to know so little German that he needs to think carefully in order to understand the German sentence used by *S*. Here, *H* could treat *S*'s behavior as a sign and hence, as an inference-basis for concluding that he meant *something or other*. For in inferring this much, he need rely only upon the knowledge he has of the "natural" signs that show somebody to be trying to communicate. But the case is altered when we try to apply *The Formula* to determine the *content* of the communication.

In order for our postulated H to "recognize" S's primary intention, he must somehow receive the *message,* the communication, *H wants me to think that it is snowing now.* Let us spell out this more complex message, in S's native language, as "Ich wünsche dass Sie glauben dass es schneet jetzt," and let us call "Es schneet jetzt" (the words actually used by S), the *kernel* of the message and its verbal context, its *hull*. Now, this entire message must somehow be communicated to H, not by way of some flash of ineffable intuition, but via the interpretation of signs or words. I have already agreed that the perception of the meaning of the "hull" raises no problems for Grice, since it can be based upon inference from the speaker's behavior; but how is the kernel, whose meaning is required for correct reception of the message, to be understood? In order for H to understand that, he must understand the very words, "Es schneet jetzt," which constituted the original message. Thus, recourse to the speaker's primary intention cannot supply H with the information he needs in order to "read" that intention. The only way in which the full intention can be communicated is in terms of an amplified message containing the original message as a kernel; so if the meaning of the kernel itself is in dispute, the procedure leads nowhere.[33]

---

[33] There is an important moral hereabouts for readers and literary critics. However useful the search for the intention behind a literary text, its only outcome can be another *text,* since the only intentions available for consideration are verbally realized ones. Now the author's own commentary, or a supplementary text supplied by the critic, may materially illuminate an obscure text. But it is clear that recourse to intention cannot in general serve as the method for establishing meaning. At some point, if we are not to be hopelessly entangled in circularity or an infinite regress, meaning will need to be ascertained in some other way than by reference to a background intention.

We might put the matter in this way: On Grice's principles, detection of the speaker's meaning requires transmission to the speaker of an amplified communication (or "message") of which the original message is a component part (its "kernel"). Now, understanding the amplified communication will either demand, as a prior condition, understanding the original message, which involves the speaker in hopeless circularity; or, the same maneuver, repeated in order to amplify the amplification, leads to a still more complex message, containing the kernel within another kernel, and so to an infinite regress.

The points I have been making in this section are obviously connected with my earlier contention that the relevant "illocutionary effect" or proximate point of a communication is its being *understood* by the hearer. In the present section, I have been arguing that, at least in situations sufficiently complex to necessitate the use of words, unless the explicit message is understood, the implied and inexplicit background of the speaker's intentions cannot be captured either. In general, Grice's view puts the semantic cart in front of the horse: it is not perception of the speaker's intention to produce certain desired effects in the speaker that allows a hearer to determine the meaning of what is being said, but, vice versa, detection of the speaker's meaning enables a suitably competent hearer, assisted by previous experience, and by interpretation of the given sign produced in the course of this speech-transaction, to infer the speaker's intention. In standard and unproblematic cases, where we are not dealing with some transposed form of speech such as irony, or a case of deception, the relevant speaker's intention is *constituted* by the meaning of what he says. As any writer can testify, the case of "How do I know what I mean until I hear what I say" is more common than the old joke would suggest.

The Unintended Object of Grice's Analysis

If the objections raised in this paper are sound, we may conclude not only that Grice's proposed analysis of speaker's meaning is defective, but also that there is no foreseeable hope of repairing its weaknesses, so long as it continues to rely upon the invocation of speaker's intention. This, I have argued, can only lead to circularity or an infinite regress, which can be masked, but not ultimately remedied, by the method of introducing qualifying clauses in response to the exhibition of counterexamples. The defects in the intentionalist approach are too radical to be cured by piecemeal tinkering, however ingenious and resourceful.

Yet if this is so, it remains true that Grice must have been offering an analysis of *something*, if not, as he supposed, of speaker's meaning. What then, in effect, was he in fact doing? An answer to this question may help to set my objections in broader perspective.

In the special case of indicative utterance, i.e., the emission of some proposition having truth-value, we might say that Grice offers a more or less satisfactory account of the successful transmission of information. That is to say, of situations in which the speaker really does wish the hearer to learn something that is claimed to be the case, *and to believe it.* This might be called a case of "persuasion," in Aristotle's generalized use of that term in his rhetoric.

In the remaining nonindicative types of cases, in which, for example, the speaker issues a request, or asks a question, and so on, it may be said that Grice's formulas provide an approximation to what is involved in a (certain kind of) cooperation. I agree with Grice that when I want another person to open a window and convey that want to him by an intelligible request, I am trying to induce him to perceive my desire and to treat such perception as a reason for complying. Plainly, such induction of voluntary compliance with a communicated desire is of the essence of the kind of coordinated effort that we call cooperation. In order for such cooperation to be possible, information must pass between the two parties: I cannot freely assist you in achieving your purpose, unless I have some way of detecting what that purpose is; and in order to do so, I must either infer that from your behavior or, in any but the simplest

cases, be *told,* what you want me to do. Now, given that cooperation, in the sense in which I am using that term, demands
successful conveyance of intentions, it is not surprising that the
whole should be taken for the part, and that a more or less
adequate explication of cooperation should be mistaken for an
explication of meaning. But to do so is as misguided as it would
be to suppose that an analysis of what it is to be a bridge partner
should count as analyzing what it is to mean something by a
bridge signal.

If the point is well taken, we can also recognize a certain
merit in Grice's approach, that my animadversions have neglected. Whatever the defects of his account of the structure of
particular speech situations, his ruling conception of a link
between intention and meaning, and consequently of a logical
connection between "cooperation" and the transmission of information, has merit as an insight into the nature of the linguistic institution that partly constitutes the behavior of
individual persons as speakers and hearers. It is inconceivable
that the kind of behavior we call speaking and understanding
could exist unless there were primitive situations in which the
intent of the speaker was recognized as being that of inducing
beliefs in his interlocutor. But to suppose that this observation
authenticates the intentionalist analysis of particular speech-acts
would be to make a mistake like that of confusing rule utilitarianism with act utilitarianism. Serving the greatest happiness
of the greatest number might well be a purpose constitutive of
moral practices and institutions in general; it does not follow
that the moral justification of a particular action depends upon
its being directly conducive to the maximization of happiness.
The same can be said about particular speech-acts, conducted
within the framework and with the ultimate support of general
linguistic institutions, that structure and constitute the individual acts properly describable in terms of such frameworks.
Even though a constitutive purpose of language in general is to
foster and render possible desired acts of social cooperation, via
the transmission and adoption of intentions, that formula

neither applies to nor serves to illumniate perfectly standard and central cases of the transmission of meaning in particular settings.

Appendix: The Endless Chain of Speaker's Intentions

I shall try to describe a series of progressively more complex situations, in each of which I manage to transmit information to a "hearer" (or "audience"). I shall try to show that the number of speaker's intentions needed, on Gricean principles, in these transactions, has no upper bound.

Case 1. As the time for preparing the departmental budget approaches, I want the chairman (H) to think that I am hard up—but without telling him so. I therefore leave, where he is bound to see it, my latest bank statement (call it U_1), showing a disturbing overdraft prominently marked. Then, my primary intention in so doing (call it i_1) is that H shall treat my "utterance," i.e., the bank statement, as a reason for thinking that I am hard up. This is, of course, the type of case that led Grice to postulate the need for a supplementary intention, in order for genuine communication between myself and H to occur.

Case 2. I write a note, as to myself (using, say, a letterhead with my name on it), as a reminder that I intend to perform the operation described in Case 1. I leave this note, as if by accident, in a place where H is bound to see it. Call this note U_2. Then, in emitting U_2, I intend that H shall recognize that I intend U_1 to induce the thought that I am hard up. So now we have, in Case 2, a more complex intention, say i_2, specifiable as the intention that H shall, on the basis of U_2, perceive my intention, i_1 and, of course, shall treat both intentions as a reason for thinking what I want him to think. (Whether the perception of my deviousness will be conducive to my purpose, I shall not discuss. The effectiveness of this roundabout way of transmitting information is not here in question.) This case somewhat resembles that of the eavesdropper, previously discussed.

Case 3. This is like Case 2, except that my deceitful "reminder" describes the procedure carried out in Case 2. Thus U_3 is produced with the intention, i_3, that H shall use it as a basis for detecting i_2, and hence also i_1. In this case, I "blow the gaff" on the procedure described under Case 2, revealing the hidden motivation of the operation there described, but concealing my ulterior motive in uttering U_3, *viz.*, that H shall find it and be led to the reasoning already described.

Case n. I leave a "reminder" to be found by H, running as follows: *"Reminder:* I intend to leave U_{n-1} and thus to create the conditions for Case $n - 1$." Here the symbols are supposed to be replaced by full descriptions of the utterance and operation required in the previous case, n. By parity of reasoning, this case reveals to H the more complex intention, i_n, which "blows the gaff" upon i_{n-1}, and thereby leads H progressively through the chain of intentions to i_1.

If this recursive procedure is followed, we shall have, in a few moves, a "message" too complex to be understood without logical calculation. Its very complexity might then arouse suspicion and defeat the overall purpose. But this "pragmatic" reflection is irrelevant—unless we wish to amend *The Formula* by adding an additional condition that the postulated structure of progressively more complex intentions shall at least be capable of detection by the intended hearer. Such a stipulation, plausible as it might be, would, I suspect, wreak havoc with Grice's final analysis.

VII

The Nature of
Representation

Some Questions

There on the wall is a painting: it plainly shows some race-horse or other, with trees that might be beeches in the background and a stableboy doing something or other with a pail in the foreground. That the picture shows all these things, that all these things and more can be seen in the painting, is beyond doubt. But what *makes* that painting a picture of a horse, trees, and a man? More generally, what makes any "naturalistic" painting or photograph a representation of its subject? And how, if at all, does the situation change when we pass to such "conventional" representations as maps, diagrams, or models? To what extent do "convention" or "interpretation" help to constitute the relation between any representation and its subject?

These are the sorts of questions that I would like to consider (though not all of them in this essay), more in the hope of clarifying the questions themselves than in the hope of finding acceptable answers. For the main difficulties in the inquiry arise from lack of clarity in such words as "representation," "subject," and "convention" that spring naturally to mind and cannot be avoided without tiresome paraphrase.

Preliminary Qualms

Are questions as imprecise and confused as these worth raising? Or are they perhaps merely symptoms of the philosopher's itch to puzzle himself about what seems unproblematic to everybody else? Well, the itch is infectious, even to laymen. And the disconcerting thing, as we shall soon see, is that the most plausible answers that suggest themselves are open to grave and perhaps fatal objections. Yet even partial answers have consequences for such varied topics as perception, cognition, the structure of symbol systems, the relations between thought and feeling and the aesthetics of the visual arts. To understand the reasons for the excessive discord that questions about representation have produced would be sufficient reward for what threatens to be an arduous, even a somewhat tiresome, investigation. My aim will be not achieved unless I can offer a plausible explanation for the excessive amount of disagreement in the field.

Some Working Definitions

When a painting—or some other visual representation, such as a photograph—is a painting *of* something, *S*, I shall say that *P depicts S;* alternatively, that *P* stands in a *depicting relation* to *S*. There is, however, room for misunderstanding here.

Suppose *P* shows Washington crossing the Delaware. Then *P* is related to Washington's actual crossing of the Delaware, in 1776, in such a way that it can be judged to be a more or less faithful, or a more or less inaccurate, painting of that historical episode. I do not want to count that historical event as a special case of the subject, *S*, introduced in the last paragraph. Consider for contrast the case of another painting that shows Hitler crossing the Hudson in 1950: here there is no actual event to serve as a control of the painting's fidelity; yet we still want to say that the painting has a "subject" that is depicted by it.

Let us call Washington's crossing of the Delaware the *original scene* to which the painting refers; and for the sake of precision let us say that the painting does not merely depict that scene but rather *portrays* it. Then the painting of Hitler's imaginary river crossing will have no original scene to portray; but it may be said to *display* a certain subject. Thus portraying and displaying will count as special cases of depicting.

The displayed subject might be conceived of as the *content* of the visual representation.[1] I shall normally be concerned with depicting in the special sense of "displaying," and correspondingly with that "subject" of a painting that is its "content," not its "original scene." Where the context is suitable and no other indication is given, the reader may take "depict" and "display" henceforward as synonymous.

It should be borne in mind that I am not initially committed to there always being an irreducible difference between "subject" and "original scene." More importantly still, I am not committed—as talk about the relation between P and S might misleadingly suggest—to the existence of the "subject" S as an independent entity in its own right. It is compatible with everything that has so far been said that *displaying-S* might turn out to be a unitary predicate, carrying no implication as to the existence or nonexistence of S. Thus, the occurrence of S in "depicting-S" might be "intensional," not "extensional."

In Search of Criteria

An ambitious investigator of our syllabus of questions might hope to discover an analytical definition of *displaying* or *displaying-S,* that is to say, some formula having the structure:

$$P \text{ displays } S \textit{ if and only if } R,$$

where "R" is to be replaced by some expression that is more detailed and more illuminating (whatever we take that to mean) than the unelaborated word, "displays." R, then, will constitute the necessary and sufficient condition for P to "display" S.

It is probably unrealistic to expect that we can find a set of

[1] There is an obvious analogy here with the sense/reference distinction connected with verbal descriptions. In the case of such a description, the "original scene," if any, corresponds to the entity or event identified by the description. The displayed subject of the painting is analogous to the description's sense or meaning, which attaches to it, whether or not it identifies any actual entity or event.

necessary and sufficient conditions conforming to this pattern. But we need not be committed to this goal, for it would already be somewhat illuminating if we could only isolate some necessary conditions. A still more modest goal, difficult enough to attain, would be to exhibit some *criteria* for the application of expressions of the form "displays-*S*," that is to say conditions that count, in virtue of the relevant meaning of "displays" and nothing else, for or against its applicability to given instances. Such criteria need not be invariably or universally relevant, always in point whenever it makes sense to speak of something showing or displaying something else: the criteria of application might vary from case to case in some systematic and describable fashion. The goal would then be partial but explicit insight into the pattern of uses of "depicts" and its paronyms, rather than a formal definition.[2] Nevertheless, although this is the program, I shall first adopt the plan of examining seriatim a number of plausible necessary conditions for "displaying." Only after we have become convinced that none of these candidates separately, and not even all of them jointly, can serve as an analysis of our quaesitum, shall I proceed to argue for a more flexible type of answer.

Somebody influenced by Wittgenstein's parallel investigations of fundamental concepts might regard our enterprise, even thus circumscribed, as reprehensibly quixotic, expecting to find the "pattern of use" too raveled for reduction to any formula. Such pessimism might be countered by recalling that "creative power" of language, as important as it is truistic, in virtue of which we can understand what is meant by something of the form "*P* is a painting of *S*" even when asserted of some painting in a new, unfamiliar, or recondite style. That we think we understand what is said in such contexts argues powerfully for the existence of an underlying pattern of application waiting

[2] Cf. the corresponding analytical task for "the concept of cause," where, in my opinion, the best to be hoped for is a similar mapping of variations of sense, based upon an exhibition of the relevant criteria of application underlying such variation.

to be exhibited. Even if this is an illusion, it would be one in need of explanation.

A Principled Objection

A search for analytical criteria of application for "displaying" naturally recalls the many abortive efforts that have been made to provide partial or complete analyses of verbal meaning. Indeed, there may be more than analogy here. Of a verbal text we can properly say, echoing some of our earlier formulations, that it is a description or representation *of* some scene, situation, or state of affairs, presented via the "content" of the text and possibly corresponding to some verifying fact (the analogue of our "original scene"). Thus questions arise that seem to parallel those about pictorial representation which I have emphasized. Some writers, indeed, try to assimilate the latter to the former, drawing their explanatory and analytical concepts from the domain of verbal semantics.

Now are there any good reasons to think that a search for a conceptual map of verbal meaning is bound to be abortive? The late John Austin seems to have thought so,[3] for reasons that do not seem to have been discussed in print.

Austin contrasts a search for the meaning of a particular word or expression with what he takes to be the illegitimate search for meaning in general. He reminds us that the first kind of question is answered when we can "explain the syntactics" and "demonstrate the semantics" of the word or expression in question. That is to say, when we can state the grammatical constraints on the expression and its ostensive or quasi-ostensive links with nonverbal objects and situations (where this is appropriate). But then Austin objects that the supposedly more general question "What is the meaning of a word-in-general?" is a spurious one. "I can only answer a question of the form 'What is the meaning of "x"?' if 'x' is some particular word you

[3] John L. Austin, "The Meaning of a Word," in his *Philosophical Papers*, ed. J. O. Urmson and G. J. Warnock (Oxford: The Clarendon Press, 1961).

are asking about. This supposed *general* question is really just a spurious question of a type which commonly arise in philosophy. We may call it the fallacy of asking about 'Nothing-in-particular' which is a practice decried by the plain man, but by the philosopher called 'generalizing' and regarded with some complacency" (p. 25) .

If Austin were right, a similar absurdity should infect our main question about the meaning of *"P* is a painting of *S,"* since we are not raising it about any given painting, but about no painting in particular. Austin's idea, so far as I have been able to follow it, seems to have been that the rejected general question about the meaning of a word in general is apt to be taken as a search for a single meaning, *common to all words.* And similarly, if he were right, our own problem would be the ridiculous one of trying to find a single common subject for all paintings. So conceived, the quest would indeed be spurious, not to say preposterously confused.

It is interesting to notice, however, that immediately after rejecting the "general question" about meaning, Austin admits as legitimate the general question "What is the 'square root' of a number?"—of any number, not any particular number. But if that is a legitimate way of looking for a definition of "square root," why should we not regard the "general question" about meaning, with equal justice, as a legitimate way of looking for a definition—or at least something relevant to the definition— of "meaning"?

Austin's reason for distinguishing the two cases apparently arises from his conviction (which I share) that " 'the meaning of *p'* is not a definite description of any entity" (p. 26) whereas "square root of *n"* is (when the variable is replaced by a constant) . I cannot see why this should make a relevant difference. It would indeed be naive to think of the search for an analysis of "displaying-*S"* as presupposing the existence of some entity indifferently displayed by all paintings. But this concession need not imply the rejection of any search for general criteria as spurious. Oddly enough, after Austin's characteristically energetic attack upon the "general" enterprise of delineating the concept of meaning, he proceeds to assign that same task an acceptable sense by taking it to be an attempt to answer the question "What-is-the-meaning-of (the phrase) 'the-meaning-of (the word) "x" '?" The corresponding question for us might be "What is the meaning of (the phrase) 'displaying-S'?" We can then proceed, as Austin recommends, to investigate the "syntactics and semantics" of that expression, without commitment to the existence of dubious entities and without nagging anxieties about the supposed spuriousness of the enterprise. It may prove impossible to reach our goal, but that remains to be seen.

How Does a Photograph Depict?

I shall now consider for a while the form taken by our basic question about the nature of depiction when applied to the special case of photographs. For if any pictures stand in some "natural" relation to their displayed or portrayed subjects, untouched photographs ought to provide prime examples. There, surely, we ought to be able to discern whatever complexities underlie the notion of faithful "copying" at its least problematic. Since photographs also provide minimal scope for the "expressive" intentions of their producers, we shall be able to bracket considerations connected with the expressive aspects of visual art (whose crucial importance in other contexts is, of course, not being denied).

What, then, is it about a given photograph, P, that entitles us to say that it is a photograph of a certain S? Here is a picture postcard labeled "Westminster Abbey": what justifies us and enables us to say that it is a photograph *of* a certain famous building in London—or, at least, for somebody who has never heard of the Abbey, of a certain building having certain presented properties (twin towers, an ornamented front, and so on).[4]

---

[4] I am here deliberately ignoring, for the time being, the distinction previously introduced between the displayed and the portrayed subject.

Appeal to a Causal History

The first answer to be considered seeks to analyze the imputed depicting relation in terms of a certain causal sequence between some "original scene" (what the camera was originally pointed at) and the photograph, considered as an end-term in that sequence. The photograph, P, that is to say a certain piece of shiny paper, showing a distribution of light and dark patches, resulted—so the story goes—from a camera's being pointed upon a certain occasion at *Westminster Abbey*, thus allowing a certain sheaf of light rays to fall upon a photosensitive film, which was subsequently subjected to various chemical and optical processes ("developing" and "printing"), so that at last *this* object—the photograph in our hands—resulted. In short, the etiology of the representing vehicle, P, is supposed to furnish our desired answer.

Reducing the causal narrative to essentials, we get the following account: P portrays S, in virtue of the fact that S was a salient cause-factor in the production of P; and P displays S', in virtue of the fact that S satisfied the description that might be inserted for "S'" (a building having towers, etc.). On this view, P might be regarded as a *trace*[5] of S and the interpretation of P is a matter of influence to an earlier term in a certain causal sequence.

An immediate obstacle to the acceptability of this account is the difficulty in specifying the "portrayed subject," S and that abstract of it which is the "displayed subject," S'. For an inference from P to circumstances of its original generation will yield any number of facts about the camera's focal aperture, its

---

For to make this distinction at once might interfere with the plausibility of the first answer now to be considered.

[5] "It will be helpful if we look at images as traces, natural or artificial ones. After all, a photograph is nothing but such a natural trace, a series of tracks left . . . on the emulsion of the film by the variously distributed lightwaves which produced chemical changes made visible and permanent through further chemical operations" (E. H. Gombrich, "The Evidence of Images," in *Interpretation, Theory and Practice,* ed. Charles Singleton [Baltimore, 1969], p. 36; cited hereafter as Gombrich, 1969).

distance from the nearest prominent physical object, perhaps
the exposure time, and so on, which we should not want to
count as part of the "subject" in either sense of that word.
There must be some way of selecting, out of the set of possible
inferences from the physical character of P, some smaller set of
facts which are to count as relevant to P's context.

An associated difficulty lurks behind the lazy formula that
identifies S', the displayed subject (and our main interest), with
a certain "abstract" of the properties of S. At the moment the
photograph was taken, the Abbey must have had any number
of properties that might be inferred from the photograph,
though irrelevant to that photograph's content. (If the picture
showed the doors open, one might correctly infer that visitors
were to be found in the Abbey's interior on that day.) Even to
limit S' to a specification of visual properties will not serve:
somebody might be able to infer correctly all manner of conclusions about the Abbey's visual appearance (e.g., that it looks
as if it were leaning on the spectator) without such items being
shown in the picture.

Some writers have thought that such objections might be
overcome by considering the "information" about the Abbey's
visual appearance at a certain moment, supposedly embodied in
the final print. Such "information" is conceived to have been
contained in the sheaf of light rays originally impinging upon
the camera's lens and to have remained "invariant" through all
the subsequent chemical transformations. What makes anything, A, a "trace" of something else, B, is just that A in this
way presents information about B. Examination of the imma-
nent "information" contained in P would thus presumably allow us to distinguish between warranted and unwarranted inference to P's etiology and so to eliminate the uncertainties
about the displayed and the portrayed subjects. I shall subject
this conception to criticism below. But we might as well notice
another difficulty at once.

Suppose the causal history of a certain photograph to be as
outlined above (pointing at the Abbey, chemical changes in the

photosensitive emulsion, and so on) while the final outcome
consisted of nothing better than a uniform grey blur. Should
we then, in order to be consistent, have to maintain that we did
indeed end with a photograph of Westminster Abbey, though a
highly uninformative one?[6] Notice that the Abbey might indeed
present the appearance of a grey blur if seen through eyelids
almost closed: perhaps the "uninformative" photograph should
be regarded as yielding only an *unusual* view of the Abbey? But
this is surely too paradoxical to be acceptable.

The moral of this counterexample is that reliance upon the
photograph's history of production is insufficient to certify it
as having the Abbey, or an Abbey, as its subject. No genetic
narrative of the photograph's provenance, no matter how detailed and accurate, can logically guarantee that photograph's
fidelity. (Of course, if the "accuracy" of the causal account is to
be determined by some other kind of test—say "invariance of
information," construed as involving no reference to any causal
history—the causal account is already shown to be insufficient.)

The causal account I have imagined, now seen to be insufficient as an analysis of the photograph's content, can also be
shown not to be necessary either.

Suppose someone invents a new kind of photosensitive paper,
a sheet of which, upon being "exposed" by simply being held up
in front of the Abbey, immediately acquires and preserves the
appearance of a conventional photograph. Would we then refuse to call it a photograph of the Abbey? We might perhaps not
want to call it a *photograph,* but no matter: it would still surely
count as a visual representation of the Abbey.

A defender of the causal approach might retort that the extraordinary paper I have imagined was at least pointed at the
Abbey, so that the "essentials" of the imputed causal history

---

[6] Some members of my audience at the lecture on which this essay is
based were willing to take this view, insisting that the etiology had over-
riding importance, no matter how disappointing the resulting "trace."
This illustrates the grip that the causal model can have—to the point of
its being accepted in the teeth of the most absurd consequences.

were preserved. After all, he might add, we are not even normally interested in the details of the particular chemical and physical processes used in producing the final print. Well, so long as we are indulging in fantasy, let us suppose that the extraordinary imprinting effect was producible only by pointing the sensitive paper *away* from the Abbey, while the result was still indistinguishable from the conventional photograph: would that disqualify the product as a visual representation and, for all we know, a highly faithful one?

Some philosophers might reply that if causal laws were violated in these or other extraordinary ways, we "should not know what to think or say." But that seems a lazy way with a conceptual difficulty. Perhaps a single odd example of the kind I have imagined would leave us hopelessly puzzled. But if the phenomenon were regularly reproducible by a standard procedure, I suppose we should be justified in saying that we had simply discovered some new, albeit puzzling, way of producing representations or "likenesses" of the Abbey and other objects. It would be easy to concoct any number of other counterexamples in which end-products indistinguishable from conventional photographs might arise from radically unorthodox procedures.

One might be inclined to draw the moral that the causal histories of photographs—or their fantastic surrogates—are wholly irrelevant to our warranted judgments that they are depictions of the Abbey. But to reject the causal view so drastically may be too hasty. Suppose we found some natural object that "looked like" a certain subject—say a rock formation that from a certain standpoint looked for all the world like Napoleon: would we then say that the rock formation must be a representation of Napoleon? (Or suppose, for that matter that objects, looking for all the world like photographs, simply rained down from the sky at certain times.) Surely not. It looks as if the background of a certain etiology is at least relevant (without being either a necessary or a sufficient condition) in ways that need to be made clearer before we are through.

An obvious counter might be that in the case of the imagined sensitive paper, and in the other examples that we might be inclined to concoct, something must be deliberately positioned in order to create, if all goes well, a representation of the subject in question. To be sure, this would exclude the supposed counterinstances of the natural objects, or the objects of unknown provenance that were simply indistinguishable from conventional photographs. But in this imagined objection, there is plainly an appeal to a very different sort of criterion, the *intention* that launched the causal process. And this deserves separate discussion. Let us first, however, look more closely at the suggestion that the notion of "information" provides the clue for which we are searching.

Appeal to Embodied "Information"

As I have already said, our puzzle about the blurred photograph would be regarded by some writers as explainable by the "absence of sufficient information" in the final print. More generally, the concept of "information," supposedly suggested by the notion thus designated in the mathematical theory of communication, is held to be useful in resolving the conceptual difficulties that we are trying to clarify.[7]

The current vogue for speaking about "information" contained in representations—and indeed, for bringing that notion into almost any kind of discussion—is certainly influenced by the supposed successes of the notion of "information" that is prominent in the sophisticated mathematical theories usually associated with the name of Claude Shannon.[8] Yet it is easy to

[7] Gombrich, influenced by J. J. Gibson's writings on perception, has suggested that instead of speaking about "interpretation" we speak rather about how "the sensory system picks up and processes the *information* present in the energy distribution of the environment" (Gombrich, 1969, p. 47). He adds that he is "fully alive to the danger of new words, especially fashionable words, becoming new toys of little cash value" (*ibid.*). But he relies strongly upon what he takes to be "the concept of information [as] developed in the theory of communication" (p. 50) throughout his article.

[8] See Claude E. Shannon and Warren Weaver, *The Mathematical Theory of Communication* (Urbana, Ill., 1949), and Colin Cherry, *On Human*

show that the two senses of "information" involved have very little to do with one another.

Let us recapitulate briefly what "information" means in the context of the mathematical theory. The first point to be made is that in that theory we are dealing with a *statistical* notion—let us call it "selective information"[9] henceforward to avoid confusion. The typical situation to which the mathematical theory applies is one in which some determinate stock of possible "messages," which may be conceived as alternative characters in an "alphabet" (letters, digits, or pulses of energy) *to which no meaning is necessarily attached,* are encoded into "signals" for transmission along a "communication channel" and ultimate reception, decoding, and accurate reproduction of the original "message." Thus individual letters of the English alphabet are converted into electrical pulses along a telegraph wire, in order to produce at the other end a copy of the original string of letters composing the complex message sent.

A rough explanation of the notion of the "selective information" associated with such a communication system would identify it with the amount of "reduction of initial uncertainty" that such a system can achieve. Suppose the various possible messages m_i are known to occur with long-run frequencies or probabilities p_i. We might say that the "information" conveyed by the receipt of a particular message, m_i, varies inversely as its initial probability of occurrence, p_i. For the higher the initial probability of transmission, the "less we learn" by receiving the message. If the message in question were, in the limiting case, certain to arrive, we should "learn nothing" by receiving it. The mathematical quantity called the (selective) information is clearly the measure of the amount of a certain magnitude—

Communication, 2d ed. (Cambridge, Mass. 1966), for explanations of the technical theory. It is ironic that experts in information theory have repeatedly protested, apparently without success, about the misleading consequences of identifying what is called "information" in the technical theory with the meaning of that word in ordinary language.

[9] See Cherry, *op. cit.,* p. 308.

roughly speaking, the reduction in the amount of initial uncertainty of reception, as I have suggested above. It is important
to stress that this has nothing to do with the meaning, if any, of
such a message, and nothing to do even with its specific content.
If I seek an answer to a question by means of a telegram, the
only two possible answers being either Yes or No, and both
being antecedently equally likely to be sent, then either answer
contains the same "(selective) information." Each answer
transforms a probability of 1/2 into certainty. An anxious suitor,
awaiting an answer to his proposal of marriage, would of course
say that the information received in the one case would be interestingly different from the information he would receive in
the other. But that is because he is using "information" in the
common or garden sense of what might be called *substantive*
information. Now the theorists of the mathematical theory have
no interest in substantive information—which is, of course,
their privilege and not a reproach. To think otherwise would be
as misguided as to make it a reproach to a theory of measure-
ment that it tells us nothing about the smell or taste of the
masses discussed in that theory.

It would obviously be pointless to think of adapting this
model to the case of representation. In place of the messages we
should have to think of the original "scenes" corresponding to
the representations, to which the long-term frequency of occurrence would have no sensible application. Even in some special
case, say that in which male and female entrants to a college
were photographed with stable long-range frequencies, the
selective or statistical information attached to any photograph
would tell us absolutely nothing about the photograph's subject
or content—which is our present interest.

A few writers who have clearly seen the limited applicability
of the statistical concept here called "selective information"
have undertaken studies of what they call "semantic information," that might seem more useful for our purpose.[10] For it

[10] See especially Yehoshua Bar-Hillel, *Language and Information* (Reading, Mass. 1964), chs. 15–17, and Jaakko Hintikka, "On Semantic Informa-

would seem that "semantic information," unlike selective (statistical) information, is concerned with the "content" or meaning of verbal representations (statements, texts). The theory of semantic information is presented as a rational reconstruction of what Hintikka calls "information in the most important sense of the word, vis. the sense in which it is used of whatever it is that meaningful sentences and other comparable combinations of symbols convey to one who understands them" (p. 3). Now this seems to be just what we are looking for: the "displayed subject" of a photograph does seem close to what common sense would call the information that could be understood by a suitably competent receiver (viewer).[11] If we follow, however, the constructions provided by Hintikka and other pioneers of "semantic information theory" we shall discover, to our disappointment, that they, too, provide something, of whatever interest, that will not help us in our present investigation. For

---

tion," in J. Hintikka and P. Suppes, eds., *Information and Inference* (Dordrecht, 1970). Bar-Hillel says, "It must be perfectly clear that *there is no logical connection whatsoever between these two measures, i.e., the amount of (semantic) information conveyed by a statement and the measure of rarity of kinds of symbol sequences* [our "selective information"], even if these symbol sequences are typographically identical with this statement (p. 286, italics in original). And again, *"The concept of semantic information has intrinsically nothing to do with communication* (p. 287, italics in original)—and hence nothing to do with the concept of information that is defined relative to communication systems. On the other hand, Hintikka says he has "become increasingly sceptical concerning the possibility of drawing a hard-and-fast boundary between statistical information theory and the theory of semantic information" (p. 263). His suggestion that semantic information theory start with "the general idea that information equals elimination of uncertainty" (p. 264), a formula that would, as explained above, fit the case of selective (statistical) information, shows the link that Hintikka relies upon—in spite of Bar-Hillel's vigorous attempt to separate the two concepts.

[11] There is, to be sure, some violence done to ordinary language here. Common sense would reserve the use of "information" for what is conveyed by the photograph about the original scene. It would be paradoxical to think of the painting of an imaginary scene as providing information to anybody—just as paradoxical as supposing that *The Pickwick Papers* contains information about Mr. Pickwick.

it turns out that the "semantic information" of a given statement is roughly the same as the range of verifying situations associated with that statement—or, more accurately, some measure of the "breadth" of that range. And here, what is finally provided is a measure of extent and not of content.

"Semantic information" is a sophisticated refinement of the common-sense notion of the *amount* of information in a statement. Just as a report of a body's mass tells us nothing about what stuff that body is composed of, so a report of semantic information would tell us nothing about what the statement in question is *about*. If we have two statements of parallel logical structure, say "My name is Black" and "My name is White,"[12] any acceptable definition of semantic information will assign the *same* semantic information to each statement. If this concept (whose interest I do not wish to deny) were applicable to paintings,[13] we should have to count distinct paintings with roughly comparable subjects (say two paintings of a flock of grazing sheep) as having and conveying the "same information." But of course the displayed subjects of two such paintings might be manifestly different.

We need a term to distinguish what Hintikka, as we have seen, called "the most important sense of information," i.e., what we mean by that word in ordinary life: let us call it *sub-*

---

[12] On the plausible assumption that the two surnames occur with equal frequency in the populations in question.

[13] I do not think that anybody has yet tried to apply the concept of semantic information to visual representations. One difficulty, and perhaps not the most serious one, would be that of "articulating" a given verbal representation in a way to correspond to the articulation of statements in a given language into an ordered array of phonemes. Unless we can regard a photograph or a painting, by analogy, as composed of atomic characters, corresponding to phonemes, the desired analogy will hardly find a handhold. Then, of course, there is the lurking difficulty behind any attempt to assimilate paintings or other verbal representations to assertions with potential truth-value. This might serve for blueprints, graphs, and other representations designed to convey purported facts ("information" in the ordinary sense!) but would hardly fit, without inordinate distortion, our prime case of paintings.

stantive information. And let us stretch the word to apply to false statements as well as to true ones (so that what would ordinarily be called "misinformation" also counts as substantive, but incorrect, information). What then could we mean by talking about the (substantive) information contained in a given photograph?

On the assumption that we have a sufficiently firm grip upon the notion of the substantive information contained in a *statement,* one might think of replacing the given photograph, *P,* by some complex statement, *A,* such that a competent receiver might learn just as much from *A* as from *P,* if *P* were to be a faithful record of the corresponding original scene. But surely there is something fanciful about this suggestion. Suppose somebody were to be presented with such a statement, *A,* and asked then to retrieve the photograph, *P,* of which it is supposed to be in some sense a translation, from a large set of different photographs. Is there good reason to think that such a task must be performable in principle? It seems to me, on the contrary, that the notion of a complete verbal translation of a photograph (and still more, the notion of a verbal translation of a painting) is a chimaera. A picture shows more than can be said—and not simply because the verbal lexicon is short of corresponding equivalents: it is not just a matter of the nonavailability of verbal names for the thousands of colors and forms that we can distinguish. But if so, the notion of information that has its habitat in connection with verbal representations (statements) will still fail to apply to the case that interests us.[14] In the end, it seems that what is picturesquely expressed by means of the figure of the "information" contained in a photograph or a

---

[14] Of course, I do not wish to deny that we can put into words *some* of the things that we can learn from a faithful photograph. If anybody wants to express this by saying that information can be gleaned from such a photograph, there can be no harm in it. But we shall never in this way be able to identify the subject of the photograph. One is at this point strongly inclined to say that in some sense the visual subject can *only* be shown.

painting comes to nothing else than what we mean when we talk about the "content" of the painting or "what it shows" (its displayed subject). There would be no objection to the introduction of a metaphor or analogy based upon information, if that provided any illumination. It seems to me, however, that this is not the case, and that reliance upon "information" on the basis of a more or less plausible analogy amounts in the end only to the introduction of a synonym—and a misleading one at that—for "depicting" or "representing." It is not unfair to suggest that "the information conveyed by a painting" means nothing more than "what is shown (depicted, displayed) by that painting."

We may, nevertheless, draw a useful lesson from this abortive digression. One caution, stressed repeatedly by theorists of statistical and semantic information alike, is that the measures of information they discuss are always *relative* to a number of distinguishable factors in the relevant situations. In the case of statistical information, the amount of information is relative to the distribution of long-term frequencies of the system of possible messages transmissible in the communication channel in question; in the semantic case, the amount of information embodied in a statement is relative to the choice of a language and, on some treatments, to assumptions about given laws constituting an antecedent stock of given "information" to which any statement not inferable from those laws makes an additional contribution. We might, therefore, be encouraged to draw a somewhat obvious moral: that however we come to identify or describe the substantive content of a painting or other visual representation, the answer will be relative to some postulated body of knowledge (concerning for instance the chosen schema of representation, the intentions of the painter or sign-producer, and so on). The idea that a painting or a photograph "contains" its content or subject as straightforwardly as a bucket contains water is too crude to deserve refutation. But ideas as crude as this have controlled some of the discussion of our present topic.

Appeal to the Producer's Intentions

I shall now consider the suggestion that a way out of our difficulties might be found by invoking the intentions of the painter, photographer, or whoever it was that acted in such a way as to generate the verbal representation whose "subject" we are canvassing. I do not know of any theorist who has based a full-fledged theory of representation on this idea, but corresponding theories of verbal representation are fairly common. Thus Paul Grice in a well-known paper on "meaning"[15] has argued that the meaning of an utterance can be analyzed in terms of certain complex intentions to produce a certain effect in the hearer.[16] Again, E. D. Hirsch, in a well-known book, has defined verbal meanings as "whatever someone has *willed* to convey by a particular sequence of linguistic signs and which can be conveyed (shared) by means of those linguistic signs."[17] Now there seems to be no reason in principle why this kind of approach should not be equally valid in connection with visual representation—or, indeed, in connection with any sort of representation at all.

The undeniable attraction of this kind of emphasis upon the producer's intention or "will" can be attributed to its tendency to remind us forcibly about the conceptual gap between the

[15] See "Meaning," *Philosophical Review*, 64 (1957), 377–388, and also his "Utterer's Meaning and Intentions," *Philosophical Review*, 78 (1969), 147–177, for the elaboration and modification of his position in reply to criticism.

[16] The details do not concern us here. The novelty in Grice's account consists in differentiating between a primary intention on the speaker's part to produce a certain belief or action in the hearer, and a secondary intention that recognition of that primary intention shall function as a reason for the hearer to comply with the primary intention.

[17] E. D. Hirsch, *Validity in Interpretation* (New Haven, 1967), p. 31. The reference to meaning as something that can be conveyed to and shared by others shows that Hirsch is not simplistically identifying the content of an utterance with the content of the speaker's intention. For elaboration of his views about this, see pages 49–50 of his book. I have no quarrel with Hirsch's vigorous case for the need to refer to an author's intentions in providing adequate interpretations of a text.

"interpretation" of some natural object (as when we infer from the characters of some trace to the properties of something that produced that trace) and the "interpretation" of a man-made object, intentionally created to have meaning or "content" of a sort that is accessible to a competent receiver. But to agree, in Grice's terminology, that the import of a painting is "non-natural" and not reducible to the termini of factual inferences from the vehicle is one thing; to suppose that the determinable subject of such a nonnatural object can be defined in terms of features of the producer's intentions is something else that is far more problematic.

There is, to begin with, the immediate objection that the producer's intention, supposing it to have existed in some uncontroversial way, may misfire. Suppose I set out to draw a horse and, in my lack of skill, produce something that nobody could distinguish from a cow by simply looking at it; would it then necessarily be a drawing of a horse, just because that was what I had intended? Could I draw a horse by simply putting a dot on paper? If the answers were to be affirmative, we would have to regard the artist's intentions as having the peculiar character of infallibility: simply wanting a painting to be a painting of such-and-such would necessarily make it so. Surely this is too paradoxical to accept. Of a botched and unrecognizable drawing we should want to say "He intended to draw a horse, but failed" as we should say, in certain circumstances, of any failed intention. The notion of intention involves the notion of possible failure.

A still more serious difficulty and one, if I am not mistaken, that is fatal to this approach, is that there is no way of identifying the relevant intention except by invoking the very notion of a subject of a possible painting that such reference to intention is supposed to clarify. Let us take the envisaged analysis in its crudest and least defensible form: Suppose the proposed analysis of "P depicts S" were to be: "M, the producer of P, intended P to be a depiction of S." In this form, the logical circularity is patent: we could not understand the proposed analysis of depicting without already having a clear notion of that relation at our disposal. Nor could the invoked producer properly have any explicit intention to produce P as a depiction of S unless *he* independently understood what it would be like for the resulting P in fact to be a painting of S: to refer back to the intention that he would have if he were to be trying to make P depict S would enmesh him in hopeless circularity.[18]

Now the situation would be less objectionable, if the proposed analysis were to take the form: "P depicts S if and only if M, the producer of P, intended E," where E is imagined replaced by some complex expression (and not a straightforward synonym of "P depicts S").[19] Then the circularity noted above would be absent. Only in order for this kind of analysis to be acceptable, E must have the same extension as "P depicts S": we have captured the right intention only if what M intended to do was necessary and sufficient for P being a depiction of S (though not expressed in those words). And if so, we can then dispense with the reference to M's intention altogether, since "P depicts S if and only if E" will, by itself, constitute the analysis we were seeking. This way of looking at the matter would also have the advantage of meeting the difficulty about the failed intention that we noticed above.[20]

[18] A similar point has been well-made by G. E. M. Anscombe (see her "On Promising and Its Justice, and Whether It Needs to Be Respected *in foro interno*," *Critica*, 3 [April–May 1969]). "If thinking you are getting married is essential to getting married, then mention of thinking you are getting married belongs in an explanation of what getting married is; but then won't an explanation of what getting married is be required if we are to give the content of thought when one is getting married?" (p. 61). With intention replacing thought, this is the structure of my own argument above.

[19] This is, in fact, the structure of Grice's analysis of nonnatural meaning, which is therefore not open to the charge of immediate circularity. One can, however, object that his analysis is in fact inadequate as not capturing what we want to count as the "speaker's meaning."

[20] It might be an interesting feature of the logical grammar of "depicts" if it were true that "P depicts S" *entailed* "The producer of P intended P to depict S." (Cf. "That counts as a move in the game only if the player intended to make that move"—which need not be circular and may indeed

I conclude that in spite of its attractions, the appeal to the producer's intention accomplishes nothing at all to our purpose.

Depiction as Illusion

We have now considered three types of answers to our prime questions as to the analysis of a statement of the form "*P* depicts *S*." Of these, one, the reliance upon the "information" supposedly embodied in the representation, *P*, seemed empty, and the two others, in appealing to a causal history and the producer's intention, respectively, invoked temporal antecedents that seemed only contingently connected with the final outcome.[21] We still need, it seems, to isolate something about *the representation itself* that will, in favorable circumstances, permit a qualified and competent viewer to perceive in the art object, without dubious inferences to antecedent provenance or partially fulfilled intentions[22] something about *P* that makes it a painting of *S* and nothing else.

The reader may be surprised that I have delayed until now in considering a famous answer that has behind it the authority of Aristotle and a thousand other theorists who have, in one form or another, endorsed his conception of art as mimesis. Let us try to formulate the conception of art as an "imitation of reality" in a way that will commit us to as little presupposed theory as possible.

---

be informative.) Unfortunately, even that is not true: the photograph may show much that its producer did not intend and would not even retroactively assimilate to his intention when he discerned it. There is such a thing as unintentional showing—as there is such a thing as unintentional speaking.

[21] This is not strictly true for the case of intention: what the artist successfully succeeded in achieving, in accordance with an embodied intention, does usually determine the intrinsic character of the product.

[22] We might say that the only intention that is relevant is the intention that the artist succeeded in embodying in the painting. Of course, a knowledge of the background—the tradition within which the artist was working, the purpose he had in mind, and other things—may well help us to "read" his painting, but the satisfactory reading must in the end be based upon what is there to be found in the painting.

Why not say that when I look at a naturalistic painting—say of a white poodle on a sofa—it is *as if,* looking through the picture frame, I actually saw an animal having a certain appearance, resting on a piece of furniture at a certain distance from me. Of course, I know all the time that there is no such poodle in the place where I seem to see it; and that is what makes the experience an illusion, but not a delusion.[23] We are not really deceived, but we have had enough visual experience to know that we see *what it would be like* if the poodle were really there. There is a suspension of disbelief on the viewer's part, as there is when reading fiction, which describes nonexistent persons *as if* they really existed. We might therefore speak of "fictive" or "illusive" vision in such cases.

The expression "as if," which I have used in my proposed formula, with its obtrusive reminder of "The Philosophy of As If," may smack of hocus-pocus. But this can be held in check, I think, and the expression treated as a harmless shorthand. To say *"A* is as if *B"* is simply to say "If *A* were the case, then *B;* but also not-*B."* In a case of illusion, the observer knows that not-*B,* in spite of appearances; in a case of deception or delusion, he believes that *A* is the case, contrary to fact. Thus the proposed analysis for our imagined case is: If there were a poodle of a certain sort and in a certain posture on a sofa at such-and-such a distance from me, I would see what I now see. And thereby I can see, here and now, what the subject of the picture is, without reference to the painting's etiology, the artist's intentions, or anything else that is not immediately present. This account must certainly have some truth in it: a

[23] For views of this sort see E. H. Gombrich, *Art and Illusion,* rev. ed. (Princeton, 1961), passim; cited hereafter as Gombrich, 1961. In view of Gombrich's sophisticated discussions of "illusion" in his great book and elsewhere, I would hesitate to saddle him with any simple view about the role of delusion in art. That he seems to assign a central, though by no means exclusive, role to such illusion seems indicated by such references as "the illusion which a picture can give" (Gombrich, 1969, p. 46). But he has always carefully distinguished, as I wish to do, "the difference between an illusion and a delusion" (p. 60).

layman in the presence of a painting by Claudio Bravo will
certainly report that it looks for all the world as if there were
a parcel behind the surface and a viewer, no matter how
armored by theoretical commitments against the role of illusion cannot avoid, if he is ingenuous, making a similar report
for other cases of *trompe l'oeil*. There is, of course, a serious
question whether an account that seems to fit this special type
of case can be extended, without distortion or eventual tautology, to fit all cases of response to visual representations that are
partially naturalistic. I think, however, that there is no serious
difficulty in stretching the view to cover cases in which the
presented subject is unfamiliar. There is no particular puzzle,
on this view, for accounting for the viewer's sight of a flying
horse or a fleshy goddess floating in the air. And the account
can even be held to fit certain "abstract" works: if I see in a
Mark Rothko painting a receding plane bounded by a con-
trasting strip, and so on, that sight is not unlike what I have
learned to see by looking at clouds. Similarly for Mondrian's
Manhattan Boogie-Woogie or other such abstractions.[24]

On this view, puzzles about how a *P* can depict a determinate
S reduce to questions about normal perception of the form
"How is that a real poodle can look like a poodle?" I am not
sure what useful sense can be ascribed to a question of this
form;[25] at any rate, it would fall outside the scope of our present
inquiry.

[24] I am not arguing that looking "through the surface" is a proper way
of looking at all abstractions: in Mondrian's case, we know it would be
contrary to his intentions. My point is only that the conception of depiction as illusion can cover a far wider range of cases than is sometimes
assumed.
[25] The undoubted interest of this type of question for psychologists such
as James J. Gibson (see for instance his *Senses Considered as Perceptual
Systems* [Boston, Mass. 1966]) arises from the need to explain how a flux
of radiant energy, reaching the eyes, can be so processed that the viewer
can correctly see the poodle as solid, at a certain distance from him, and
so on. But answers to this kind of question, important as they are, are not
our concern here. Cases of veridical experience are sufficiently familiar to
be used as explanations for the more problematic cases of seeing *as if*.

Let us now consider possible objections. The first type consists in effect of the objection that the "illusion" is not, and is not intended to be, complete. As we shift our position with respect to the canvas, we do not get the systematic changes in appearance that would occur if there really were a live poodle in the indicated position: a painted canvas does not even produce as much "illusion" as a mirror. Furthermore, the presented visual appearance is "frozen," does not show the slight but perceptible changes to be seen in even a "still life" and so on.[26]

The second type of objection draws our attention to the perceptible distortion to be noticed even in the most "realistic" paintings: in all but special cases, the sensitive viewer will see the brush strokes and will be aware, after all, that what he sees is not "very much like" the real thing.[27]

The undoubted presence of interfering and distorting features, even in the most "faithful" of paintings, is, up to a point, not serious for a defender of the theory that identifies depiction with illusion. Illusions need not be perfect and we have plenty of experience in genuine perception of discounting variations in appearance[28] and, on the other hand, of dis-

[26] "As the eye passes over the picture, across the frame, to the wall on which it is placed, it cannot but become aware, however the cunning the painting may be, of a discrepancy or discontinuity, which is fatal to the illusion" (Richard Wollheim, "Art and Illusion," *British Journal of Aesthetics*, 3 [January 1963], 25) . This assumes, without justification, that unless an illusion is total, it is not an illusion at all. Imagine an open aperture through which I could see an actual landscape outside: then what happened as my eye passed over the walls and so on would not prevent me from saying that I saw the landscape.

[27] Cf. the reaction of Roy Campbell on first seeing snow, having seen only paintings of it before: "From paintings I had imagined it to be like wax, and snow flakes to be like shavings of candle grease" (quoted from Gombrich, 1961, p. 221) .

[28] Cf. the famous "constancy phenomenon" (for which see, for instance, Julian E. Hochberg, *Perception* [Englewood Cliffs, N.J.: Prentice-Hall, 1964], p. 50) . We see a poodle—indeed the same poodle, from different angles, at different distances, and in various lights. Then why should we not be able to see the poodle through whatever distortions are due to the

tinguishing between imperfections of the eye (floating specks, effects of myopia, and so on). Once we have learned *how* to look through the partially distorting medium of paintings and photographs, we shall simply see the depicted subjects as if they were really present.

But the real difficulties are concealed in the deceptive phrase, "once we have learned how things look," for this concedes in effect that in many cases there is a sense in which the subject does *not* look in the painting as it would if it were really present behind the canvas-plane—and such large deviations from ordinary vision cannot be written off by means of the retort we have just envisaged. If Picasso's women are to be seen *as* women (seen as if they were women behind the canvas) we shall have to learn a key of interpretation for which there is no analogue in normal perception. For instance, we shall have to learn to distinguish between a "faithful" painting of a green face and a green painting of a white face. But once we allow, as we must, for such prior induction into the "technique of representation," the equation of depiction with fictive representation or "illusion" loses its attraction. Instead of saying *"P* is a representation of *S* because seeing *P* is, with some reservations for incompleteness and distortion, like looking at *S* (seeing *P* is as if one were seeing *S*)," we now have to say something like: "In general, *P* is a representation of *S*, if *P* looks like *S*, according to the conventions embodied in the artist's style and technique." And now, one wonders how much work the surviving reference to "looking as if *S* were present" really does. Given a case of extreme distortion, is it still necessary to say that we see, and are required to see, something that looks as if it were behind the canvas? Is this not perhaps only a misleading way of making the obvious point that if we have learned how Picasso in his cubistic period painted a woman,

---

artistic medium and the artist's handling of it? If we can recognize the poodle in moonlight, or even in a trick mirror, then why not when it is, as it were, seen through a painting darkly?

we shall *know* that the painting is of a woman?[29] Is anything added by the insistence that we also "see the painting as if" it were something really there? I am inclined to think that by the time the theory has been stretched so far it has degenerated into useless mythology.

Finally, we might notice that the view under examination can be regarded as reducing "depicting" to "looking-like." For instead of saying that *P* is seen as if *S* were present, one might as well say that *P* "looks like *S*" (although we know that *S* is not present). Most defenders of an illusion theory have indeed supposed some view concerning resemblance between a picture and its subject to be at its foundation. But this deserves separate examination.

Depiction as Resemblance

We have seen that any tenable conception of depiction as involving a sort of illusion (seeing the painting's subject *as if* it were present) must provide room for the observable differences, ranging all the way from selection to outright distortion, between the subject as represented and as it would appear if actually present. Only when the purpose is delusion or deception, is the controlling aim of the artist, an aim never fully achievable, that of total "imitation." Now a favored way of allowing for the element of unlikeness in even the most "faithful" visual picture is to invoke a notion of *resemblance:* the picture is not conceived now as "looking as if" the subject were present, but rather as looking as if something *like,* something resembling, the subject were present.

A typical statement of this standpoint is the following by Monroe Beardsley: " 'The design *X* depicts an object *Y*' means

---

[29] Even in a very distorted representation, we can sometimes analyze the particular elements that are operative, picking out one outline or color patch as the face, another as the arm, and so on. (But it does not seem necessary that we should always be able to do this.) And reliance upon such clues, if that is what they should be regarded as being, does not fit easily into the conception we are here examining.

'X contains some area that is more similar to the visual appearance of Y's than to objects of any other class'."[30]

On a certain rather simplistic conception of similarity or resemblance (which I take to be synonyms in the present context), it is easy to launch devastating objections to any attempt to make resemblance central to the relation of depiction. For one thing, a photograph or a painting, considered as physical objects, are really not at all like horses or trees or oceans, and there is something askew in supposing a "design" is more "similar" to a tree than to an ocean. (Cf. asking whether a postage stamp is more similar to a person than to a piece of cheese.) But if we take Beardsley's formula as a careless way of saying that the *look* or appearance of the "design" has to be "more similar" to the *look* of a tree than to the look of an ocean, we are at once enmeshed in all the conceptual difficulties that attend any conception of comparisons between such dubious entities as "looks."[31]

But we need not enter upon this controversial range of questions, since the superficial logical structure of the verb "to resemble" makes any resemblance view excessively implausible. To take only a single point: we tend to think of the relation of resemblance or similarity as symmetrical. If *A* resembles *B,* then necessarily *B* resembles *A,* and both resemble one an-

---

[30] Monroe C. Beardsley, *Aesthetics* (New York: Harcourt, Brace, 1958), p. 270. I do not wish to saddle Beardsley with some version of the depicting-as-illusion view. An adherent of the conception that the essence of faithful naturalistic depiction is to be found in some relation of resemblance need not be committed to any opinions about the resulting "illusion," although the two conceptions fit well together.

[31] The archetypical situation for our crudest conceptions of resemblance, as arising from comparisons of objects, is that of having the two objects side by side and looking at each in turn, in order to "perceive" relevant resemblances. But then the "comparison" of appearances would require a kind of second-order looking at looks. Perhaps this can sometimes be achieved. But it seems remote from what happens when we see something in a painting as a horse. We do not in the mind's self-observing eye compare the look of what we now see with the look that we should see if we were faced with a horse: saying "That looks like a horse" refers surely to some more primitive operation.

other.[32] But if we take this seriously, we shall find ourselves committed to saying that any tree is a representation of any naturalistic picture of a tree. And since nothing resembles a painting so much as a reproduction of it, the absurdity lurks close at hand of identifying the subject of any picture with its copy.[33]

Further Objections to a Resemblance Model

The well-known objections, restated above, to regarding resemblance as the basis of naturalistic depiction, might well leave us unsatisfied. We might have an uneasy feeling that appeal to the surface grammar of "resemblance" is too summary a way of disposing of a putative insight. To be sure, if we treat resemblance as symmetrical and transitive, we shall be saddled with paradoxical consequences; but is there not, after all, we might still think, *something* to the notion that a naturalistic photograph "resembles" or "looks like"[34] its subject? And if so, could we not modify the superficial implications to preserve this insight? If ordinary language commits us to saying, for instance, that in some sense of resemblance a painting resembles nothing so much as itself, is it beyond the wit of man to establish a more appropriate sense of the crucial expression? It will be worth our while to probe more deeply.

---

[32] It is important that these logical features are not always exemplified in the ordinary language uses of "looks like." When *A* looks like *B*, *B* need not look like *A*, and the two need not look alike. It is this kind of point that makes any easy reference to resemblance or similarity (as a substitute for the less pretentious but more relevant notion of looking-like) so unsatisfactory.

[33] This kind of objection has often been made before. "An object resembles itself to the maximum degree but rarely represents itself; resemblance, unlike representation [= depiction, in this context] is symmetric. . . . Plainly, resemblance in any degree is no sufficient condition for representation" (Nelson Goodman, *Languages of Art* [Indianapolis and New York: Bobbs-Merrill, 1968], p. 4).

[34] I do not mean to imply that these two expressions can always replace one another. Indeed, I shall soon argue that the associated patterns of use show important differences.

Our common, simplifying, conception of "resemblance" is controlled, I would like to suggest, by one or more "pictures"[35] or idealized prototypes of application.

Consider the following simple examples of clear cases of "resemblance":

1. A writer is buying a new supply of typing paper in an unfamiliar shop. He *compares* a sheet that is offered him, with one from his old and nearly exhausted stock. "That is *rather like* what I want; but that is better; perhaps that *resembles* what I need sufficiently closely."

2. A housewife goes to a shop to buy some extra material for a dress she is making: she compares the material *in imagination* with what she already has. "That *looks almost* like what I need; it resembles it very closely; I think it will do."

3. A film producer needs a stand-in for his principal actor in some dangerous sequence. He *compares* the two men, deciding whether the substitute sufficiently *resembles* the star so that the audience will not detect the substitution.

4. A historian compares the careers of Hitler and Stalin for *"points of resemblance."*

5. In trying to sway a judge, an advocate offers a previously decided case as a precedent, but is met with the objection, "I don't see sufficient 'resemblance' between the cases."

---

[35] I am using this word here in somewhat the way that Wittgenstein often did in his later writings. Cf. such a characteristic remark as "The *picture* of a special atmosphere forced itself upon me" (Ludwig Wittgenstein, *Philosophical Investigations* [Oxford: Basil Blackwell, 1953], p. 158). Wittgenstein's notion of a "picture" deserves more attention than it has yet received. Many of our key words are associated with what might be called semantic myths, conceptions of exemplary and archetypical cases in which the use of an expression seems to be manifested in excelsis. Such an archetypical situation is not merely a paradigm but, as it were, a paradigm of paradigms, wherein we think we can grasp the essence of the expression's meaning in a single flash of insight. It is as if the extraordinary complexity of the expression's actual use were compressed into a dramatic and memorable fiction. To the extent that we are dominated by such a primeval myth, we are led to procrustean conceptualization—a cramping, because oversimplified, conception of the word's meaning. (Of course, Wittgenstein has said this far better than I can.)

Such examples and the many others that could easily be produced suggest the following reflections:

(a) The notion of resemblance is closely connected with the notions of *comparison* and *matching* (also with that of *similarity*, which I shall here ignore). In some of the cases, but not in others, the ideal limit of the scale of relative resemblance is that of indistinguishability: if the writer could not tell the new paper apart from the old, he would surely be satisfied, though would be willing to accept something less satisfactory. And similarly, *mutatis mutandis,* for cases 2 and 3.

(b) In other cases, the degree of "resemblance" in the things compared turns upon point-to-point correspondences, so that there is an observed *analogy* between the things compared, while indistinguishability is not in question (cases 4 and 5).

(c) What determines the choice of specific criteria of degree of resemblance in a particular case is determined by the overarching purpose of the process of matching or analogical comparison: sometimes it is a question of finding an acceptable *surrogate,* with respect to appearance, durability, or other properties; sometimes a matter of finding a justification for applying general concepts, dicta, maxims, or principles (cases 4 and 5). In short, what counts as a sufficient degree of resemblance, and the respects in which features of resemblance are treated as relevant, is strongly determined by the overall purpose of the process. To put the point negatively: in the absence of such a purpose, any proposed process of comparison is indeterminate and idle. If I am asked to compare *A* with *B,* or to say how much resemblance there is between them, in the absence of any indication of what the comparison is to be used for, I do not know how to proceed. Of course, if politeness requires me to make some response, I will invent some purposive context, trying to assimilate the task to some familiar case, and hence seeking for points of color resemblance, or similarity of function, or whatever else ingenuity may suggest.

Of the points I have singled out for emphasis, the first two serve mainly to remind us of the great variety of procedures that are covered by the umbrella term "resemblance": that compendious label covers a large variety of processes of matching and analogy drawing, performed in indefinitely many ways and for indefinitely many purposes, with corresponding variety in what counts as appropriate and relevant to the comparison procedures. But the third point, stressing the relativity of comparison with relation to some controlling purpose, is the crucial one for the present inquiry. It is quite opposed in tendency to the picture we have of "resemblance" being constituted by the sharing of common properties, as if we could decide the question whether one thing were or were not similar to another *in vacuo,* without any reference to the aim of the exercise. (Cf. asking whether *A* is better than *B,* which also demands a comparison, in the absence of further determination of the question's sense.)

Let us now apply these elementary reflections to our prime case of the painting and its subject. The first obstacle to using either pattern of resemblance (the search for an approximate match or the search for an analogical structure) is, as we have already seen, that the "subject" is normally not available for independent scrutiny. When the painting is "fictive" there can be no question of placing it side-by-side with its subject in order to check off "points of resemblance." But let this pass, though the point is far from trivial: it remains that the determining purpose of the imputed comparison is left unstated. What is the *point* of my looking first at a portrait of Queen Elizabeth and then at the Queen herself, "in order to find points of resemblance"? Here, there can be no question of the painting being a surrogate for the person, as in some of our exemplary cases. Nor can it be a matter of being able to make corresponding statements about the two, though that *might* be the point, if the portrait were to be preserved in some historical archive to supplement and amplify some verbal description. We are left with nothing better than the empty formula that the painting should "look like" the sitter. But that is merely to substitute the unanalyzed expression "looks like" for our problematic expression "resembles." And here again, the point about the absence of determination of purpose is relevant. Given that for some purposes and in some contexts the most naturalistic *trompe l'oeil* portrait will look conspicuously like a person, what is to *count* as "looking like"? Whatever merits the resemblance view might have, it cannot provide answers to these questions.

My chief objection to the resemblance view, then, is that when pursued it turns out to be uninformative, offering a trivial verbal substitution in place of insight. (In this respect it is like the view of depiction as the expression of "information" previously discussed.) The objection to saying that some paintings resemble their subjects is not that they don't, but rather that so little is said when only this has been said.

"Looking Like"

I have agreed that stress upon "resemblance," however philosophically uninformative in the end, does at least serve the useful purpose of reminding us how the fact that a painting resembles something *in the sense of looking like it* may be relevant. It would be a willful violation of common sense to say, for instance, that whether a photograph "looks like" a tree, a man, or whatever the case may be, has *nothing* to do with its function as a picture. Certainly a picture may "look like" its subject, but the problem is to see whether we can say anything useful about what "looking like" amounts to. So it should be worth our while to look somewhat more closely at the notions connected with the expression "looking like" or its grammatical variants.

Here we shall immediately find, as in the case of the words connected with "resemblance," that there are paradigmatic uses that need to be distinguished. So let us begin again with some examples.

(1) We are meeting somebody at the station. Pointing to someone approaching in the distance, you say "That looks like him."

(2) On meeting two twin brothers, you say "Tom does look very much like Henry, doesn't he?"

(3) Of a cloud: "Look at that: doesn't it look like a bird?"

(4) We might say of a man: "He looks very much like a wolf."

The first type of case might be identified as one of *seeming*. It can sharply be distinguished from the others by the possibility of substituting the phrase "looks as if," with corresponding adjustment in the rest of the utterance. Thus, in case 1, little if any difference would result from saying "That looks *as if it* were him." Two other grammatical points may be made: If we try to insert adverbial qualification, as in "That looks *very much* like him," we may justifiably feel that we are shifting to another use: thus to the latter remark, but not to the original one I have imagined, it might be natural to reply "I don't see the resemblance." A connected point is the difficulty of negating the original remark: If I want to disagree with "That looks like him," in the intended use, the best I can do is to say "No, that does not look like him" or "I don't think so"—while "No, that looks unlike him" has, in context, the feel of playing on words. For present purposes, we may think of this first use of "looks like" as connected with qualified assertion: the whole utterance has the force of expressing a weak truth-claim with the implication of lack of sufficient and conclusive reason. (Cf. the form "That might be him.") I note this use only to exclude it from further consideration, since it obviously has no application to our prime subject: there is normally no occasion to make qualified assertions about the subject of a painting or picture.[36]

---

[36] An exception might be a case in which we were trying to identify the sitter of some portrait or the actual scene of some landscape. In such special case we might say "It looks like Borgia" or "It looks like Salisbury

The second type of case is the one already discussed, in which explicit and even point-by-point matching is present or in the offing. Here, reference to "resemblance," in uses close to some that we previously listed, is appropriate.

In the third case (the cloud "looking like a bird"), I should want to argue that the attempt to assimilate it with full-blooded matching would be a distortion. For one thing, we seem here to be engaged in some kind of indirect *attribution,* rather than in some implicit comparison. For instance, a supplementary question of the form "Like *which* bird?" would be rejected as stupid, unless taken to be a request for further specification of the attribute, (an eagle, rather than merely a bird). Here it is worth emphasizing that recourse to "points of resemblance" will seem particularly out of place; indeed the form of words "Look at that cloud: doesn't it *resemble* a bird?" will feel like a shift to the previous type of use.[37] One might say that, in certain cases of this type, the speaker is more or less indirectly describing the situation *before him.* It is as if, given the task of describing the cloud in terms of an animal, he were to say "If I *had* to describe it as some kind of animal, the only one that would fit would be 'a bird'." There are some obvious analogies here to the use of metaphor, as contrasted with the use of simile: *looking-like* in the context of attribution, rather than comparison, is closer to metaphor than to simile.

Finally, there are cases like the last ("He looks like a wolf") where the suggestion of comparison, which is admittedly still present, is so far suppressed as to have almost no effect. Saying

---

Plain," with the sense of there is some visual evidence for supposing that that man or that scene was represented.

[37] An obstacle to making this kind of point persuasively is that use of the words I am discussing is more elastic and variable than I may seem to be contending. I do not doubt that "resembles" can sometimes and without impropriety or ambiguity be used as a contextual synonym for "looks like." Yet, if I am not mistaken, the differences in use that I am trying to emphasize really exist and could be fixed more sharply in a longer and more laborious investigation.

of a man that "He looks like a wolf" or, alternatively, "He has a wolfish look" may be a way of recording an immediate impression, with no thought of being able to specify points of resemblance—or, in some cases, of being able to specify *any* ground for the description. In such cases we might be said to be dealing with *nonexponible* metaphor or catachresis. On being challenged as to the propriety of our description, perhaps the best we can say is that it seems to fit—which is, of course, saying very little.

The chief moral that I wish to draw from this brief examination of some related uses of "looks like" is that if we had to position in our schema the use of such a sentence as "That looks like a sheep" (said while pointing to a picture), we should do well to choose the last of our four types. If one says of a painting, or part of one, "That looks like a man," one is normally not saying that there is partial but incomplete evidence for its being a man (which would be preposterous), nor that there are exponible points of resemblance between that patch of painting and a man (which is highly implausible and, in the absence of any assignable point to the comparison, idle), nor attributing a property to that patch as one might, by way of simile, call a cloud birdlike, but rather saying something about that very thing before us, as we say of a man that he has a wolfish look, intending to say something directly about him— and not about a certain imputed relation to wolves. If so, the sense in which a realistic painting "looks like" its subject still resists analysis. One might even be inclined to say, indeed, that that expression ought to be avoided, as tending to have misleading suggestions.

If a child were to ask how one could learn to find out whether a canvas "looks like" a man, perhaps the best we could say is, "Watch a painter at work on his canvas and then, in the end, perhaps you will really *see* a man when you look at the painting." But if that is the best that we can say (as I believe) it looks as if the fruits of our analytical investigation are, after all, very meager.

A Landing Place

I have now completed the task of examining the credentials of plausible candidates for the role of a necessary condition for the holding of the relation of "depiction." I have now satisfied myself, and perhaps the reader also, that none of the criteria examined will supply a necessary condition.

Appeal to the "causal history" of a photograph or a naturalistic painting came to look like the invocation of contingent factual circumstances that may in fact be needed for the production of a terminal visual representation, but do not determine its character as a picture by virtue of logical or linguistic necessity. By considering extraordinary, but logically possible, cases in which deviant causal histories might produce pictures indistinguishable from our paradigms of faithful likenesses, we were able to eliminate appeal to a causal history of a special kind as a necessary or a sufficient condition. And the same verdict, however disappointing, was all that emerged from our examination of the other criteria. Reference to the imputed intentions of the picture's producer seemed enmeshed in hopeless circularity, since the very specification of such an intention required independent specification of what would count as fulfilling the producer's intention. The seductive model of "information," factitiously borrowing prestige from an irrelevant mathematical theory, proved a will-o'-the-wisp, amounting in the end to no more than a linguistic rechristening of the problematic concept of "depiction." Finally, reliance upon the attractive notion of "resemblance" between a picture and its "subject" left us, once we had unraveled the skein of criteria concealed by the deceptive surface unity of the abstract label of "resemblance," with nothing more than our original problem, under the guise of questions as to what it really means to say that a picture "looks like" what it represents, in the crucial cases in which "looking like" cannot properly be assimilated to point-to-point matching with some independently given object of comparison.

Are we then left empty-handed? Should we confess that the investigation we undertook has been a complete failure, with no hope of improvement? Such conclusions would, in my judgment, be too hasty. For the point needs to be made, and with emphasis, that the qualification of some proposed condition as a necessary and sufficient criterion by no means shows that condition to be *irrelevant* to the application of the concept in question.

It would, for instance, be quite wrong to suppose that knowledge of how photographs are regularly produced, and of the perceptible changes that occur in the series: displayed scene, negative, and final positive, have *nothing* to do with our ultimate judgment of the photograph's representative content. On the contrary, our mastery of the skill of interpreting or "reading" photographs depends essentially upon our schematic knowledge of how such photographs are *in fact* normally produced.[38] It is through our knowledge of the photograph's provenance that we understand what the photograph "shows." And in cases of mysterious provenance, as when a layman looks at an X-ray photograph, the absence of relevant factual knowledge of etiology obnubilates comprehension. Indeed, in disputed or ambiguous cases, specific reference to the circumstances of production may be necessary in order to determine *what* the subject is.[39]

---

[38] One might conjecture that a factor in the alleged inability of members of primitive culture to understand photographs on first meeting them may be partly due to such ignorance of the mode of production. If these bewildered would-be interpreters were allowed to follow through the stages of production, with a chance to compare the negative with the external world, they might begin to have a clue to what Erik Stenius has called the "key" of the relevant system of representation (cf. his *Wittgenstein's 'Tractatus'* [Oxford: Basil Blackwell, 1960], p. 93, where the useful term "key" is, however, used in a somewhat more restricted sense). For reports of the inability of primitives to "understand" photographs, see for instance Marshall H. Segall; Donald Campbell; and Melville J. Herskovits, *The Influence of Culture on Visual Perception* [Indianapolis and New York: Bobbs-Merrill, 1966], pp. 32–34.

[39] Some interesting examples will be found in Gombrich 1969. We should, for example, not know what to make of his illustration of the

Similar remarks apply to the currently discredited appeal to the producer's intentions.[40] Although we cannot define "depiction" or "verbal representation" in terms of intention, without vicious circularity, it may be altogether proper, indeed sometimes essential, to refer back to the producer's intentions in order to be able to read the very picture in which his intentions, to the extent that they were successful, were ultimately embodied. Here, as before, to pretend that we could ever learn to understand photographs or paintings without repeated reference to what photographers and painters were trying to achieve, would be unrealistic.

Finally, similar points can be made about "resemblance" and "looking-like." Our justified qualms about the capacity of these to provide defining conditions for the overall concept must not be allowed to obscure the utility, at times, of relying upon point-to-point comparisons or—to jump to something different—to the "way the picture looks" or simply to "what we inescapably see in the picture."

The proper moral to be drawn from the initially disconcerting outcome of our investigation is that the notion of "depicting" is what has been called, a "range concept" or a "cluster concept."[41] The criteria we have considered—and perhaps oth-

---

"Tracks of an oyster catcher" without the accompanying commentary (pp. 35–36)—which explains, *inter alia,* that the bird shown was superimposed on a photograph by an artist. Our knowledge of this unusual causal history materially influences our "reading." Consider also the cases, discussed by Gombrich in the same paper, in which we need to "interpret" photographs of deliberately camouflaged objects (pp. 37 ff.). I agree with Gombrich that "knowledge, a well-stocked mind, is clearly the key to the practice of interpretation" (p. 37). But I think it is also *a* key to the very mastery of the relevant *concept* of interpretation.

[40] This is hardly the place to discuss the so-called "Intentional Fallacy" that has been memorably castigated in William K. Wimsatt, Jr. *The Verbal Icon* (Lexington, Ky.: University of Kentucky Press, 1954). Professor Reich makes the useful and commonly overlooked point that Wimsatt (and his collaborator Monroe Beardsley) "carefully distinguished between three types of intentional evidence, acknowledging that two of them are proper and admissible" (Hirsch, *op. cit.,* p. 11).

[41] For the general methodology of handling such concepts see Max Black, *Problems of Analysis* (London: Routledge & Kegan Paul, 1954), ch. 2.

ers we have overlooked—form a skein, none of them being separately necessary or sufficient, but each of them relevant in the sense of potentially counting toward the proper application of the concept of depiction. In perfectly clear cases, all of the relevant criteria point together toward the same judgment, whether we rely upon what we know about the method of production, the intentions of the producer, or the sheer "look" of the picture as it appears to a competent viewer, with a previous experience of the tradition within which the picture is placed.[42]

A reader who might agree with this kind of moral might still perhaps wonder why, if "depicting" is properly to be viewed as a "range-" or "cluster-concept," just *these* criteria should have been "clustered" together. One answer might be to invite such a questioner to undertake the *Gedankenexperiment* of imagining conditions in which the criteria were disassociated.[43] The point of *our* concept of depiction—the "only concept we have"—might then become plainer. But such an answer, whatever its pedagogical merits, is somewhat evasive.

There is something of the first importance lacking from our account, namely all consideration of the purposes of the activities in the course of which, what we, in our culture, recognize as "pictures" are produced. And no account of the concept of depicting, or of the various related concepts bundled together under that label could be adequate without some examination of such purposes.

This weakness in our discussion might even be felt in con-

---

[42] Hard cases of "interpretation" typically arise when there is a real or apparent conflict between the defining criteria. When, for instance, we have firm evidence of the producer's intentions and of the means for realizing his intentions within the tradition to which he adheres, but cannot yet "see" the desired embodiment in the picture itself and do not know whether to blame the artist or ourselves.

[43] For instance, by imagining, *in full detail*, what the situation would be in a "tribe" (that convenient mental construct) whose members were keenly interested in "seen" likenesses, in total disregard of the intentions or modes of productions of such objects.

ception with our account of how photographs depict. Photographs have been talked about in this essay as if they were objects having no identifiable uses and consequently no intelligible interest. But we are obviously keenly interested in photographs, and for a variety of reasons. If we focus upon one such interest, say that of *identifying persons* (as in passport photographs), we shall not find it difficult to see why some of our criteria harmonize with that purpose. Of course, it is by no means easy to formulate, with any show of thoroughness, the many purposes that photographs serve in our culture; and when we pass to the more difficult realm of art objects, the difficulties multiply. But the moral to be drawn is that clarity about the basic notion of artistic representation cannot be expected to be reached by a process of logical analysis alone, however sophisticated in its apparatus of "cluster concepts" and "family resemblances," but will call for a less tidy and more exacting inquiry into the production and appreciation of art objects as "ways of life." But this is hardly the place for what is already too long and labored a discussion.[44]

[44] One of the great merits of Wollheim's stimulating little book on aesthetics (Richard Wollheim, *Art and Its Objects* [New York: Harper & Row, 1968]) is that he initiates such discussion.

VIII

The Structure of Symbols

Introduction

Nelson Goodman's important book *The Languages of Art*[1] runs a serious risk of being misunderstood and consequently undervalued. The arrangement is unorthodox, weaving together discussion of specific problems in the philosophy of art with an ambitious outline of a general theory of symbolism. Furthermore, there is presupposed throughout an original and far-reaching metaphysical position that is assumed rather than fully explained.

The very title is somewhat misleading, as Goodman, with typical candor, confesses. " 'Languages' in my title," he says, "should, strictly, be replaced by 'symbol systems' " (p. xi) . For his main purpose is to supply "an approach to a *general theory of symbols*" (p. xi; emphasis added) . He is especially concerned with the neglected field of "nonverbal symbol systems, from pictorial representation on the one hand to musical notation on the other [in the hope of furthering] comprehensive grasp of the modes and means of reference and of their varied and pervasive uses in the operations of the understanding" (p. xi) . This is a welcome and exciting undertaking, which deserves close study.

Goodman's preliminary declaration of intent is still perhaps misleading in its emphasis. For it is clear that, however strongly interested in a *general* theory of symbol systems, he also has his attention sharply focused upon certain key problems in the

---

[1] *Languages of Art: An Approach to the Theory of Symbols* (Indianapolis, Ind., 1968) ; hereafter referred to as Goodman, 1968.

theory of the arts: to read his book mainly for the light it throws upon certain fundamental issues in aesthetics, as many readers are bound to do, would not be a willful distortion of the author's intentions. Goodman's discussions of topics related to aesthetics are among the most provocative and valuable contributions of his book.[2]

Within the intricately woven fabric of Goodman's argument, we can distinguish the following strands: (1) contributions to a general theory of meaning, and, notably, an original account of the nature of "expressive symbolism," (2) a general theory of "symbol systems," and of the special kind of such systems called "notations," (3) relatively independent discussions of certain special topics in the theory of art: among them, the theory of linear perspective, and the problem of authenticating works of art, (4) applications of the general theory of symbol systems and notations to the reclassification and reordering of art forms, (5) some philosophical morals concerning the relations between "aesthetic experience" and "cognitive experience." The reader needs to be warned again that Goodman's thought is dominated, to an extent altogether exceptional in writers on similar themes, by a metaphysical position—his own distinctive brand of "nominalism," making its influence felt throughout.[3]

The logical relationships between the above-identified strands are roughly as follows. The general theory of symbols—the author's main interest according to his introductory statement —depends strongly upon his general theory of meaning. The applications of the general theory to art forms requires much

[2] The book is certainly destined to become a classic, which it would be folly to ignore and impertinence to praise. Let me state, once and for all, my admiration and gratitude for a work that is continuously illuminating —perhaps especially so when it provokes disagreement. It has rare distinction of style, showing throughout the impress of a keen intelligence that can indulge in epigram and wit without sacrifice of seriousness.

[3] It is a pity that Goodman omitted from this book any explicit statement of his "nominalism," leaving its detailed character to be gathered from his previous writings.

additional and independent assertion concerning the characters of the various arts. (Thus, reservations about such applications are not necessarily damaging to the general theory.) The concluding philosophical morals are rendered plausible by much that precedes, but use additional epistemological premises that are perhaps insufficiently elaborated. Finally, Goodman's discussions of specific aesthetic questions stand on their own feet, and could survive even if the rest were rejected.[4]

Behind this imputed logical order, one can discern a somewhat different structure of motivation. A reader will soon detect hostility, on Goodman's part, to any position that draws a sharp distinction between verbal and nonverbal symbolism and an allied rejection of the popular view that some works of painting have a "natural" relation of "resemblance" to their subject matter. Because he regards these popular views as mischievous prejudices, he sees the need for a revolutionary reordering of the language that we use in talking and thinking about symbol systems. In his treatment, puzzles about the nature of linear perspective, or about how to distinguish spurious from authentic works of art, function as more than exercises, providing on the one hand reinforcement for the rejection of "naturalism" and on the other a strong motivation for an emphasis upon the identifying role of a notation that dominates his general theory of symbols.

It would be impossible to do justice to this fascinating book without occupying time which might be better spent in grappling with the original. I shall confine myself to remarks and tentative criticisms that might help the kind of reader that Goodman deserves. In what follows, I shall discuss Goodman's views roughly in the order in which I have listed them above, but with a prefatory consideration of the general ontological position that underpins them.

---

[4] They impressed me as provocative and interesting, but I shall not discuss them in this study.

Goodman's Nominalism[5]

A Universe of Individuals

Stated quite badly, Goodman's conception of the universe is that it consists only of "individuals" and of certain properties of and relations between such individuals. Goodman says, "Nominalism [in his special sense, that might have surprised some medieval nominalists], then, consists of the refusal to countenance any entities other than individuals. Its opposite, Platonism [again, in an idiosyncratic sense of that word], recognizes at least some 'nonindividuals' " (1951, pp. 33–34). Or, more simply still: "For me, as a nominalist, the world is a world of individuals" (1956, p. 15). It will be noticed that Goodman says nothing so far about the admissibility of properties or relations of individuals.

But what is an "individual"? Goodman claims that we have a rough layman's understanding of that word, from which, however, he deviates fairly sharply for his own theoretical purposes (1956, p. 15). As clarification of his technical usage, he offers the following formula: "to treat entities as individuals for a system is to take them as values of the variables of lowest type in the system" (1956, p. 17). For present purposes, I think, it might be enough to think of an "individual" as whatever is irreducibly nameable in a given system (although this is *not* the way that Goodman puts it). I call an expression such as "the average man" a reducible name or designation, because it could be eliminated, in principle at least, by means of contextual definitions.

It is important to observe that the conditions for something to be an individual, conceived in so abstract a way (using

[5] The main source is Goodman's treatise, *The Structure of Appearance* (Cambridge, Mass., 1951; hereafter referred to as Goodman, 1951). But see also the valuable reply to criticism entitled "A World of Individuals," in *The Problem of Universals* (Notre Dame, 1956). This relatively inaccessible paper—hereafter referred to as Goodman, 1956—has now been reprinted in Goodman's collection of essays, *Problems and Projects* (Indianapolis and New York, 1972).

either Goodman's formula or my own), allow a wide range of choice of the individuals—the ultimate building blocks, as it were, of the universe. In *Structure of Appearance,* Goodman chose a certain kind of phenomenalism, recognizing as his ontological atoms the so-called "qualia" (a term originally suggested by C. I. Lewis)—that is to say, roughly speaking, certain perceptible characters of experience. I suppose some kind of primitive Pythagorean, who thought that numbers, conceived as irreducible to other entities, were the stuff of which the universe was made, could still count as a "nominalist" in Goodman's sense. Nothing in his commitment requires the individuals to be "concrete" rather than "abstract."[6]

Since Goodman's earlier adoption of a sophisticated phenomenalism plays no part in the book here under discussion, we shall not distort his position if we couple "nominalism" with materialism and think of the ultimate elements as bounded regions of space-time.

Where Goodman departs rather sharply from ordinary usage is in allowing the sum of several such separated individuals (as Pakistan is the sum of East and West Pakistan) to count as a single individual. This device is indispensable for him. For, roughly speaking, the familiar relation of subject and predicate (or member and containing class) is replaced in his system by the part-whole relation between individuals.

Goodman's nominalism is notably tolerant to the presence of any kinds of predicates or relation-words applying to the chosen individuals—provided only that such terms are not treated as further names (i.e., provided they are not available for quantification). "The nominalist may use whatever predicates of individuals he likes" (1951, p. 35)—that is to say, provided that they are treated as "syncategorematic."[7]

---

[6] "I do not look upon abstractness as either a necessary or sufficient test of incomprehensibility" (Goodman, 1956, p. 16).

[7] "In building a system, we must consider carefully what terms we are willing to interpret as denoting and what terms we want to interpret syncategorematically" (Goodman, 1956, p. 17).

For Goodman, what he forbids is perhaps even more important than what he will permit. He objects to such allegedly occult entities as properties or classes[8]—and perhaps especially the latter.[9] So, throughout Goodman's book, we should beware of thinking that a word is some abstract entity or "type" having phonological embodiment, or even the class of such a word's actual and possible inscriptions; it is, however, admissible to conceive of the word "red," say, as the superindividual composed of the sum of all its actual occurrences or "inscriptions." And similarly, we must not let ourselves be seduced into thinking that to a predicate such as "red" there answers some "property" of, say, redness; the universe contains only the predicate (the sum of the corresponding inscriptions, themselves individuals) and the individuals to which that predicate applies (the particular things that are red) .

Comment

Ontological commitments are forbiddingly hard to submit to rational assessment, if only because they are intended to have large-scale theoretical consequences. If Goodman can provide a general conceptual framework, on such a self-denying basis of fundamental assumptions, purging the universe meanwhile of classes, powers, possibilities, and the like, an onlooker can only wish him well and await the detailed results.[10] I confess to some qualms as to whether a universe thus delineated is properly describable as a "world of *individuals*." Common sense might wish to object that the admissible predicates of individuals must surely correspond to "something in the world"

[8] "Some of the things that seem to me inacceptable without explanation are powers or dispositions, counterfactual assertations, entities or experiences that are possible but not actual, neutrinos, angels, devils and classes" (Goodman, *Fact, Fiction and Forecast*, 2d ed. (Indianapolis, Ind., 1965), p. 33; hereafter referred to as Goodman, 1965.

[9] "Nominalism for me consists specifically in the refusal to recognize classes" (Goodman, 1956, p. 16) .

[10] One needs to read *The Structure of Appearance* all the way through to appreciate Goodman's extraordinary inventiveness and resourcefulness.

—to speak with intentional crudity—even if the objective correlates of such predicates are distinct from "individuals." (This
I take to have been the position of Frege with respect to the
functions that he regarded as "unsaturated," or syncategorematic, and therefore unavailable for independent designation.)
Given Goodman's hospitable attitude to abstract entities, I
can see little reason why he should balk at allowing something
"out there" to answer to a predicate. (No doubt he would regard this last sentence, with its use of "something," as incoherent.) To be sure, anybody who accepts Quine's dictum
that to be is to be the value of a variable will retort that, in
the presence of a prohibition against quantifying over predicate-
correlates, such alleged correlates cannot be said to exist. But I
have never found that dictum self-evident or persuasive.

For the purpose of assessing Goodman's general theory of
symbols, it might seem that such thorny ontological issues can
be by-passed (which would be fortunate for any reader who
felt incompetent to cope with them). In a conciliatory mood,
Goodman is willing to allow his "Platonistic" opponents to
"countenance" properties if it gives them any satisfaction.[11] He
claims that any moves he makes must be acceptable to Pla-
tonists,[12] so that their additional ontological commitments are
idle myths.

It is an attractive and irenic suggestion that Goodman's conception of the universe is a kind of minimal ontology, to which
all can subscribe, for a start. (Ontological underclothes, as it
were, to which additional garments can be added at will.) I
think, however, it is underrating the intellectual consequences
of ontological commitments, in the style of Goodman or another philosopher, to suppose that they can be adopted quite
so innocently. Goodman's ontology, as I shall later try to show,

---

[11] In less tolerant moments, he refers to the recognition of properties as
"a prissy prejudice" and as "pussyfooting" (Goodman, 1968, p. 87).

[12] "Every device he [the nominalist] uses, every step he takes, is acceptable to his opponents; he makes no move that is not entirely legitimate
by platonistic standards" (Goodman, 1956, p. 31).

enforces or at least strongly encourages certain preferred ways of reorganizing and structuring a complex subject matter. He has himself well said that "symbolization . . . is to be judged fundamentally by how well it serves the cognitive purpose: by the delicacy of its discriminations and the aptness of its allusions; by the way it works in grasping, exploring and informing the world; by how it analyzes, sorts, orders, and organizes; by how it participates in the making, manipulation, retention and transformation of knowledge" (1968, p. 258). Now Goodman's theory of symbol systems and their relation to art forms is itself a proposed novel "symbolization," requiring a new terminology that reflects a new pattern of discriminations, allusions, and linkages. It would be surprising indeed if a shift from, say, regarding the universe as composed of atomic facts to regarding it as composed of individual space-time regions in part-whole relations had no consequences for such conceptual restructuring. I believe the contrary to be the case: Goodman's nominalism does have consequences. That is one reason why it is important.

The Linguistic Springboard
Against Mimesis

Goodman is inveterately opposed to what might be called a "disparity view" of the relations between verbal representation and pictorial depiction, that is to say a view to the effect that words and pictures symbolize[13] in radically different ways. Common sense thinks there is an immense difference between showing a lion in a photograph, or in a naturalistic painting, and talking about him; we look into a picture, seeing the depicted scene there and then, but we have to understand the story,

[13] Wherever a word, an expression, a sentence, a picture, a diagram, a model, etc. may be said to "stand for" something, or mean something, or signify something, I shall speak of "symbolization"; I shall call whatever is thus symbolized the "import" of the symbol in question. This is approximately how Goodman uses "symbol" and "symbolize," although this use of the deliberately neutral word "import" is my own.

guided by arbitrary conventions that connect the words with their import. Pictures supply knowledge-of, narratives, knowledge-about; the first aim at fidelity, the second at truth. So far the voice of "common sense" and, with modifications, the principled convictions of a long line of philosophers of art, headed by Aristotle, who have assigned a central role in their theories to "imitation" or "mimesis."

Now Goodman is a resolute enemy of any such "disparity view."[14] Looking beyond obvious superficial dissimilarities among pictures, stories, and other types of symbols, such as graphs or musical notations, he undertakes to reveal general principles of classification and comparison that cut across the distinctions that underpin a disparity view. He argues that the notion of a "natural" or "nonconventional" symbol is a chimera, and a dangerous one. All symbolization, in whatever medium, and using whatever special devices, requires the imposition of conventions that are arbitrary, in the sense of being only contingently determined by given human purposes and the customs and traditions in which such purposes are manifested: they are *not* required by some independently existing subject matter that is to be "copied" or "reflected" or "imaged." Hence, all pictures, whether "naturalistic" or "nonrepresentational" and all symbols without exception, need to be "interpreted" with the aid of appropriate conventions: all symbols must be read.

Language as a Paradigm

The starting point for this attack upon disparity prejudices is the special kind of symbolism we call language.[15] Here, in

[14] I shall not say more about Goodman's objections, for which see especially (1968, p. 4). I think he ties the object of his criticism too closely to a crude notion of "resemblance" that he is able to demolish by a few rather obvious counterexamples. But Goodman's views about the nature of pictorial symbolization can in any case stand on their own feet.

[15] That is why, so far as the book is about pictorial symbolization, it might have been called "A Picture Theory of Language." Cf. Goodman's interesting remark in an earlier essay: "I began by dropping the picture

this exemplary and paradigmatic case, Goodman roots his main explanatory concepts, such as "denotation" and "reference" (although with some eventual extension of these terms). His thought moves, by generalization and extrapolation, from language to other modes of symbolization.

A Nominalistic Approach to Meaning

The most striking overall feature of Goodman's metalinguistic apparatus is its extraordinary economy. Everything that might preanalytically be brought within the scope of "meaning" or "signification" is, in Goodman's presentation, somehow assimilated to the single notion of "detonation," or to some logical transformation of that notion.

We are provided with no explicit explanation of "denotation"—but the point of departure is clear enough. Consider the case in which a general word such as "man" (or perhaps, more strictly for a nominalist, the sum-individual composed of all the actual tokens of that word) denotes each and every actual man, past, present, and future: then the common "label" (a favorite word with Goodman) is conceived to stand for or to refer to each person to whom it is timelessly applicable. Next, the very same relation of denotation is also held to be present in the link between a proper name or a veridical definite description with its actual bearer: denotation (and the layman's "meaning" for which it is the technical surrogate) is assimilated to reference. Nothing—or almost nothing—is said about any other semantic relation accompanying and determining reference: a notion of something like "connotation," in Mill's fashion, or of "sense," in Frege's, is uncongenial to Goodman. (It would presumably lead us to recognize the existence

theory of language and ended by adopting the language theory of pictures" ("The Way the World Is," *Review of Metaphysics*, 14 [1960–61], 56; hereafter referred to as Goodman, 1960–61). He explains that he is reacting against "a certain absolutistic notion concerning both picture and language" (*ibid.*, pp. 55–56), the view that symbolism must reflect or mirror a preexisting structure of "the world," as in Wittgenstein's *Tractatus*.

of properties—a category that, as we have seen, the nominalist cannot "countenance.") No distinction is drawn between the meanings of words and sentences,[16] and none between syntactic and semantic aspects of meaning; nor is any attention given to the commonplace contrast of speaker's meaning and lexical meaning—indeed the systematic aspects of meaning are almost totally ignored.[17] Goodman's silence on these topics is deafening.

Nevertheless, exclusive reliance upon denotation as an explanatory concept is, and is intended to be, distinctive of Goodman's approach throughout. When he comes to speak of the "representation"[18] to be found in painting or sculpture, he says forthrightly, "Denotation is the core of representation" (1968, p. 5) and adds, "The relation between a picture and what it represents is thus *assimilated to the relation between a predicate and what it applies to*" (1968, p. 5; emphasis added), so that "representation is a special kind of denotation" (1968, p. 5). Of course, only in exceptional cases, such as those of portraiture, can a picture be assimilated to some veridical definite description such as "the general who crossed the Rubicon." Hence a prime obstacle to be overcome, on the view under discussion, will be that of how to understand "fictive" representation (for which see the next section).

---

[16] It is forbiddingly hard to see how a plausible account of the meaning, even of a true sentence, can be given by invoking reference or denotation alone. Goodman would certainly not want to follow Frege in supposing that sentences are names of The True or The False; but I fancy he would not be much happier in considering them as referring to facts or states of affairs. I cannot find a theory of truth either in the present book or in any of Goodman's other writings.

[17] There are occasional and welcome exceptions, as when Goodman says, in connection with metaphor, "a label functions not in isolation but as belonging to a family" (1963, p. 71). But this idea receives little elaboration.

[18] "Representing," as Goodman uses that word, is short for "pictorially representing" and is in regular contrast with "describing," which is reserved for verbal symbolization. A typical remark illustrating these usages is: "What we have done so far is to subsume representation with description under denotation" (1968, p. 42).

Comment

At first blush, it seems willfully paradoxical to think of a painting as standing to its subject, the person or scene depicted, in the same relation that the predicate "man" stands to each thing properly called a man. Nor is the impression of paradox removed by Goodman's ultimate extension of the scope of "denotation," when he finds it advisable to use the word "somewhat more broadly than is usual, to cover a system where scores are correlated with performances complying[19] with them, or words with their pronunciation, as well as a system where words are correlated with what they apply to or name" (1968, pp. 143–144). Has "denotation" preserved its original sense in this radical extension of application? "Offhand indeed," Goodman says, "the relation between a term and what it denotes appears quite different from that between a score and its performances or between a letter and its occurrences; but no very clear principle seems to underlie this difference" (1968, p. 200). But do we need a "clear principle" to restrain us from "assimilating" things that look so obviously different?

One might be tempted, at this point, to treat "denote" as a mere stylistic variant upon "symbolize," as I am using it, i.e., as a neutral label for the relation between a symbol and whatever it symbolizes, implying no theoretical analysis of the relation in question.[20] But to do so would be to misconstrue Goodman's undertaking. The point of his notion of denoting (the

---

[19] "Compliance" is Goodman's technical variant for the converse of denotation, used to mark his extended uses of the latter term: "I shall use 'complies with' as interchangable with 'is denoted by,' 'has a compliant' as interchangeable with 'denotes,' and 'compliance-class' as interchangeable with 'extension'" (1968, p. 144).

[20] Goodman's *general* label for symbolization is "reference," of which denotation is a species. Cf. such remarks as "a picture, to represent an object, must be a symbol for it, stand for it, refer to it" (1968, p. 5) and "a picture must symbolize, refer to, what it expresses" (1968, p. 52). In such contexts, as throughout, "refer to" is not an innocent and neutral alternative to "stand for," but is still bound to the dominating conception that only actual individuals can be "referred" to.

substitute for the common concept of "meaning" in his investigations), whether in connection with predicates or proper names, or in its extended application to symbol systems, is the commitment that the things denoted shall actually exist. Of course, one is bound to wonder how Goodman will surmount the problem of accounting for the fact that so many works of art, if they represent at all, seem *prima facie* to be symbolizing something fictitious or imaginary. Let us consider his solution.

The Prevalence of Unicorn-Pictures

Given that "unicorn" and "centaur" apply to no actual individuals, have no extensions, are we to say that they have no "denotations" and therefore mean the same thing, that is to say nothing? Obviously, Goodman cannot accept this—not because it violates common sense, for which he has little respect, but because, given the fictitiousness of what is represented in pictorial art, it would reduce his theory to vacuity. Even Oscar Wilde might have balked at saying that all art says the same thing—nothing! Goodman's way out is ingenious.[21]

Words of null-extension, such as those cited above, sometimes occur as parts of compounds having genuine, nonnull, extensions. There do exist pictures of unicorns ("unicorn-pictures" for short), and also pictures of centaurs ("centaur-pictures"), and the two sets of pictures do not coincide. Likewise, in cases of terms that do not refer to visibles, say "even prime greater than two" and "perfectly good man," there do exist different "descriptions" (treated, by analogy, as verbal pictures, so to speak). The compound description "prime greater than five and less than seven" is not the same *description* as "perfectly good man now alive," examples which suffice to show that "prime-greater-than-five-description" and "perfectly-good-man-

[21] See his paper, "On Likeness of Meaning," *Analysis,* 10 (1949), 1–7; hereafter referred to as Goodman, 1949, and also his "On Some Differences about Meaning," *Analysis,* 13 (1953), 90–96; hereafter referred to as Goodman, 1953, which contains rebuttals to the lively criticisms evoked by the earlier paper and some welcome elaboration of his own standpoint.

description" both denote actual, but different things. Goodman says, therefore, that "unicorn" and "centaur" have different "secondary extensions," inasmuch as compounds containing them, like "unicorn-picture" and "centaur-picture," have different primary extensions (= denotations). The final formula proposed is: "Two terms have the same meaning if and only if they have the same primary and secondary extensions" (1949, p. 5).

It follows at once that there are no genuine synonyms in language. Take "quickly" and "swiftly," for instance: the compound predicates "quickly-description" and "swiftly-description" certainly have different extensions, so the original words must be nonsynonymous, according to the proposed analysis. More simply still, we might rely upon the differences in extension between "quickly-label" and "swiftly-label," and so in general. Whenever we have two terms, T_1 and T_2, alleged to be synonymous, we can be sure that the corresponding compound predicates "T_1-label" and "T_2-label" will have different extensions, and so the paradoxical result follows.[22]

This remarkable result—which plainly gratifies Goodman's pleasure in shocking common sense—is, however, not the center of his interest. If some way could be found to alleviate the paradox—perhaps by distinguishing between various kinds of contexts in which vacuous predicates can occur as parts—nothing would be lost. All he wants is a use of, say, "unicorn," which treats it as syncategorematic—as a mere auxiliary component in a genuinely denoting predicate constructed with its assistance.[23]

[22] Goodman does not use this argument, but it should be acceptable to him.

[23] It might be objected that this makes no provision for the use of "unicorn" and other vacuous predicates in primary extension. I suspect that Goodman would have to count the assertions "Unicorns are part horse," "Unicorns are part tiger," and the corresponding assertions with "centaur" replacing "unicorn," as being indifferently true. This difficulty, if it is one, should be added to other obvious cruxes for any theory of meaning relying exclusively upon denotation: that no two persons can

Goodman seems to assume that his treatment of vacuous predicates must not allow a compound predicate such as "picture-of-a-unicorn" to be regarded as a semantic function of the predicate "unicorn"; for else we should have to concede that "unicorn" had an independent meaning, determined apart from its occurrence in compounds. That is why he insists that " 'picture of Pickwick' and 'represents a unicorn' are better considered unbreakable[24] one-place predicates or class-terms, like 'desk' and 'table' " (1968, p. 21). And just before that remark he says, "Much as most pieces of furniture are readily sorted out as desks, chairs, tables, etc., so most pictures are readily sorted out as pictures of Pickwick, of Pegasus, of a unicorn, etc., *without reference to anything represented*" (1968, p. 21; emphasis added). One might perhaps say that, according to Goodman, a unicorn-picture is no more to be regarded as a picture *of* a unicorn than a ship is to be considered as having something to do with a hip—or a bullseye with bulls.

But something is surely wrong here. The plausibility of "secondary extension" as a test for synonymity depends upon the nonaccidental presence of "unicorn" in such compounds as "picture of a unicorn"; while, on the other hand, it is no indication of difference in meaning between "in" and "up" that "pin" and "pup" do have different extensions.

----

normally attach the same meanings to the predicates they use; that what the meaning of "horse" is must be a contingent fact as to which individual things are horses; that the intended meaning of "horse" can never be known; and so on. Goodman's resourcefulness would, I suspect, be equal to the task of explaining such difficulties away. But too many *ad hoc* dodges tend to discredit a general theory.

[24] In reply to criticism, Goodman has admitted that "unbreakable" was an unfortunate choice here. "I did not mean to restrict our freedom to treat such predicates as conjunctive," he said, and, "Since such predicate-splitting is not prohibited, the epithet 'unbreakable'—intended merely to reinforce 'oneplace'—is misleading and should be omitted" ("Some Notes on *Languages of Art*," *Journal of Philosophy* 57 [1970], 564). The sole point that Goodman wishes to emphasize is that "*p* is a unicorn-picture" must not be taken as implying that there *exists* some unicorn of which *p* is a picture.

I see nothing in Goodman's general position that would forbid the recognition of linguistic operators with regular semantic roles generating, for instance, a predicate of the form "picture-of-X" from a given predicate "X." Such recognition would be compatible with denying the kind of analysis that would parse "picture of a unicorn" as implying the existence of a unicorn, and would serve Goodman's purpose without unnecessary overcommitment. It would, to be sure, entail recognition of another way in which linguistic units contribute to meaning; but that would be an advantage. Nor need it be, so far as I can see, inconsistent with nominalistic commitments. Given that predicates, for Goodman, already have a kind of syncategorematic function that does not require them to denote out of context, why should we not recognize higher order syncategorematicals, having a similar function?

In order for this device to work, we should, to be sure, need to be able to specify in some way the linguistic uses of a denotatively vacuous term such as "unicorn," without invoking the totality of its occurrences in compounds. In so doing, however, we should not be committed to acknowledging the existence of a "connotation" in some objectionable sense. It would suffice to recognize certain privileged assertions containing the word "unicorn" (those that we should commonly admit as definitions or partial explanations of meaning) as expressing linguistic truths about unicorns. Then the uses of some, but not all, compound predicates would be derivable from such rules of use. And thus we could settle questions about synonymy (which, however, are generally somewhat underdetermined in the absence of information about which features of use count as relevant) by reference to just the privileged compounds in which the putative synonyms occur.

All of which, to be sure, is at some distance from Goodman's conception. But in the absence of some such supplementation, the relations between compound predicates and their components, or between the use, say of "unicorn," in "No unicorns exist" and in "That is a picture of a unicorn" remain mysteri-

ous. It is ultimately unsatisfactory simply to regard the applications of simple and compound labels as a brute fact, or at any
rate one that is no concern of a theorist of symbolism.

The Riddle of Expression

A different kind of task for Goodman's approach is constituted by what is commonly called "expression." What is at stake
can perhaps be elucidated by drawing a contrast between what
I shall call "external" (or: remote) meaning as contrasted with
"internal" (or: proximate) meaning.

In cases of real or fictitious representation, there is usually
an obvious difference between the symbol and its import: A
painting known as *The Laughing Cavalier* depicts some real or
imaginary man; the verbal expression "The Laughing Cavalier"
refers to a painting. In each case, the symbol is one thing, its
import another. Even in cases of self-reference, the same holds.
When a sentence starts with "The opening words of this sentence . . . ," those words do indeed refer to themselves, but
only *per accidens:* the start of the sentence leads us, if we understand it, to something (its reference) which turns out to be the
starting point. When a symbol is thus distinct from its import
or only contingently identical with that import, I propose to
speak of *external* meaning.

On the other hand, there are many familiar cases where we
are initially reluctant to recognize a corresponding gap between
the symbol and its import, and wish to say, however obscurely,
that the symbol "manifests" or "bodies forth" or "displays" its
meaning. We say that the *Funeral March* is sad, and would find
it far-fetched to claim that it stood for or referred to sadness;
or we may describe a smile *as* happy, and not as an indicator
or index or sign of happiness, although it may also be those
things. In such cases, there seems to be no hiatus between the
symbol and its import; in grasping the one we think that we
necessarily grasp the other. When a symbol necessarily contains
its import or a part of it, I propose to speak of *internal* mean-

ing. (Of course, the contrast proposed might turn out to be illusory.)

Now it is natural to confine expression, in at least one important sense of that versatile word, to cases of "internal meaning." The music, we say, expresses sadness, the smile expresses happiness, the loser's outburst expresses his disappointment, and so on. Whether we can speak in the same way of a painting expressing harmony, or grace, or a balance of forces, is one of aesthetics' many tantalizing and unsolved questions.

Current uses of "expressing" and its cognates inevitably suggests a kind of "toothpaste theory," as of import being vented or squeezed out into its symbolic manifestation. But this suggestion can be suppressed. Whether or not an integral part of the import exists antecedently to its expression (a question interesting enough in its own right) is subordinate in importance to questions about the genuineness of the imputed immediacy of "expression." Should we, for instance, recognize two markedly different modes of symbolization, or should the imputed "immediacy" be explained away as an interesting, but theoretically unimportant, variation upon general features of symbolism? This seems to me the chief unresolved conceptual puzzle about expression. But the topic remains disconcertingly obscure. One may agree with Goodman that the available answers are no better than a "chaos" (1968, p. 94) in which expression appears "either as sacredly occult or as hopelessly obscure" (1968, p. 94).

Goodman needs to be able to give some analysis of expression in order to achieve his goal of a general theory of symbols. For the segment of his theory so far discussed will accommodate at best only instances of "external" symbolizing, in which the picture or the narrative point to something other and distinct from the symbol, or only contingently identical with it. But to stop there would be to abandon the vast range of cases in which the communicative or aesthetic point of an utterance, a gesture, or a work of art is not that of referring to something else, but rather (if our intuitions are not mistaken) to *presenting* an import with that mysterious immediacy we have in mind when speaking of "expression." The case of music, which transmits no independent "message," is, of course, crucial; but even in cases of apparently realistic or naturalistic art, the "expressive" aspects are at least as important as the representational ones.

Goodman's solution has a breath-taking simplicity and audacity. A simplified account might run as follows: First, when we find a smile sad (to use Goodman's own example) the smile really *is* sad, *but only in a figurative or metaphorical sense.* So far we have only an instance of "metaphorical exemplification" —as, say, when a cloud is called angry, or a man's remarks nebulous, or a painting fidgety. But now suppose that the smile in question is also being used to refer to or to symbolize sadness (as when I answer a question about my feelings by smiling at you in a certain way); then the smile stands for what it also metaphorically exemplifies, and we do have, according to Goodman, a clear case of expression. On this view, in short, expression is figurative exemplification together with reference to the exemplified: "If *a* expresses *b* then: (1) *a* possesses or is denoted by *b;* (2) this possession or denotation is metaphorical; and (3) *a* refers to *b*" (1968, p. 95).

So far, I have been reporting in the "Platonizing" style that Goodman regards as a "prissy prejudice." His official story is complicated, as the reader will now expect, by his need to think of an expressive symbol as referring not to some allegedly occult property of sadness, but rather to the corresponding predicate, "sad." And, similarly, what the smile possesses or exemplifies is, on the full view, not the property of sadness but rather the corresponding predicate. A further slight complication is needed in order to accommodate cases in which the relevant predicate would not, strictly speaking, be "sad" but some synonymous label, whether in the same language ("mournful") or in another ("triste"). So the final answer, in brief, runs: "The picture [expressing sadness] metaphorically exemplifies sadness if *some label coextensive with 'sad'* is referred to by and metaphorically denotes the picture" (1968, p. 85; emphasis added). And *mutatis mutandis,* the same applies to expression.

Comment

Goodman claims that the *Funeral March* does not express sadness unless it refers to the predicate "sad" or some synonym of "sad." That is too much to ask anybody to accept who is not already irrevocably committed to Goodman's variety of nominalism. For remember that the predicate in question is, on his view, the set of all the marks and sounds that are tokens of the type-word "sad" (or, on another interpretation, the individual composed of all those inscriptions as parts). One wants to object that even if the imputed reference to sadness (to speak with the vulgar again) were to be allowed, one would find it hard to construe that as a crypto-reference to marks and noises. Surely the reference could not be to such "inscriptions" as mere physical things, but at least to them in their role or function of meaning sadness? (Cf. speaking, in a more plausible case, of "The Black King" in chess; surely we are not referring to certain pieces of wood and ivory merely as physical objects?) But let this difficulty pass. It might prove upon examination that Goodman here, as elsewhere, is being less paradoxical than he seems and that what he says can be read, by "bracketing" his ontological commitments, as a learned restatement of common sense. It is in any case a pervasive difficulty, stemming from his rejection of talk about properties, and not peculiar to this special department of his investigation.

A more specific difficulty is that Goodman's analysis seems, on the face of it, to be restricted to expressive symbolizing. Yet normally, we would want to recognize clear cases of "expression" in which, so far as I can see, there would really be no question of the gesture, say, as symbolizing something as abstract as a predicate (or the corresponding composite-inscription-individual). When a woman answers a question about her feelings by looking sadly at her interlocutor, she might reasonably be said to be referring to sadness by her gesture; but what if she merely weeps *in* misery? Should we then deny that her tears are expressive, and indeed expressive of misery? It looks as if here we have a case of expression that is not a case of expressive symbolism. Of course it is Goodman's privilege to restrict the scope of his analysis in this way, since he is after all primarily interested in symbolization and not in expression per se, if there is such a thing.

But considered now solely as an analysis of expressive symbolization, the account offered seems to rely too heavily upon the problematic and dubiously explanatory notion of metaphor. Whether the smile expresses sadness, Goodman says, depends upon whether the smile is properly called "sad" in some metaphorical sense. (He insists that the sadness really is possessed, even if the attribution is metaphorical or figurative.) But, how are we to tell whether this is so? In the case of stock metaphors, linguistic usage may provide a determinate answer to the question, though even then I would be less confident than Goodman in identifying cases as clearly metaphorical. Is it a metaphor to call the smile sad, or a number high? I should have thought it at least as plausible to say that we are dealing with secondary literal senses of the words in question.

In his wide-ranging discussion of metaphor, which is illuminating in detail but does not, for one reader at least, cohere to form an integrated whole, Goodman relies rather strongly upon transfers of application that involve not merely new denotations, but rather the shift of a whole system of connected labels belonging to the same linguistic family or field (a "schema" in his terminology). "Metaphor typically involves a change not merely of range but also of realm" (1968, p. 72). And again, "A whole set of alternative labels, a whole apparatus of organization, takes over new territory. What occurs is a transfer of a schema, a migration of concepts, an alienation of categories" (1968, p. 73). But this seems more apt for sweeping, systematic, or profound metaphors, than for the case of the sad smile. Does that involve a transfer of "a whole apparatus of organization"? The answer will depend upon our view concerning the initial organization of "sad" and its paronyms. If we count the application of the word to gestures and facial expressions as literal, we shall not admit that any such shift has occurred. It looks as if any applicable criterion of the metaphorical is enmeshed in circularity.

Goodman will retort that the existence of hard cases does not invalidate his analysis, any more than the existence of border-line cases of the application of "horse" invalidates a biologist's definition of that animal. The difficulty I find is that in proportion as we move toward clear cases, the proposed analysis loses rather than gains in plausibility. It would be clearly metaphorical to describe a straight line segment as, say, "striving toward perfection" (because it could never be completed as a whole line). Suppose then that somebody consciously striving toward perfection chooses to wear a button displaying such a line segment; would that be a prime case of expression? It does not seem so.

A curious feature of Goodman's account is that the emphasis upon the metaphorical or the figurative, which is central to it, tends to diminish rather than to stress the imputed "immediacy" or "internality" which was our point of departure. For, as he himself rightly recognizes, one strong indication of the presence of an authentic metaphor, rather than something so-called only by courtesy, is the conflict between the known background of accepted literal sense(s) and the specific figurative application. "Where there is metaphor, there is conflict: the picture is sad rather than gay even though it is insentient and hence neither sad nor gay. Application of a term is metaphorical only if to some extent contra-indicated" (1968, p. 69). But somebody who does not see "sad" or "gay" as initially restrained from application to the insentient would regard the illustration as question-begging. And even when the "conflict" is genuine, there would be to that extent, I should think, a diminution of the perplexing "immediacy" that generated the riddle. At best, I think, Goodman's discussion, ingenious as it is, attaches only to that interesting subclass of cases that might be called "metaphorical expression" and leaves the paradigm cases of expression still awaiting further illumination.[25]

The Nature and Functions of Notation
The Point of Departure

One reason for Goodman's attempt to clarify the concept of a notation seems to have been his interest in the special problem of distinguishing fakes and forgeries from authentic works of art.[26] An admirable discussion of such questions as, "Why should we reject fake paintings? Why do we attach so much importance in such cases to the authenticity of the work of art?" leads Goodman to reflect upon the differences between what he calls "autographic" and "allographic" art (a useful distinction that ought to enter the general vocabulary of discussions of art). An autographic work, such as a painting, is one whose history of production is constitutive of its identity, so that anything produced in other circumstances, however similar in its qualities, could not count as the same work. By contrast, an allographic work, such as a musical composition or a novel, admits of replications or "performances." This is why autographic works, identified by their history, admit of counterfeit, while the notion of a fake allographic work is an absurdity.[27]

But then what is it that makes an "allographic" work what it is? What are the constitutive, rather than the accidental, properties of a sonata or a poem? At this point, the idea suggests itself that "an art seems to be allographic just insofar as it is

[25] Of course, there is nothing in his general theory to preclude a different theory of expression—which, if it could dispense with the dubious notion of metaphor, he might welcome. It is worth repeating that no better theory of expression is now available.

[26] But his interest must soon have generalized to attach itself to general questions about the possibility of supplying notations for art forms. Thus "the possibility of notation for the dance was one of the initial questions that led to our study of notational systems" (1968, p. 211). Goodman concludes that dance notation *is* possible, cf. for instance (1968, p. 213).

[27] For some necessary refinements and qualifications, see for instance Goodman (1968, p. 119, n. 12).

amenable to notation" (1968, p. 121) and we are off on the search for an analytical grasp of notation that will occupy us for a hundred pages. For, "What is wanted now is a fundamental and thoroughgoing inquiry into the nature and function of notation in the arts" (1968, p. 123).

Identification and Identity

It deserves to be emphasized that Goodman is not merely seeking for criteria by which authentic works of art can be identified but rather for what, in more traditional language, would be called the "essence" of such a work.[28] He is explicit on the point: "The problem of developing a notational system for an art like music [in the early days when such notations were being constructed] amounted to the problem of arriving at a *real definition* of the notion of a musical work" (1968, p. 197; emphasis supplied). And so Goodman's incidental interest in the special problem of whether dance admits of notational representation is to be construed as nothing less than a search for a "real definition" of the dance. Here, and throughout, Goodman is in effect aligning himself with those many writers on art who have thought a satisfactory answer to the question "What *is* the work of art?" to be of prime importance.

A "real definition" of an (allographic) work of art has to be contrasted with "an arbitrary, nominal definition of 'work', as if it were a word newly coined" (1968, p. 197). The distinction is important to Goodman, for he shows that a notation can always be arbitrarily imposed upon an art (even upon such a paradigmatically autographic one as painting) if we are content to ignore antecedent understandings concerning individuation and classifications. The introduction of a notation, whose prime function is to establish "a distinction between the constitutive

---

[28] He even uses the word "essential" at one point, but I fancy inadvertently: "The function of a score is to specify the *essential* properties a performance must have to belong to the work" (1968, p. 212; emphasis supplied). With this exception, Goodman prefers to speak of "constitutive" properties.

and contingent properties of a work" (1968, p. 121, and in many
other places) must follow, so far as is practicable, "lines antecedently drawn by the informal classification of performances
into works and by practical decisions as to what is prescribed
and what is optional" (1968, p. 121). The "real definition"
which Goodman seeks is to be "consonant with antecedent practice" (1968, p. 198). I shall reserve comment.

The Anatomy of a Notation System

Let us now consider how Goodman elaborates and distinguishes the various conditions that any art must satisfy in order
to be amenable to the imposition of a "notational system."

By way of preliminary orientation, it will be enough to say,
somewhat imprecisely, that Goodman understands by a "notational system" a special kind of sublanguage whose well-formed
expressions or "characters" have a peculiarly stringent relation
to their references. In ordinary language even an unambiguous
name or description has a many-one relation to its reference:
Churchill is describable indifferently as "a man," "a politician,"
and in many other ways. In a "notational system," however, the
relation between a notational expression and what it symbolizes
must be one-one: the notational "character" that fits a given
object of reference is uniquely recoverable from that object.
(A simple example would be any of the chess notations now in
general use, in which a certain formula uniquely identifies a
given move, while a move, in turn, uniquely determines its
proper notational record.)

Goodman takes very seriously a certain condition, which I
propose to call the *conservation condition,* which, if he is right,
must hold between the notational record (in his terminology,
the "score") of an allographic work of art and its various
instantiations (or "performances"). Let us call a passage from
the notational record (say the composer's original manuscript)
to an instantiation of the work (say an actual concert performance) in A-step; let us call the passage from an instantian-
tion to the record (say an accurate report in musical notation

of an actual performance) a *B*-step; and let us call the step from one performance to another performance of the same work a *C*-step. Finally, call any finite sequence of *A*-, *B*-, and *C*-steps a transposition[29] of the work in question. Then the "conservation condition" can be stated concisely as follows: In every "transposition" of a given (allographic) work, strict identity of the work must be preserved. As we pass from a score to a performance, then perhaps to another performance that "copies" the first in essential respects, then back to a notational record of that performance, then to another performance, and so on for any number of steps, the very same work must be in question. "Otherwise, the requisite identification of a work from performance to performance would not be guaranteed; we might pass from a performance to another that is not of the same work, or from a score to another that determines a different— even an entirely disjoint—class of performances" (1968, p. 129) .

Goodman emphasizes that this "conservation condition" (a spelling out of the basic idea that the relation between score and performance must be one-one) is "a strong one" (1968, p. 130) , but he thinks it inescapable. Certainly it is strong enough to generate consequences that will seem startling to common sense. For it leads him, in the end, to argue consistently that a single wrong note in a performance turns it into an instantiation of a different work: "Since complete compliance with the score is the only requirement for a genuine instance of a work, the most miserable performance without actual mistakes does count as such an instance, while the most brilliant performance with a single wrong note does not" (1968, p. 186) . If this condition were relaxed, all individuating distinctions between works would be lost: ". . . by a series of one-note errors of omission, addition, and modification, we can go all the way from Beethoven's *Fifth Symphony* to *Three Blind Mice*" (1968, p. 187) . In the case of difficult works, one might therefore conclude,

[29] The terminology introduced in this paragraph is my own, not Goodman's.

common sense to the contrary notwithstanding, that the work in question has never been played, since no "perfect" performance has ever been produced.

Goodman knows that he is running counter to "ordinary usage," but is satisfied that ordinary usage "here points the way to disaster for theory" (1968, p. 120, n. 13). Nor is he disturbed by what he expects to be the indignant protests of musicians. This turns out to be a case where the "real definition" has to be accepted, in face of the reluctance of those engaged in the "antecedent practice" that is supposed to constrain it.

It is not hard to see the consequences of the conservation condition for any notation in which it can be satisfied. Let us follow Goodman's terminology. The notation will consist of (atomic and composite) *characters,* each of which will be a class of *marks;* to each such mark (and so indirectly to each character to which the mark belongs) there will correspond a class of *compliants* or a *compliance class.* Roughly speaking, therefore, we shall have, in the notation itself, a set of *mark classes* (each such class constituting a character) and, in the realm to which the notation refers, corresponding compliance classes. It does not need much argument to see that in order for the conservation condition to hold, the mark classes must be mutually exclusive or "segregated" from one another, so that no inscription may belong to two characters at once; a parallel condition must hold for the compliance classes, so that no compliant can belong to two different marks in the notation. Moreover, if the notation is to be usable, it must be "theoretically possible" to determine whether a given mark does in fact satisfy the first (syntactic) segregation condition, and whether a given object does in fact satisfy the second (semantic) segregation condition. Adopting a term of Goodman's and borrowing one that is used in a somewhat similar sense in logic, I shall say that a system that satisfies the first two conditions is (syntactically and semantically) *articulate* and one that satisfies the third and fourth is *effective.* Finally, in addition to *effective articulation,* Goodman requires ambiguity of the notation to be excluded, so that the relations between the characters and their compliants are timelessly invariant. To sum up: a genuine notation must be unambiguous and effectively articulate; and a character or "score" will satisfy the conservation condition if and only if it belongs to a genuine notation.[30]

Some Consequences

Any distinctions that are not willfully imposed may help to organize a realm so seemingly heterogeneous and so disconcertingly variegated as that of symbolism. At the very least, Goodman's terminology will help henceforth to emphasize and mark certain important formal affinities between cases that might otherwise seem hopelessly disparate. (The full value of his conceptual apparatus can be appreciated by following his illuminating discussions of such varied instances as cardiograms, records of analog computers, as well as of paintings, musical scores, and literary texts.) But any ambitious and thoroughgoing conceptual reorganization is liable to change the perceived structure of the realm to which it is applied. What is of most interest for the present purpose is to notice the conceptual restructuring that results from Goodman's analysis.

It will be remembered that Goodman sees the main purpose of a notation as that of identifying works of art (or, rather of those "allographic" works that are susceptible to notational record) by highlighting their "constitutive" properties. Given the severity of Goodman's "conservation condition" and the five detailed specifications entailed by it, one might expect some rather surprising readjustments of the informal criteria we antecedently use for identifying works of art. And this is indeed so.

---

[30] It will be convenient at this point to mention a couple of interesting features that are not constitutive of the notion of a notation, but serve to distinguish special cases. A symbolic system is syntactically dense "if it provides for infinitely many characters so ordered that between each two there is a third" (1968, p. 136). Finally, a symbol is said to be "replete" according to the degree to which physical features of the symbol-inscriptions are constitutive rather than contingent properties of that symbol (1968, pp. 229–230).

We have already seen that Goodman counts the occurrence of even a single wrong note in a musical performance as making that occasion count as the performance of a different work. What is equally striking is that indications of tempo (and, one might add, of rhythm and of what is popularly called the "feeling" of the musical composition) cannot count as "constitutive" (or, dare one say, "essential") properties of the work in question. Here, as always, Goodman is admirably candid and bold in accepting the consequences of his theoretical commitments: "No departure from the indicated tempo disqualifies a performance as an instance—however wretched—of the work defined by that score. For these tempo specifications cannot be accounted integral parts of the defining score, but are rather auxiliary directions whose observance or nonobservance affects the quality of a performance but not the identity of the work" (1968, p. 185). So, we might conclude, a Handel *Largo,* played allegro and fortissimo on an electric organ, with all the stops out, still counts as a performance of Handel's composition, albeit the "quality" of the performance has been "affected." Something has surely gone wrong here—perhaps the lurking presuppositions about what the function of a musical score can reasonably be supposed to be.

Of more general theoretical importance is the new look received by the old question from which we departed, about the differences, if any, between allegedly "representational" works, such as naturalistic paintings, and such contrastingly "abstract" works as those of music or nonrepresentational painting. Given the conceptual apparatus for the analysis of notation and symbolism now at hand, the distinctions that are bound to appear prominent and therefore important cut right across the conventional ones. When we classify symbolisms in terms of such formal criteria as "articulateness" and "denseness,"[31] "the distinction between the representational and the diagrammatic [becomes] a matter of *degree*" (1968, p. 230; emphasis in original)

[31] See n. 30 above.

and in any case, relative. "Nothing is intrinsically a representation; status as representation is relative to symbol systems. A picture in one system may be a description in another; and whether a denoting symbol is representational depends not upon whether it resembles what it denotes but upon its own relationships to other symbols in a given scheme" (1968, p. 226). Even the apparently obvious distinction between the verbal and the nonverbal now comes to look relatively unimportant. "Descriptions are distinguished from depictions not through being more arbitrary but through belonging to articulate rather than to dense schemes; and words are more conventional than pictures only if conventionality is construed in terms of differentiation rather than of artificiality. Nothing here depends upon the internal structure of a symbol; for what describes in some systems may depict in others. . . . Thus does heresy breed iconoclasm" (1968, pp. 230–231). Goodman rather glories in such "open heresy" (1968, p. 230), but heresy is no better for being heretical than dogma is for being dogmatic. The only question of moment is whether the new conceptual scheme, heretical or not, really does serve the purposes of conceptual illumination. About this I remain somewhat skeptical.

Some Qualms and Caveats

I shall now try to assemble a number of reservations that have grown upon me in following Goodman's fascinating investigations of notational systems. Some concern points of comparative detail, not integral to his main enterprise; others may call into question much of his methodological orientation.

1. We have seen that much of Goodman's discussion of notational systems turns upon a search for conditions of identity. It will be remembered, indeed, that he sees as the "primary function" of a "score" and hence of any character in a notation, "the *authoritative identification* of a work from performance to performance" (1968, p. 128; emphasis added) and at many places he speaks of such authoritative identification as being the "basic purpose" of a notation (e.g., 1968, p. 132).

Now one would think, offhand, that one could distinguish two problems in connection with identity conditions for a given category of objects: (a) the finding of an adequate test for identification, and (b) the determination of what is thereby identified.[32] We can identify persons by means of their fingerprints, but one would hesitate to say that difference in fingerprints is what makes two persons different. Of course, the difference in fingerprints is sufficient to constitute difference, but we regard the former difference, in some sense hard to render precise, as merely "accidental." If we could comfortably use the language of "essential properties," we could say that difference in fingerprints is not an essential criterion for personal difference and identity. At the start of his inquiry into notation, Goodman does emphasize that he is hoping to treat a notation as a "test," but it is to be a test of "the constitutive properties" of the work in question (1968, p. 122). It seems to me, therefore, that he assumes at least part of the time that identity of notational symbolization (narrowly construed in accordance with his rigorous conditions for what counts as such) is not merely a necessary test but also a sufficient condition. That is why, one might suppose, he does not count variations of tempo and "expression" in a performance as disqualifying it from being an authentic instance of the composition in question. Not only *must* a performance be describable as conforming to the notes of the *Moonlight Sonata*'s score but that also *suffices* —however many oddities by way of arbitrary tempo, syncopa-

---

[32] Cf. the following remarks by V. C. Chappell: [An ontologist] "may also ask, regarding something whose being is not in dispute, just *what it is;* he wants to know its nature, or how to categorize it. Supposing there is such a thing as water, what sort of a thing is it? Is it one thing or many? If many, what are the many severally which constitute it? If one, is it a universal or a particular? These are questions to which philosophers have in fact given different answers" ("Stuff and Things," *Proceedings of the Aristotelian Society,* 71 (1970–71), 61; emphasis supplied). Philosophers and art critics will continue to ask parallel questions about works of art; it may well seem to them that Goodman's analysis implies certain answers to *such* questions.

tion, etc., may be present. And similarly, not only must a novel be identified as having a particular verbal text, but the novel *is* that text. So far as the structure of the argument goes, this seems to me no more plausible than saying that because a man can be identified by his fingerprints, he *is* his fingerprints. I can see, in both cases, no objection to treating notational symbolization as an adequate test of identity; but I would be reluctant to go further.

2. In any case, one wonders whether "identification," as Goodman construes it, has quite the importance that he attaches to it and (in the case of allographic arts) to the notation by which it is achieved, when he repeatedly stresses that the "basic purpose" of a score is to identify the performances as instances of a given composition. The purposes to be served by a notational record may vary widely according to circumstances and our changing interests. A faithful notational record may be decisively important in determining whether a chess player has overstepped the time limit, and a verbatim report of a speech may be equally important when a case for alleged slander is in the offing. But in other instances, we are satisfied with less stringent criteria—and why not? It would be disconcerting to attend a concert in which Serkin was to play the *Hammerklavier* and find him playing *Three Blind Mice* instead, but that is surely because we hope that he will be guided by the score in question, and our expectation that he will try to play the right notes is not sharply separable from the expectation that he will try to be faithful to the composer's intentions in other equally important ways. (Cf. saying after a performance by some beginner, "That was no performance of the *Hammerklavier* but a parody of it"—which may be a just comment even if every note was played "right." There is more to playing the piano than hitting the right keys in the right order.)

Altogether, it seems to me that Goodman's analysis encourages, no doubt unintentionally, a simplistic conception of the relation between an interpreter and the score from which he works—as if that consisted of predetermined instructions to which the player must "correctly" conform.[33] One wonders what the effect of Goodman's position is, in the end, intended to be. He concedes that nonphilosophers, whether players or hearers, will find it convenient to go on talking in their ordinary "loose" way about performances of the same work even in cases where wrong notes intrude; then what is to be gained by the "strict" view? It is as if one were to say that a man is, strictly speaking, a different person each day and then proceeded as if nothing had changed.

3. Goodman is explicit about his analysis being independent of judgments of aesthetic value: in saying that one performance differs, strictly speaking, from another, we are not prejudging the question of whether it is aesthetically better or not. But one wonders whether it is possible to contrast "constitutive" properties so often with "contingent" ones, without some value judgments creeping in. If the notes, and they alone, are constitutive of the musical performance, is it not tempting to treat the rest as relatively unimportant? (Isn't what counts as "essence" what, in the end, we count as relatively important—e.g., personality rather than fingerprints?) And surely the effect upon our comprehensive vision of the arts will inevitably be, if we follow Goodman's "approach," to attach an excessive importance to notation? (Even in chess, where the relation between performance and notation, as we have seen, is as tight as it could possibly be, the game is the thing and the record merely auxiliary.) It seems to me that the tactic of what might be called "verbal ascent" (passing from the material to the formal mode) to which Goodman is committed by his ontological principles, with its distrust of such allegedly occult entities as attributes,

---

[33] Contrast the anecdote of the pianist Coenraad Bos and Brahms' "Vier Ernste Gesaenge," where the player ventured to change some awkward figurations in the published music and was congratulated by Brahms himself after the concert for having "marvellously" solved a technical problem. This anecdote, which only the foolish would treat as an invitation to unbridled interpretational freedom, seems to me a better paradigm of the interpreter's relation to the score than the one suggested by Goodman's insistence that a single wrong note deindividuates the performance.

leads him to bestow an undue prominence upon notation and symbolization and so to foster what, in the end, is a distorted perspective of the arts.

4. I am less impressed than Goodman is by the need to satisfy what I earlier called the "conservation condition," from which his austere and demanding conception of notation inevitably flows. The argument that by changes of single notes we could pass from any performance to any other is, for one thing, altogether too reminiscent of the ancient sophism that undertakes to show that all men are bald. But the sophism of the *falakros* shows only, what is no longer surprising if it ever was, that the terms of ordinary language—or, for that matter, of science, also—so far as they express empirical concepts, are "loose" in having no fixed and determinate boundaries. But that does not impair their usefulness or impugn their indispensability, so long as the "fuzziness" of their borders is remembered and, where necessary, corrected. Now why should we not be equally liberal for such expressions as "the same performance"? Why not here follow ordinary usage, which may have more reason behind it than Goodman would concede, and restrain a zeal for absolute precision which engenders paradox?[34] I believe, indeed, that Goodman's valuable analysis of the varieties of symbolic systems would survive intact, with this kind of accommodation. The extreme precision of pure geometry does not require us to apply it with absolute literalness to ordinary life, and perhaps the same attitude might be in order for a "pure" theory of notation. (It would be legitimate to regard Goodman's theory of notation as analogous, *mutatis mutandis,* to a geometry.)

[34] It might be worth trying to locate the looseness of fit between a score and a performance in the relation between the performer and the work he is trying to interpret. That relation is certainly gradable as being more or less faithful, appropriate, congruent with the composer's imputed intentions, and so on. On this approach, we could avoid Goodman's paradox of the single wrong note. I suspect that this alternative would be repugnant to Goodman because it would necessarily imply some use of obscure and controversial notions such as those of intending, copying, and the like.

Conclusions

A summary verdict on the outcome of Goodman's continuously stimulating investigations might run somewhat as follows: The analysis of a notational system, and the attendant set of distinctions and technical terminology: wholly successful, and a pioneering contribution to an important subject. The application to works of art of a nominalistic theory of meaning (meaning as confined to reference): ingenious and resourceful, but in the end unconvincing. The identification of works of art as constituted by their relations to appropriate symbol systems: unproven and, in my judgment, based upon at best a partial and at worst a distorted conception of the character and function of works of art. The light thrown upon traditional aesthetic questions:[35] provocative, but still unpersuasive.

I should be sorry if these qualms were to leave the intending reader in any doubt about the value of Goodman's remarkable investigations. If Goodman had achieved nothing else, he would have succeeded in formulating with memorable force some of the severe difficulties that still beset any effort to improve the conceptual apparatus with which we discuss the arts. Right or wrong, he has shown the pitfalls in the path. Anybody, like myself, who thinks that a theory of language cannot afford to restrict itself to the single fundamental mode of "reference" will be obligated, with as much painstaking search for accuracy and clarity as Goodman constantly manifests in his book, to distinguish and delineate the various modes of meaning proposed as alternatives. And so, *mutatis mutandis,* for all the basic and immensely difficult topics that Goodman discusses. If in the end

---

[35] I spare the reader of this excessively long discussion any detailed reflections upon the concluding 25 pages where the author argues for the cognitive functions of the emotions and offers some "symptoms" of the aesthetic, involving his concepts of syntactic density, semantic density, and relative repleteness (see 1968, p. 252). Of such remarks as "aesthetic and scientific experience alike are seen to be fundamentally cognitive in character" (1968, p. 245), one can only say that they encourage the reader to hope that Goodman will write another book on this theme.

one has to judge that he supplies only a partial view—why, after all, *le plus beau système ne peut donner plus ce qu'il a.*[36]

[36] I am much indebted to discussion with Nelson Goodman, who has been generous in answering my questions.

IX

Paradigm Cases and
Evaluative Words

Introduction

The so-called "Paradigm Case Argument" (hereafter *PCA*)
has received more attention from philosophers than it deserves.
Exaggerated claims for its efficacy have arisen from taking it to
be a knock-down way of refuting certain varieties of philosophical skepticism: if a skeptic doubts whether material objects
exist, show him a stone; if he disbelieves in the possibility of
motion, invite him to look at a horse race. But philosophical
skepticism is too stubborn to be so easily put down: Berkeley
knew that the world was littered with things that the vulgar
called material objects and Zeno must have seen as many races
as any other Greek. Only they thought they had profound logical and metaphysical reasons for rejecting common usage.

Yet one feature of the *PCA* is valuable, no matter if it leaves
the skeptic unmoved. When, as so often happens in philosophical controversy, a dispute turns partly upon confusion in the
use of key terms, an important first step can be to find instances
on which the disputants can provisionally agree, no matter how
much they eventually differ about the analysis and implications
of the illustrated usage. Considered as an attempt at partial
clarification of the meaning of contested terms, the "Appeal
to Paradigm Cases" (hereafter *APC*), as I shall call it, is a promising way of bringing philosophical disputation down to earth
by providing some initial agreement, however modest. Where
disputants can agree about paradigm cases there is some pros-

pect of their talking about the same topics—some hope, therefore, of fruitful disagreement.

It is therefore disquieting to find J. O. Urmson, in a well-known paper[1], contending, without subsequent dissent, that a *PCA* is severely limited in its application to what he calls "evaluative terms," connoting some approval or disapproval on the part of their users.[2] Although Urmson expresses high regard for the *PCA*, his criticisms of it markedly restrict its usefulness. For his objections are independent of his own debatable view of the nature of "evaluation" and apply, if correct, to any terms having "nondescriptive" features. Since many of the terms that interest philosophers are of this sort, it is worth considering whether Urmson has established his case. I believe that his arguments are defective. I hold that the *APC*—or, for that matter, the *PCA*, where that is in point—applies to so-called "normative" or "performative" expressions no less than to "descriptive" ones.

Urmson denies that paradigm case arguments can provide instances of *valid* deductive, inductive, or "ethical" reasoning. I think he is wrong with respect to the first two: there are paradigmatic instances of valid deductive reasoning and correct inductive reasoning. (If I do not say as much for "ethical reasoning," that is because I doubt whether it is desirable to recognize any such distinct category.)

In what follows, I shall explain how I am using the term "paradigm case." After that I shall try to summarize and criticize Urmson's main contentions and I shall end with some independent remarks on the important issues raised by him.

[1] J. O. Urmson, "Some Questions Concerning Validity," *Revue Internationale de Philosophie*, 7 (1953), 217–229, reprinted in A. Flew, ed., *Essays in Conceptual Analysis* (London, 1956). In referring to Urmson's paper, I shall use the pagination of its first appearance.

[2] Throughout this discussion I shall rely upon the oversimplified conception of "evaluation" to be found in Urmson's original paper. For a more sophisticated and more plausible analysis, see the same author's later discussion in his book, *The Emotive Theory of Ethics* (London, 1968). My conclusions also substantially apply to Urmson's later view (though he does not consider its bearing upon the *PCA*).

My purpose is not to convict Urmson of error, but rather to throw more light upon what, in spite of its limitations, remains a productive philosophical method.

The Intended Meaning of "Paradigm Case"

Let us begin with some examples. A child wants to know what I mean by a "swastika," so I draw him one. Somebody who is unfamiliar with the meaning of the word "beige" asks me to explain its meaning. I show him a painted card saying *"That* is a case of beige, if anything is!" Again, a philosopher agrees with Karl Popper that induction is an illusion. In trying to change his view, I present a simple statistical syllogism, saying, once again, *"That* is a case of a sound inductive argument, if anything is." In trying to become clearer about the meaning of "making something happen," I once described a simple episode involving this term: "You are thirsty, but there is a glass of beer within easy reach: you stretch out your hand, bring the glass to your lips and drink."[3] Of this example, I still feel justified in saying *"That* would be a case of making something happen, if anything is!"

In the light of such examples, I offer the following provisional explanation of the expression "paradigm case." By a "paradigm case" of the application of a given word W, I mean some actual or possible thing, produced or merely described, of which it is correct to say "That is a case of W if anything is!" I shall make the following preliminary comments before proceeding to offer some criteria for using the expression "paradigm case."

(i) Appeal to a paradigm case does not require the exhibition of some actual individual or situation: a clear description suffices. Unlike other writers, I do not restrict an appeal to paradigm cases to the exhibition of *existing* entities or situations. The thing or episode presented as a paradigm case must, however, be *able* to exist, i.e., its description must be of some-

---

[3] *Models and Metaphors: Studies in Language and Philosophy* (Ithaca, N.Y., 1962), p. 153.

thing whose existence is logically possible: there are no paradigm cases of round squares or infinite integers. But a paradigm case of a perpetual-motion machine can be described, and the only obstacle to invoking paradigm cases of centaurs is their lack of firm specification. (Can a centaur be a mule?) Here we have a link between the "paradigm case argument" and the "appeal to paradigm cases." Where use of the latter requires description or production of some *existing* thing or situation, the two procedures coincide. For, in such a case, partial explanation of a term's meaning also shows that an instance of its application *exists*. Thus, successful production of an actual case of a sound inductive argument should serve as a preliminary counterexample to wholesale skepticism with respect to inductive reasoning.

(ii) I do not restrict the uses of an *APC* to so-called "ostensive" terms, such as "red," whose meaning is partly determined by "pointing" to features of perception.

(iii) In choosing a paradigm case of inductive reasoning, above, I have anticipated my later contention that an *APC* is applicable to so-called "evaluative" words or expressions.

(iv) Finally, I am not assuming that a word or expression having a clear use in the language must necessarily have paradigm cases of application.

Some Criteria for Paradigm Cases

A paradigm case should be (i) *clear* or central (as opposed to *borderline*); (ii) plain or *obvious* (as opposed to only *inferentially* a case of *W*); (iii) *uncontroversial* (not *problematic*); (iv) exemplary or *standard*—a case by reference to which a question whether something else is a case of *W* might properly be decided. Moreover, these conditions must be satisfied solely in virtue of *W*'s *meaning*. These mutually consistent criteria are not intended to be logically independent.

To illustrate: in presenting a paradigm case of a chair, it would be foolish to describe a "deck chair" or one of those odd water-filled objects now enjoyed by connoisseurs of the bizarre.

In seeking a "plain" or obvious case of a material object, one would be well-advised to avoid invoking a pulsar or an electron. The standard meter rod, preserved in Paris, would be an obvious choice for a paradigm case of "meter"; an uncontroversial instance of a valid mathematical proof should not be a proof involving the controversial "axiom of choice."

I assume throughout that the prime purpose of an *APC* is to serve as the partial explanation of a feature of the meaning of the word or expression in question.

I shall deliberately avoid any invocation of speculative child psychology. Nothing is implied here about how we learn language. Nor am I supposing that speakers who agree in their use of the term under discussion must necessarily be antecedently acquainted with the proffered paradigm cases. All that is required for agreement of meaning is that, once the paradigm has been accurately described, both speakers shall then agree that it *is* a paradigm. In case such agreement is lacking (and not because of any uncertainty about the intended meaning of "paradigm case") that shows that the speakers are using the disputed expression in different senses. If you cannot treat my paradigm case of sound inductive reasoning as a clear, obvious, uncontroversial, and exemplary instance of such reasoning then, unless I have blundered in my choice, you must mean by "sound inductive reasoning" (and hence, also, by "inductive reasoning") something different from what I mean.

Urmson's Caveats

The course of Urmson's argument is approximately as follows:

(i) He considers examples of *PCA*'s in connection with deductive, inductive, and "ethical" reasoning, treating them as intended to establish that there are *valid* instances of each of these types of reasoning.

(ii) He argues that "valid" is, at least in part, "evaluative in meaning" (p. 223), since to use that label is "to signify approval" (*ibid.*) of an argument to which it is applied.

(iii) He claims in effect that a *PCA* can yield only a "classificatory" formula, such as " 'valid' means the same as 'of the same logical character as certain standard arguments such as a syllogism in Barbara' " (this formula being modeled upon a comparable discussion of the use of a *PCA* in connection with "solid" at p. 218; see also p. 223).

(iv) It seems to him illegitimate to equate in this way a classificatory expression with an evaluative one (pp. 223, 224). Hence a *PCA* for an evaluative expression fails to capture its distinctively *evaluative* features.

(v) An important consequence for Urmson is that a *PCA* involving an evaluative term does not determine whether the paradigm case *should* be favorably evaluated. In the case of "valid," for instance, the question "What good reasons have we for evaluating arguments as 'valid'?" (pp. 226–229) remains *open*. Here, according to Urmson, a *PCA* settles that a syllogism is valid, but leaves open for further discussion whether and why the syllogism should be "approved."

Comments and Criticisms

(i) *Urmson's examples of deductive, inductive, and ethical reasoning.* It is ironic that, for all of Urmson's respect for the paradigm case argument, he spares himself the trouble of actually providing cases of the three types of reasoning to which he refers. One might wonder about the desirability of recognizing a special category of "ethical reasoning." But valid *deductive* reasoning is chiefly in point: since cases of such reasoning can be easily supplied, there is no need to linger here.

(ii) *Urmson's contention that "valid" is, in part, "evaluative."* What Urmson means by "evaluative" in his essay is unclear, except that he takes it to imply at least that the term in question "signifies approval."

Is Urmson right in thinking that users of "valid" "signify approval"? In making up one's mind about this, it is important to distinguish whether utterances concerning validity do *in fact* signify approval, and whether, on the other hand, such approval, if present and communicated as part of the speaker's meaning, is part of the meaning of what is said in virtue of *linguistic convention.*

Consider the following case. It would be generally agreed that to call a knife sharp is, normally, to signify "approval" of it. It would be a mistake, however, to claim that sharpness was part of the meaning of "knife." For if that were so, the expression "a blunt knife" would be self-contradictory.

Urmson says that "Once stated it is obvious that 'valid' is an evaluative expression" (p. 223) . It does not seem obvious to me. To be sure, Urmson does proceed to offer an argument for what he takes to be obvious, but it is too weak to serve his purpose. He says, "To speak of a good argument is in most cases equivalent to speaking of a valid argument" (*ibid.*) . But what does "equivalent" mean here? A plausible answer would be that a competent hearer would normally suppose somebody speaking about a good deductive argument to be referring to an argument that was at least valid. (But the converse is untrue.) If this is enough to establish the point in question, it looks as if Urmson has overplayed his hand. For the word "argument," without a qualifying adjective, would also quite properly in many contexts be taken to be "equivalent" to "good argument." It would be far-fetched, however, to argue that the term "argument" *simpliciter* is on this account "evaluative" and it seems clear that this is not Urmson's contention.

But should we say, after all, that "valid" is by linguistic *convention* a term of approbation or commendation? This is like asking whether "checkmate" is a conventional term of approval. Certainly, the object of chess is to produce checkmate, and one object of deductive reasoning is to produce valid argument; but these banalities are far from identifying an evaluative component of the word's meaning. In the case of any functional word, W (referring to something serving an identifiable purpose, and hence something of which "good" or "satisfactory," etc., can normally be predicated) , its use is normally, but not invariably, taken to indicate an intended reference to a *good* thing of the sort in question. Furthermore, if a necessary condition for a *W* to be good is its having a certain good-making property, *P,* then a user of *W* is normally and properly taken to impute the presence of the good-making character, *P.* "Knife" refers to something to be used *for cutting;* thus a good knife must at least be one that cuts (is sharp). So, if somebody asks for a knife, it would be ridiculous to ask whether he wants one sharp enough to cut. But it does not follow that "sharp" is evaluative per se. We can provide a neutral account of what is meant by calling a knife sharp, without omitting anything relevant to the meaning of "sharp."

Consider the parallel case of the word "anesthetic." An anesthetic, *qua* pain-killer, is an instance of the application of a functional term. Imagine somebody who systematically disapproves of reducing pain. Then, whenever *he* uses the word "anesthetic," he would be expressing *dis*approval, unlike the vast majority of those who use the word. But that would by no means show that he misunderstood it. For if that were so, no normal person could argue or disagree with a thoroughgoing sadist.

(iii) *Urmson's contention that a PCA can yield only a "classificatory" formula.* Urmson claims that the contention that something, say *A,* is a paradigm case of the application of a term, say *T, entails* that *T means the same as* "like *A* in certain respects (to be specified)." This seems to me a mistake. For one thing, in the case of "red," which Urmson himself uses as an exemplary instance of the application of the *PCA,* it would be impossible to specify the "respects" in question. Thus Urmson's formula is too restrictive.

Consider another case, more to the point, in which the relevant "respects" can be specified. Suppose we say that Alekhine's Defense is an exemplary and paradigm case of a chess opening. It would be quite implausible to claim that "chess opening" *means the same as* "like Alekhine's Defense in such and such respects." For a man could very well understand the meaning of "chess opening" without knowing Alekhine's Defense. Furthermore, once the "respects" included in Urmson's formula were specified, the reference to the particular illustration would be otiose. In general, in order to understand your use of *A*, I need not know your paradigms in advance: I need only accept them as paradigmatic after you produce them.

(iv) *Urmson's contention that successful uses of the paradigm case argument leave open questions about evaluation.* Because Urmson thinks that the best we can get from a paradigm case argument is a "classificatory formula," yielding "criteria" for the application of the term, he thinks that we shall always be left with an important question of the form exemplified by "What good reasons do we have for evaluating arguments as 'valid'?" (pp. 226–229). This certainly seems an odd verdict in the case of valid deductive reasoning. Suppose we do have a certain criterion for recognizing a particular kind of argument, say the classical syllogism, as valid. Let this criterion be *K*. Then, presumably, we have discovered that any syllogism having *K* is valid. What sense remains in raising a further question whether we have good reasons for evaluating such syllogisms as valid? The position seems to be that we have *found out* that any syllogism possessing *K* is necessarily valid: this seems, surely, to be about as good a reason as one can hope for.

I suspect that Urmson may have harbored a certain confusion connected with his special views about "evaluation." If one thinks, as he seems to do in this paper, that no amount of *information* concerning things or events can entail an evaluation, it will seem plausible that, after all the relevant information has been obtained, there remains an open question as to whether to "approve" of the thing or event in question. But, whatever one may think of Urmson's views about evaluation, this kind of application of it is unacceptable. Suppose we have reliable information that a particular knife is sharp enough for our purpose and, if one cares to add other criteria, that the price is fair, within our means, and so on. Could one then reasonably ask whether we have good reasons for evaluating such a knife as "good"? The answer seems to be plainly no.

Conclusions. If I am right in the foregoing criticisms, Urmson's line of thought fails to establish what he thought it did. For all he says, it remains possible for an evaluative expression to have perfectly straightforward paradigm instances. This question, however, deserves independent discussion, to which I now turn.

Independent Discussion

The question is whether a term or expression that is "evaluative" in Urmson's sense, i.e., one that *conventionally* signifies approval, can have paradigm cases.

There seems to be no difficulty in principle in providing examples of nondescriptive terms having paradigmatic instances. Consider, for instance, the use of clapping as a conventional gesture of applause (that this example concerns a nonverbal conventional gesture is immaterial). If some galactic tourist were puzzled about how *we* use clapping, it would be easy enough to show or to describe a case where the gesture is used in a standard way. Were Yehudi Menuhin's brilliant rendering of some Beethoven sonata to bring an audience to its feet, clapping furiously, it would be perfectly clear, I should think, that they were using the gesture correctly to convey "approval"—if that is not too weak a way of describing the situation.

In order to gloss such a case we should, of course, have to describe "subjective" features of the situation, such as the pleasure and delight of those clapping—but there is no harm in that. Whether in this type of case, the performance really should count as *worthy* of applause, would indeed remain an "open question."

Consider now, for the sake of contrast, a situation, easily describable, which would be a paradigm case of somebody making a promise. Is it really arguable whether, other things being equal, a man making a promise is *binding* himself to do what he promises? Surely the answer must be that one fails to understand some central uses of "promise" if one remains uncertain whether a person making a promise in a standard situation is under any obligation to perform.

These considerations can readily be generalized. There is an absurdity in asking, from the standpoint of somebody accepting an institution, such as the promise-making institution, whether the subjects of that institution are committed to consequential actions by their performative utterances. Pursuit of the relevant goals, such as truth-telling, being reliable, etc., is constitutive of the practice in question.

Of course, it by no means follows that one must "play the game" in question by using such words as "promise" or "valid" in the standard ways. One can try to modify or cancel the standard meaning by making the "speaker's meaning" deviate from the "standard meaning" (as in irony and sarcasm). More drastically, one can emulate Nietzsche in "transvaluating" values by using key words in novel senses to express heterodox, possibly revolutionary, notions concerning the relevant purposes, goals, and obligations. But for all this, it would be perverse to think of the use of a partially nondescriptive term such as "promise" somewhat as follows: The word "promise" stands for such-and-such "neutral" features; and it is just a sociological fact that people of our subculture happen to value promise-keeping—as they may also happen to like ice cream.

Promising belongs to a ritualized system of activities whose object is to increase the reliability of undertakings, to hold people to account in cases of violation, to internalize such obligations, and so on. Hence, to use such a term as "promise" in situations where the hearer can properly be expected to count on agreement between the "speaker's meaning and the standard meaning is to be *ipso facto* committed to the goals and purposes of the promise-making and promise-keeping activity. (Similarly, to use words such as "foul" or "offside" on the football field is to count as being committed to the purposes of *that* game. It would be absurd to import an alienated spectator's standpoint into the verbal comments that go with playing football—to say, as it were, whenever I say "foul" I simply mean just, and no more than, "what others mean by 'foul.' ")

I have been contending in this essay that "valid" does not have an evaluative dimension and that therefore Urmson's attack upon the appeal to paradigm cases, to the extent that it relies upon the specific case of the uses of "valid," misses its mark. Nevertheless, there is no difficulty in finding words which are "evaluative" in Urmson's sense—or at least partially non-descriptive. With regard to such partially nondescriptive words or expressions, I have tried to show that there is no difficulty in principle in using an appeal to paradigm cases. When an appeal to paradigm cases, however, is made in connection with words or expressions having a conventional evaluative component, the full description of the paradigmatic case typically involves some reference to the background of related terms within the language and, notably, the linguistic practice or practices in which that word plays a crucial role. It is in this way that readiness to use an evaluative term commits its user to conventional evaluations and obligations. Even in the simplest cases, as when somebody recognizes that a colored sample is a paradigm case of "red," he must also *ipso facto* understand that it is a paradigm case of "not blue," "not green," and so on. So here, as elsewhere, partial delineation of a word's meaning involves reference to a linguistic subsystem.

It is easy to be misled by an oversimple model of what naming consists in. For example, Bruce Goldberg, in his paper on "The Linguistic Expression of Feeling,"[4] makes much of the allegedly arbitrary and noncommital features of assigning a name to a single thing or event. According to him, if I call my desk *A* (i.e., attach an arbitrary label to it), it remains completely open what other things I may and can want to call by the same name. He argues also that there is no escape from this in relying upon similarity, because use of the same label determines the similarity in question and not the other way round. The kind of "naming" that Goldberg discusses (something like pinning a label to a thing or producing a gesture in the thing's presence) is, however, a caricature of naming. Naming, like other linguistic performances, has a systematic aspect. In general, the point

[4] *American Philosophical Quarterly*, 8 (1971), 86–92.

of appealing to a paradigm case is not to be smugly satisfied with having found an illustration, but rather to use it as a jumping-off point for establishing the relevant rules and conventions. Thus, even in its most naive forms, the appeal to paradigm cases has an implicit generality.

It seems then, that appeal to paradigm cases is less simple and straightforward than some of its ardent advocates have supposed. It does have the advantage of bringing philosophical discussion concerning controversial concepts down to earth, by drawing attention to instances about which the disputants can agree. It is, therefore, a starting point for agreement. It also has the advantage of being quasi-inductive, by not committing the investigators to any presupposed analysis of a controversial concept or its encompassing conceptual system. Such a prelude, however, to fruitful philosophical discussion can be no more than a modest beginning. And even the "commitment" to conventional evaluations which, as I have argued, may emerge as a result of the requisite linguistic analysis, is less drastic in its consequences than might be at first supposed. For, unless the background linguistic practice is basic enough to implicate such fundamental concepts as intelligibility or rationality, the analyst remains free to abstain from the use of the crucial expressions and in this way to remain outside the linguistic practice in question. Nobody who agrees with my sketch of the appeal to paradigm cases in connection with evaluative words need feel that his precious freedom to say what he pleases and to mean what he likes is thereby restricted.

X

Questions for Chomsky

Noam Chomsky's stimulating and provocative views about linguistic theory deserve more elaborate and systematic discussion than I can here provide. I offer the following remarks, in no spirit of carping criticism, with the hope of highlighting some of the main questions that are likely to need attention in a sympathetic evaluation of the position of transformational linguistics. Many of these questions have, of course, already been considered by Chomsky and his associates.

1. *What is the task of a formal grammar of a language?* One way of conceiving it is as follows. We start with an infinite class of sentences or, more generally, an infinite class of linear "strings," constructed from a finite stock of atomic constituents (words, or other elements, treated as indivisible for the sake of the grammatical analysis) . We now look for a simple and necessarily finite way of characterizing the members of that class of strings. That is to say, we search for some set of necessary and sufficient conditions for membership in the given class. More specifically, we hope to end with some finite set of rules for generating just those strings that belong to the class. For simplicity, I will here ignore the equally important and fundamental task of generating the "phrase structure" of the strings, i.e., of showing the internal structures of the subelements of a given sentence and the morphological categories to which those subelements belong.

A simple analogy may help. Suppose the initial class of strings to consist of linear sequences of the symbols *a* and *b*, with repetitions allowed, limited only by the condition that "triple sequences" of the form *XXX*, where *X* stands each time for the same subsequence of symbols, shall not occur. Thus *a, bb, aaba, ababa* are members, while *bbb, baaa, abababa,* and *bbabbabba* are not. We ask for a set of rules to generate just those strings of *a*'s and *b*'s that belong to the class described. (The solution, even in this very simplified illustration, is by no means obvious.) Here the occurrence of a "triple sequence" corresponds to the occurrence in a natural language of *ungrammaticality.* Criteria for ungrammaticality are, of course, immeasurably more complex than the presence of a triple sequence.

2. *What kind of task is set by a specific formal grammar?* In my simple analogy, the task is plainly one for pure mathematics. The problem of finding an adequate set of generative rules can be solved without concern for any possible use for the strings of *a*'s and *b*'s, or any attention to physical representations of the abstract structures investigated. In writing a generative grammar proper, however, matters are less simple. Whether a string of morphemes shall be regarded as grammatical (admissible) is determined not by a simple formal criterion, as in the illustration, but rather by the verdict of a suitably competent user of the language in question—often the investigator himself, acting as his own informant. Here, there is a link with some kind of extraneous verification.

The resulting grammar can therefore, quite plausibly, be regarded as a mathematical theory of a class of well-defined empirical phenomena. Some grammarians like to compare a descriptive grammar with a simple physical theory. Grammar is to speech behavior as, say, Kepler's laws are to planetary motions. Both are theories about the actual world; if both traffic in idealizations and abstractions, they are equally subject to strict, though indirect, control by empirical facts.

3. *How much idealization is involved?* Chomsky wishes to characterize the behavior of an ideal speaker, having perfect command of syntax and morphology, and free from the memory lapses, slips of tongue, and other irregularities and inconsistencies that distinguish actual "performance" from ideal "com-

petence." This much idealization seems no more suspect in principle than physicists' talk about ideal gases or perfect fluids. Yet it may be important to recall how far from grammatically people speak, even in such relatively formal performances as speeches and lectures. To listen to a typical conversation is to be vividly reminded of the great gap between ideal competence and actual performance.

A more troublesome kind of idealization enters through the simplifying assumption that allows sentences to be arbitrarily long and to have any degree of internal complexity. The extent of what might be called "theoretical distance" thus introduced may be important. The very concept of a sentence is already something of a grammarian's artifact: it is by no means easy to chop up speech into sentences without relying upon some antecedently available grammar. And actual utterances are bounded, however, indeterminately, even when produced by speakers as long-winded as Faulkner. A speaker can no more produce an indefinitely long utterance than a man can walk an indefinitely long distance. Pragmatic constraints limit the length and complexity of speech episodes: if you make your utterances too long you will violate the tacit understandings needed to maintain a viable speaker-hearer relationship. Were I to say, in any natural context, "Caesar and Nelson and Atilla and . . . ," with the extraordinary intention of using a hundred proper names in the subject-phrase, my hearer would soon fail to understand what I was doing. It may be a useful theoretical fiction to say that the grammar "describes" the speech-behavior of idealized speakers, but we need to be clear about how far we are thereby departing from direct empirical confirmation. The assumption of unbounded length of sentences might be compared with an assumption of the infinite indivisibility of matter (or the assumption, in certain forms of probability theory, of infinitely long runs of trials with pennies or other random devices). Both are useful as simplifying the initial tasks of theory; both raise similar problems of verification.

4. *How is a descriptive grammar verified?* In the light of what

has been said, it would be wrong to think that the generative rules of a grammar straightforwardly predict speech-behavior. Kepler's laws can properly be taken to predict certain planetary motions, because the orbits are there to be observed. But statements about indefinitely long sentences are like statements in probability theory about the "long run." In the long run, as Keynes reminded us, we are all dead; in the long run, also, we are all silent.

The position seems to be that the empirical controls for a grammatical theory are not so much what people say in the object-language in which they talk about ships and sealing wax as what they say in a grammatical metalanguage, speaking as amateur grammarians. The question about my centipedal sentence's grammaticality has to be settled by appeal to an informant acting as a grammatical judge: the test is not how he *would* respond to the long sentence itself, but how he *does* respond to its short description. The appeal is to a referee, not to a player—even if the same man plays both parts.

It seems to me, therefore, that in such cases we are checking the grammarian's proposed set of generative rules against another untidier set of embryonic and half-explicit rules. The verification route is from rules to rules, not from rules to hypothetical and idealized performance. Now of course we should like to do more than this, by providing a theory of the language itself, not a theory of users' ideas about the language. But how is this to be done? Is there perhaps the risk of merely reviving and extending a set of rules previously taught in the classroom? The kind of verification involved seems to me interestingly different from what arises in the case of physics. We cannot ask a planet how it thinks it ought to behave in situations that don't arise: yet this seems to be what we are doing when we consult a native "informant."

5. *Does a particular grammar explain anything?* Whatever their value, Kepler's laws do not explain the planetary motions, in any useful sense of "explain": they replace a crude and unsystematic description ("those orbits out there," or "the orbits

conforming to these readings") by another description concisely presenting some mathematical properties of the orbits. The same applies, *mutatis mutandis,* to the rules constituting a specific generative grammar. Our initial crude "intuitions" as to what should count as grammatical or the reverse are replaced by a set of precise and explicit rules that (approximately and with idealization) generate a corresponding classification. This provides valuable insight into structural connections: it may be said to provide intelligible reasons for what we previously seemed to be doing by a kind of instinct. But "explanation" hardly seems the right tag. If we use that word here, what are we to reserve for our attempts, at deeper theoretical levels, to account for the superficial grammatical rules themselves? Are we to talk about explaining an explanation?

A generative grammar can, from another standpoint, be regarded as equivalent in theoretical efficacy to an axiom-system. I would not myself regard an axiom-system for plane Euclidean geometry or, for that matter, for the voting behavior of committees, as *explaining* anything. But if we do call this explaining, we shall do well to recognize that it is not of the disparity-reducing kind that arises from the attempt to solve a puzzle, nor the causal sort common in the natural sciences.

The process, I would suggest, is really one of *codification.* The descriptive grammarian is like somebody undertaking to provide the rules of a game, whose players have no explicit code to which to appeal: he is the Hoyle of speech behavior. Or he is like the legal theorist who undertakes to provide a legal code for some land where claimants and prosecutors have long behaved *as if* they were controlled by explicit rules.

I do not know how pregnantly Chomsky would wish to use the terms "rule" and "rule-governed behavior." A radical distinction between a rule and a regularity, which seems to me desirable on other grounds, would reinforce the point I have been making about the special types of verification and explanation in question.

6. *What are the constraints on the choice of a grammar?* It

should be immediately obvious that the illustrative puzzle of the *a–b* strings can be solved in indefinitely many ways. For any set of rules can always be transformed into some other set, having the same logical power. Some solutions will appear simpler than others, but nobody has yet given a plausible analysis of what simplicity means in such connections.

Let us call two different sets of rules that generate the same sets of admissible sentences *productively equivalent*. We can see that the codification of the grammar of a given language might produce indefinitely many different but productively equivalent systems of grammatical rules. It is well known that an axiom system for plane Euclidean geometry can be formulated by using as a primitive only the notion of a circle, or alternatively, only the notion of a line (with corresponding changes in the axioms) ; analogously, since the reasons are quite general, there will be many alternative but different ways of presenting a grammar. In particular, the very notion of a rule is dispensable: in order to segregate the grammatical from the ungrammatical and to reveal the grammatical structure of admissible sentences, we could use sets, or functions, or a number of other organizing ideas that a professional mathematician could produce with ease. Mathematical organization is never uniquely determined by extramathematical data.

So long as we confine ourselves to the theoretical interests of grammarians, the choice between these alternatives will be dictated by convenience, ease of use, and heuristic fertility. The linguist will choose a grammar that he finds easy to work with, useful in field work, suggestive of experiments, and so on. How we describe celestial motions is, of course, a matter of indifference to the planets themselves: if we find it less cumbersome to use conic sections rather than circles and epicycles, or integral equations rather than differential ones, that is our affair. But in speech, where rules are, in some sense hard to render precise, acknowledged by the speakers themselves, the case is different. Some rules, that might provide elegant codifications of grammatical relations, would be unusable by normal speakers. Chomsky has never supposed that the normal speaker constructs his sentences by following the canonical representation of grammatical structure. The ordinary speaker does not, except in very special cases, start with the category of sentence, proceeding by bifurcation into subject and predicate, and onwards to noun-phrases, verb-phrases, and so on, to end only after many intermediate steps with desired words in a proper order.

We seem to be faced then with the ticklish problem of reconstructing grammars that are actually used by speakers and hearers. The nature of such a task is by no means sufficiently clear. Yet the attempt will need to be made if we want the theorist's grammar to be something more than a device for "saving the appearances." We shall need to make the transition from the algebra to some psychological "reality," whatever we mean by that dubious but indispensable word.

7. *How can we pass from mathematical grammar to psychology?* A transformational grammar, I have argued, can be regarded as a piece of mathematics, suggested by selected grammatical verdicts of qualified informants. So, Chomsky's main premises, which I accept on trust as well-founded, look to me like mathematical ones, having the form: such-and-such will just suffice to generate such-and-such a class of sentences (abstract structures, suggested by utterances that competent speakers would certify as "correct"). Yet Chomsky ends with *psychological* and *epistemological* conclusions. If his reasoning is sound, some psychological and epistemological premises must have been introduced in order to warrant the transition: I am unclear as to what these additional premises are. No doubt they could be found in Chomsky's numerous discussions of his position, but I cannot see them as sharply as I should like.

8. *Must we be rationalists?* The most challenging conclusion that Chomsky draws from his conception of language and the appropriate methodology for linguistic science is the need to return something like the position of classical rationalism. But we never swim in the same tradition twice: the rationalism that Chomsky recommends differs in important respects from the

position of such paradigmatic rationalists as Descartes, Leibniz, or Kant.

As I understand them, these ancient advocates of a doctrine of "innate ideas" typically regarded the intellect as a source of *necessary* principles, supposedly required for the organization and cognitive mastery of the external world. Just because such principles were held to be "intuited" with certainty, they were judged to be logically independent of experience. If experience yields only the tentative and corrigible, and if we find ourselves in the possession of apodictic truths, there must be some other nonexperiential and infallible source of knowledge. The rationalists' conviction of irrefutable knowledge of the necessary truth of such principles as universal causation, the three-dimensionality of space, etc., was their main reason for denying the sovereignty of experience. This is far removed from Chomsky's climate of thought.

Chomsky is a rationalist with a difference: he cannot think that the principles of "universal grammar" (still waiting, so far as I can see, to be laid bare) are known, in anything like the classical sense. They are supposed to operate at a level so far below awareness that we have a hard time formulating them, let alone recognizing them as authoritative. Nor does Chomsky regard the basic principles as necessary in the logical sense, since he insists upon the existence of many conceivable, but unused, alternatives.

Given such far-reaching differences in doctrine, it seems to me somewhat willful, from a historical point of view, to appropriate the tattered label of "rationalism" for a philosophical standpoint so transformed in content and intention. I suspect that this unnecessary bit of pseudohistorical affiliation is mainly introduced *pour épater les empiristes.*

The more genuine dispute between Chomsky and his critics is as to the proper allocation of the responsibility for language acquisition between learning and antecedent biological endowment. (Roughly speaking, how much can we expect from the genes?) Chomsky is a "nativist" rather than a rationalist.

Now, expressed in the most general terms, the old dispute between nativists and empiricists is quite without interest. Everybody can agree that the notion of a perfect *tabula rasa* is an absurdity and the notion of a *machina immaculata* as much so. Even a blank sheet of paper will not permit anything whatever to be inscribed on it! The only question of interest is *how much* a child can learn from experience and *how much more* must be imputed as biological endowment in order for such learning to be possible.

I must say that it looks to me as if Chomsky pits an old-fashioned and unresourceful empiricism (roughly speaking, the sensationalism of Hume, or its modern survival in stimulus-response psychology) against an up-to-date and sophisticated "rationalism" that Leibniz would disown. Of course, the poorer one's conception of experience, the more tempting it will be to succumb to nativism or rationalism. But learning from experience need not be construed on the simplistic model of association, by contiguity and resemblance, of logically independent sense-data; nor need the generalizing power of the organism necessarily be restricted to Baconian induction. Perception of spatial relations, and the emergence of concepts, inherently productive, because applicable to novel instances, are at least as much to be found in "experience" as immediate recognition of patches of color. I should hesitate to locate any aspects of experience, thus generously construed, "in the organism" without substantial evidence.

Such evidence will certainly be hard to find, since on Chomsky's views the latent dispositions, already at least one remove from direct observation, themselves need to be activated by suitable experience. Since we can at best observe certain complex patterns of behavior (including a productive generalizing capacity) demanding previous training, it is hard to see what work the assumption of innate structures really does. In natural science, reference to dispositions and powers is usually a promissory note, to be cashed by some identifiable internal structure: if we seriously attribute elasticity to a piece of metal, it is because we expect to find inside it some relatively stable configuration that will reveal the dispositional term as something more than convenient shorthand for if–then connections between impressed forces and reactions. But there is no serious question at present of finding such internal configurations in human organisms: we hardly know what we should be looking for, or where to look. So far as stimulation of research goes, "nativism" looks to me like a dead end, while "empiricism" (the provisional attribution of learning to something, however complex, detectable in antecedent training and learning) suggests programs of investigation that may be expected to uncover interesting data. Chomsky may be sinning against that special version of Occam's razor that runs "Innate endowments are not to be multiplied beyond necessity." I am yet to be convinced of the necessity.

9. *How good is the evidence for linguistic nativism?* The evidence offered by neonativists is classifiable as follows: (*a*) the presence in all languages of certain "universals"; (*b*) the ease with which young children learn language (including a command of grammar) and the comparative difficulty with which adults learn it; (*c*) the difficulty of accounting for these facts upon any "inductive" conception of the learning process.

Now as to the existence of language universals, I am somewhat skeptical about the strength of the available evidence. For one thing, there is a risk of tautology in the argument from examination of known languages. The "universals" we fancy we find may simply be part of our criteria of what is to *count* as language. Consider the strikingly particulate character of all known language, at the levels of phonology and morphology. We can choose to exclude other modes of communication, e.g., by continuously varying gestures, as nonlinguistic: but is that more than arbitrary definition? It would certainly be implausible to argue from some component of a definition, or from the partial analysis of a concept, to a general empirical truth about human beings. And the fact that human beings do without exception, it seems, use particulate linguistic systems may perhaps be explained more plausibly on the ground of the obvious efficiency of such systems than by invoking a corresponding biological predisposition. The use of levers is almost universal among mankind, but it would be a hardy thinker who postulated a corresponding specific endowment.

The examples of linguistic universals that Chomsky, at least tentatively, regards as innate, seem to me rather unplausible in themselves. One might expect any such principles that might emerge to be special cases of more general ways of responding to and structuring experience. Are there perhaps universals of symbolism?

The evidence for childish facility in acquiring language is no doubt stronger. But neglecting such inessentials as correctness of accent, is the evidence as good as it is usually supposed to be? Very little is know at present about how much grammar children really acquire in the formative years. But suppose, for the sake of argument, that there is a period in early infancy when children can learn to talk more easily than in later years; what would this show? Young children can probably learn to swim faster than adults; yet in this case the nativist inference looks unpalatable. An antinativist might try to argue that variation in external facilitating conditions, such as the obvious advantages of learning the first language, the influence of adults, etc., suffice to account for the imputed difference in learning rates. That an antinativist could reply in this way, or in some elaborated version of such a defense, suggests that the dispute is not straightforwardly empirical after all. It may be a conflict between two methodologies rather than a dispute between two theories.

Finally, it might be held that the difficulty of accounting for language acquisition on the basis of inductive analysis of data (given the highly fragmentary and "degenerate" examples of linguistic performance that the child is exposed to) makes any explanation but the possession of innate endowment impossible. This argument has all the weakness of any conclusion *ab ignorantia rationis*. "What else *could* explain this?" is too often a sign of the questioner's lack of imagination to inspire much confidence. Suppose we found a stone so intricately streaked that we were at a loss to conceive how environmental influences could have produced it: it would be a bold leap to hold something in the stone itself responsible. Now the argument from incapacity to understand how induction could serve the learner's needs may be no stronger than this: Is the fault perhaps with the crudity of our conception of induction or, more generally, with our conception of experience?

10. *A possible incoherence?* I will end with a qualm, connected with a point I have already made about the logical contingency of the imputed principles of universal grammar. Chomsky is able to tell us some of the alternative principles (or modes of organization) that are *not* used in the languages we know. Let us call such principles *unnatural*. Are we asked to believe that human beings cannot *in fact* use unnatural principles, at however much inconvenience, and still make themselves understood? If so, I doubt whether we can know it, without a trial. But suppose it turned out, as it might, that we could speak and make ourselves understood by employing unnatural principles. Then, on Chomsky's approach we would have to postulate some higher-order disposition for modifying the first-order dispositions that produce the "natural" linguistic capacities. Which looks suspiciously like a *reductio ad absurdum*. Chomsky seems to me to be in the position of other theorists (such as Karl Mannheim and Whorf) who have claimed to discover general limitations upon human powers: in the course of describing the limitation, they show by their own discussion how to escape from it.

It may be possible, therefore, to find an empirical disproof of Chomsky's position, by teaching children or adults to violate the principles of universal grammar. Since human beings seem to be rather good at breaking grammatical rules, I think it not impossible that such an experiment would succeed. At least, it would be interesting to try.

11. *No simple resolution?* My list of questions has probably

made the issues between transformational grammarians and their critics look simpler than they really are. Chomskyites will, I suspect, retort that I am expecting too much of a theoretical reorientation, in asking for piecemeal empirical verification. The test must be global theoretical adequacy, as against available alternatives. I am sympathetic with this reply. The current vogue of transformational grammar is symptomatic of a revolt among linguists, at least in America, against the somewhat doctrinaire neglect of theory by an older generation strongly under the influence of such giants as Boas, Sapir, and Bloomfield. For all the enormous merits of the empirical research inspired by these pioneers in scientific linguistics, one cannot deny that it too often emphasized the descriptive at the expense of the explanatory. Whatever may be its weakness in details, the point of view outlined in Chomsky's paper has had the great merit of reviving interest in such long-neglected but fundamental issues.

XI

Some Aversive Responses to a Would-Be Reinforcer

The spectacle of a convinced determinist *urging* his readers to save the human race is bound to be somewhat comic. But B. F. Skinner is very much in earnest in his latest book,[1] and no traces of the irony and self-deprecation that occasionally enlivened *Walden Two* are here allowed to mollify the urgency of a call to behavioristic salvation. For, "we have the physical, biological and behavioral technologies 'to save ourselves'; the problem is *how to get people to use them*" (p. 158, emphasis added). That a requisite "technology of behavior" (p. 5) is already at our disposal may be doubted. Whether Skinner can say consistently with his own principles that we should work to achieve such a technology, I shall discuss later.

Skinner's call to action, if that is what it is, is marred by endemic ambiguity, repeatedly manifested in his uses of the key terms of his vocabulary of exhortation. Thus, survival, according to him, demands "control" of the "environment"; but equivocation upon both of these terms makes it doubtful whether radical changes are in question.

Consider the following characteristic remarks: "A scientific analysis of behavior dispossesses autonomous man and turns the *control* he has been said to exert over to the environment" (p. 205, emphasis added here and in the following quotations). (Here, it should be explained that "autonomous man" refers simply to the "myth" of men's responsibility for their actions.

[1] B. F. Skinner, *Beyond Freedom and Dignity* (New York, Knopf, 1971).

We notice that "control" is to be assigned, characteristically, to a supposedly impersonal environment.) "To refuse to *control* is to leave *control* not to the person himself, but to other parts of the social and non-social environment" (p. 84). "When we seem to turn *control* over to a person himself, we simply shift from one mode of *control* to another" (p. 97). "Attacking *controlling* practices is, of course, a form of *countercontrol*" (p. 181). "Good government is as much a matter of the *control* of human behavior as bad, good incentive conditions as much as exploitation, good teaching as much as punitive drill" (p. 180). And so on.

It seems, then, that "control" is ubiquitous in social relations and any attempt to change oneself or others, whether by conditioning, persuasion, or argument, is sure to count as "control." In this loose and obfuscating usage, "control" means no more than "have some effect upon," and the admonition to facilitate human survival by "control of the environment" becomes vacuous and somewhat fatuous, since it urges us to do anything we please, with the assurance that we shall thereby be controlling our environment. Of course, this is emphatically not Skinner's intention, as we shall see.

A similar shift from a natural and restricted sense to a vacuously inflated one will already have been noticed in connection with the term "environment." One might reasonably gloss it as "*physical* environment," since this is the sense that Skinner needs, but he repeatedly renders his call for human conditioning persuasive by stretching the word to cover *persons*. Thus, "setting an example" also counts as changing the environment, and so as controlling those influenced by the example (p. 92). In this expansive sense, changing others and ourselves, by whatever means, will count as changing the "environment."

Since "control" and "environment" are used in these reckless ways, it is unsurprising—though, to be sure, unintentionally amusing—to find Skinner speaking of the "control" exercised by a laboratory animal on his handler. "His apparatus exerts a conspicuous control on the pigeon, but we must not overlook *the control exerted by the pigeon.* The behavior of the pigeon has determined the design of the apparatus and the procedures in which it is used" (p. 169, emphasis added). It reminds one of the old joke about one pigeon boasting to another of how it had conditioned Skinner to provide food whenever it pecked a button.

Skinner might seem to have anticipated such objections in admitting that "the text will often seem inconsistent" (p. 23). But he misses the point when he goes on to say that "English, like all languages, is full of prescientific terms which usually suffice for purposes of casual discourse." His own preferred technical terms, being theory-laden only in a very weak sense, are scarcely more than common expressions in fancy dress (so that a "response," for instance, is nothing but a bit of behavior under a physical description), and he *needs* the ordinary senses of "control," "reinforcement," and the like for his message to sound plausible. As for his promise that "acceptable translations" (of "mentalistic expressions") "are not out of reach" (p. 24), we shall see later that that is merely a bluff.

The increased and more effective control advocated by Skinner is not merely the taking of whatever measures may improve society: he really intends the special and controversial modes of control known as "classical" and "operant conditioning," and especially the latter. He is able to equate whatever needs to be done with conditioning because he holds that *only* conditioning will be effective.

Operant conditioning consists basically of the application to animal subjects of carefully planned schedules of positive or negative "reinforcements," by which the subjects' favored responses are "shaped and maintained" (p. 169), or "strengthened," by being rendered more likely to occur. To such procedures, the term "control," in its dictionary sense of "exercise restraint or direction over," does apply without dilution or extension of meaning. A Skinnerian psychologist, engaged in conditioning a pigeon or a man, is quite literally shaping, restricting, directing, in short controlling his subject's responses.

We must remember that, on Skinnerian principles, what the subject thinks about the routines imposed upon him is causally irrelevant. (Sometimes, however, Skinner seems willing to admit the efficacy of the subject's "interpretation" of the situation, with the usual promissory gesture in the direction of an eventual translation in behavioristic terms.) Skinner regards serious reference to such allegedly "mentalistic" factors as motive, intention, and the like as being at best Aesopian, and strictly speaking inadmissible in a truly scientific account. So, it is reprehensible in the end even to talk about "mental" features, and unwarranted to assign causal efficacy to any of them. The pigeon, we may presume, cannot reflect upon his conditioning and, if a man under conditioning knows what is being done to him, that makes no difference to the administered reinforcements.

Given the postulated irrelevance of the subject's awareness of his training, and hence also the irrelevance of his knowledge and consent, a better label for the procedure would be *"involuntary* control," or its more familiar variant, "manipulation." Skinner's true doctrine, barely veiled by his habitual equivocation, calls for the wholesale manipulation of human beings, willy-nilly, for their own good or rather for the survival of the species.

Skinner will retort that men are controlled anyhow, whether by propaganda, the threat of force, education, indoctrination, or love. Well, all these things affect us, to be sure, but that hardly amounts to control, in the sense of manipulation. Common sense would hold that men are sometimes manipulated and sometimes not. The differences, turning crucially as they do upon the knowledge and consent of those involved, are crucial. To ignore them is to leave "control" without any clear sense.

In its familiar and proper use, "control" implies a controller or controllers. Skinner's right to control pigeons is sanctioned by our society's tolerance for scientific research. But who is to choose the Grand Manipulators of all of us? And what is to be their authority to manipulate us without our knowledge? This question Skinner repeatedly dodges, by using his favorite device of speaking of control by the "environment," as if the envisaged display of "reinforcers" were not to be designed and employed by hidden managers. It is a safe, if somewhat pessimistic, rule of thumb that unintended consequences of technological innovations are likely to turn out badly. Skinner himself says that "what is needed is more 'intentional' control, not less, and this is an important engineering problem" (p. 177). He might have added that it is also an important political and moral problem. For if a manipulator stands behind each "engineered" environment, his moral and political restraints are of keen interest to his "subjects."

Skinner has a short way with the question of control over the social controllers. He tells us that "such a technology [the extension of deliberate human conditioning] is ethically neutral" (p. 150). Here lurks the old fallacy that the introduction of "technology," even when its human consequences can be reasonably foreseen, is from the moral standpoint neither good nor bad. We need some assurance that wholesale conditioning will not have results as deplorable as the introduction of some stupefying drug. Skinner says that "the great problem is to arrange effective countercontrol and hence to bring some important consequences to bear on the behavior of the controller" (p. 171) but seems to regard this as a mere technical hitch: he is conveniently vague about who is to exert the requisite "countercontrol" (anglice: restraint). For the rest, we get the ritual obeisance to democracy: "In a democracy the controller is found among the controlled, although he behaves in different ways in the two roles" (p. 172). Indeed he does, as the case of Joe McCarthy may remind us. The promoter of the Great Lie is not deceived (or if he is, so much the worse) and the controller of the Great Social Conditioning Experiment is likely to have enough sense to stay out of the Skinner box. In evaluating what are, properly understood, political proposals, we need specific descriptions of the envisaged political and social institutions, and the restraints under which they will operate. Faced with Skinner's skeleton design, we can only be reasonably sure that manipulation will be more congenial to an authoritarian than to an imperfectly democratic form of society—if only because dictatorships, as we know, pride themselves upon "efficiency." Mussolini boasted of making the trains run on time; a Skinnerian dictator may be expected to have all of us running on time.

As for the allegedly "scientific" basis for these far-reaching recommendations, a lay observer can perhaps do no more than register an impression of implausibly sweeping generalization from a narrow empirical base. Suppose Skinner and his associates to have been conspicuously successful in training pigeons and other experimental animals: does it reasonably follow that similar methods will be equally effective with human beings? The scope of conditioning may well be wider than common sense suspects, but that is something yet to be established—and if necessary, guarded against.

Suspicions of unwarranted generalization are roused by finding Skinner using the technical term "reinforcer" (roughly speaking, any event that increases the likelihood of occurrence of some associated item of antecedent behavior) in ways unsanctioned by his own self-denying methodology. One finds him freely using "reinforcement" for social approval (or, strictly speaking, the noises and gestures by which such approval is expressed), money, friendship, the joy of achievement, love, indeed anything that we should ordinarily regard as a reward. If "institutions may derive effective reinforcers from events which will occur only after a person's death" (p. 135) (a neat trick, from the standpoint of operant conditioning) we are certainly a long way from the pigeon in its controlled apparatus. Similar doubts arise when Skinner claims that "the accidental appearance of a reinforcer strengthens any behavior in progress and brings it under the control of current stimuli" (p. 176). That what Skinner calls "superstition" is quite so universal in its incidence may well be doubted. And is there really enough evidence to show that "how people feel about facts is a by-product" (p. 113) ? Does Skinner know this? Does he have reasonable grounds for believing it? I very much doubt it. The extent to which feelings (and intentions, motives, ideals, and so on) are in fact causally effective in particular situations is a question for detailed empirical investigation. Common sense tells us that feelings sometimes make a difference, sometimes not. (The anger felt by the father of a child killed by a reckless motorist may lead to murder.) Pending the presentation of relevant evidence to the contrary, uninstructed common sense may reasonably continue to think that what men feel and believe *does* often make a substantial difference, and is not a mere "by-product."

When scientists, professionally committed to cautious and well-hedged hypotheses, indulge in universal generalizations that denigrate entire categories of entities as fictions, one may well suspect some metaphysical bias. That Skinner has such a bias against "mentalism" is abundantly clear from his writings. Consider such a revealing remark as: "The world of the mind steals the show. Behavior is not recognized as a subject in its own right" (p. 12). Can the original sin of "mentalism" be its setting bounds to the inferences drawn from empirical associations between what have been called "colorless movements"? At any rate, extensive debates in the past between behaviorists and their philosophical opponents have made it very clear that science cannot, on the basis of the historical record of scientific achievement, be identified with the mere correlation of observables: the introduction of suitable theoretical terms, ultimately but only indirectly linked with observation, deserves to be regarded as of the essence of scientific method. Skinner's inveterate propensity to identify his favored methodology with "scientific analysis" is simply unacceptable. There is also by now an impressive body of testimony to the severe difficulties that must be overcome by anybody committed to behavioristic translations of the commonplaces of ordinary life, for which such terms as "intention," "goal," "attitude," and "feeling" still seem indispensable.

The last point is amusingly illustrated by Skinner's exercises in translating some "mentalistic" assertions. The assertion that "there is nothing he [a college student] wants to do or enjoys doing well, he has no sense of leading a purposeful life, no sense of accomplishment" is to be translated, according to Skinner, as "he is rarely reinforced for doing anything" (p. 147). (The man in question might console himself by the reflection that reinforcement of some sort is always in progress, as we have seen.) "He feels guilty or ashamed" becomes "he has previously been punished for idleness or failure, which now evokes emotional responses" (*ibid.*); and "he experiences an identity crisis" is paraphrased as "he does not recognize the person he once called 'I'" (*ibid.*). One wonders what this unfortunate man (like the old woman in the nursery rhyme who complained "This is none of I") now calls the person he once called "I"? Does he perhaps refer to himself as "He"—or even as "K"? Skinner disarmingly says that the "paraphrases are too brief to be precise" (*ibid.*). Well, some of them don't even have the charm of brevity. There are weighty reasons for thinking that no such paraphrases, long or short, will be satisfactory, and that the vocabulary of ordinary life and of literature has a genuine point.

Given Skinner's theoretical commitment to behaviorese—or at least to ordinary language that is to be ultimately translated into the new jargon—it is perhaps unsurprising to find him belittling what he pejoratively calls "the Literature of Freedom and Dignity," that is to say any discourse that imputes responsibility and choice. It is, however, disconcerting to find him displaying such open and steady animus against what, under a more persuasive description, is merely the common language of ordinary life, literature, and history. (After all, the members of *Walden Two* were great readers.) How are we to explain such remarks as "[There is a] threat posed by the literature of freedom and dignity" (p. 177)? Perhaps the answer is to be found in the following remark: "What we may call the literature of dignity is concerned wih preserving due credit. It may oppose advances in technology, including a technology of behavior, because they destroy chances to be admired and a basic analysis because it offers an alternative explanation of behavior for which the individual himself has previously been given the credit" (pp. 58–59). So the prime mistake made by humanists is to attach blame and praise ("credit") to persons. We might say, on Skinnerian principles, that the fault is not in ourselves, dear Brutus, but in our re-inforcers. That we are on the right track is shown by another remark: "A scientific analysis shifts the credit as well as the blame to the environment, and traditional practices can then no longer be justified" (p. 21). Or, again: "It is in the nature of an experimental analysis of human behavior that it should strip away the functions previously assigned to autonomous man and transfer them one by one to the controlling environ-ment" (p. 198). Here is that ostensibly impersonal "environ-ment" again, presented now as a bearer of praise and blame. Skinner might more consistently have placed praise and blame on the index. (I seem to recollect that nobody praises, blames, or even gives thanks in *Walden Two*.) Once the myth of personal responsibility has been rejected as superstition, not even the controllers can count as responsible. For this is what is really at stake in Skinner's polemic against the humanistic standpoint. It is disingenuous on his part to depict the "litera-ture of dignity and freedom" as a device for flattering its readers, for he knows as well as all of us how often the teach-ings of history and literature have been derogatory and pessi-mistic. The blunder of humanism, according to him, is to hold men to account for their deeds. It would be interesting to hear a good, or even a persuasive, argument that absolved Skinner from responsibility for the book under discussion.

Skinner claims that purging the "myth" of responsibility (my description, not his) will be a step forward. "What is being abolished is autonomous man—the inner man, the homunculus, the possessing demon, the man defended by the literature of freedom and dignity. His abolition is long over-due. . . . Science does not de-humanize man, it de-homunculizes him, and it must do so if it is to prevent the abolition of the human species" (p. 200). Here, at least, is one place in which Skinner agrees that ideas (the myth of responsibility) make a difference. Would it be "a step forward" (p. 215) to be in a "behavioral environment" arranged by skillful hidden manipulators, in which the very language of responsible action had been expunged by effective conditioning? Would this be a sanitary removal of some obfuscating myth? We might justifiably regard the end-product as a dehumanization, in which men were no longer accorded the dignity of being treated as persons. A world of well-controlled bodies, emitting physical movements in response to secret reinforcements might perhaps seem hardly worth preserving. It may, after all, be better to be dead than bred—like cattle.

Throughout these comments, I have been regarding Skinner as a reformer who offers admonitions having the form "You (we) *should* do such and such." That he does wish to "control" us in this way seems plain enough. Given the inconsistency of his language, it is hard to determine whether he really wants us to do much or little. But let us suppose that he does wish his readers to approve of certain actions, and to work toward them—perhaps by instituting managers trained in Skinnerian conditioning techniques and licensed to condition all of us to the hilt. Call the advocated actions, *A*. Then how, from the perspective of a radical behaviorism, are we to understand the admonition "You should do *A*"? For it is not, on the face of it, a statement of fact of the sort that Skinner admits.

Skinner provides us with the materials for an answer when he says that we might translate a "value judgment" of the form "You should (you ought to) tell the truth" into "If you are reinforced by the approval of your fellow men, you will be reinforced when you tell the truth" (p. 112). Since the reference to truth-telling is only illustrative, we may take it that, in urging us to do *A*, Skinner would be content to have us understand him as saying "If you are reinforced by the approval of your fellow men, you will be reinforced when you do *A*." Taken as a conditional statement, this last statement may well be false. Even the parallel behavioristic surrogate for the injunction to tell the truth is false, if it refers to the reinforcement of *all* "fellow men," since lying is approved by thieves, schoolboys, advertisers and politicians. The commandment should presumably be relativized to run: "If you are reinforced by those who approve of truth-telling, you will be reinforced when you tell the truth."

To which one wants to reply, "Of course!" The translation proposed is saved from tautology only by the weak presupposition that the man addressed will in fact be in the presence of the approvers of truth-telling. Grant that and the truth of the conditional follows at once. In that form, it can be cheerfully affirmed, by habitual truth-tellers and liars alike. Ananias might readily have agreed that *if* he was reinforced by the approval of the approvers of veracity, he would try, like other liars, to appear as a truth-teller in the presence of veracity-approvers. But Ananias might have been *negatively* reinforced by the approval of veracity-approvers, preferring the approval of Sapphira. Given the falsity of the antecedent in the doctored command, it then gets no grip upon him—which is perhaps why Peter needed to intervene with so drastic a negative reinforcement. In this example, Skinner seeks to reduce the motive force of the "should," in a way that is clearly unsuccessful to a hypothetical prediction about the effects of other persons' approval.

We are entitled to make parallel responses to Skinner's own recommendations, on his own interpretation of what he is saying. "If you are reinforced by the approval of those who approve my recommendations, you will follow them." I think I am not deceiving myself in claiming not to be "reinforced" by Skinner's recommendations or by the approval of those who agree with him, but rather the reverse. So, I can agree with his hypothetical prediction—and do nothing at all.

It would be wrong to suppose that this argument *ad hominem* disproves the possibility of some more sophisticated behavioristic reduction of "should"-statements. But the most plausible candidate for naturalistic interpretations of such statements invoke the concept of attitude, which is beyond Skinner's behavioristic ken. Enough has been shown, I think, to demonstrate at least the incoherence of Skinner's position.

Such incoherence can be found throughout the book. Skinner's arbitrary identification of science with the procedures of operant conditioning, his unsupported and dogmatic rejection of the notion of human responsibility and hence of human agency, his extravagant testimonials to a "behavioral technology" which is happily still no more than a future threat—all this *mélange* of amateurish metaphysics, self-advertising "technology," and illiberal social policy adds up to a document that is a disservice to scientists, technologists, and to all who are seriously trying to improve the human condition.

If the book has here received more attention than it deserves on its merits, the excuse may be that it has received wide circulation. In this, there is little cause for alarm: few of those who buy the book will read it, fewer still will understand, and even fewer will change their actions in consequence. If some who favor manipulation are "reinforced" by Skinner's approval, that need not disturb us much either. For those who wish to manipulate and dominate can always find some "justification" or other when they think it politic, even while they decry the very notion of justification as an absurdity.

XII

Some Tasks for the Humanities

1. *In search of defining criteria.* Considered as a general term, the pretentious and now somewhat shopworn label of "the Humanities" has the defect of lacking any clear criteria for membership. Indeed, the traditional label, for all its self-congratulatory connotations, has now degenerated into a mere umbrella-word for whatever cannot conveniently be assigned to "Science" or the "Fine Arts." It may still be useful, however, to search for some criteria that serve to distinguish "the Humanities" from other studies and disciplines.

There can, I think, be no hope of finding an Aristotelian definition *per genus et differentiam:* the various humanistic studies are too variegated and share too many features in common with the natural and social sciences to admit of neat classification. But we can still hope for glimpses of some unifying conception, some good reasons for a contrast with Science and Technology.

I shall use "humanistic studies" throughout to refer to second-order activities of "placing," interpreting, criticizing, and evaluating primary "humanistic" texts, works of art, and related artifacts, institutions, and practices. Correspondingly, I count, for the purpose of this discussion, a "humanist" as a student, teacher, or investigator working at this "second-order" level—a literary critic, not a poet; a musicologist, not a composer; and so on.

2. *The concept of "the Humanities" is an "essentially contested" one.* I borrow the useful notion of an "essentially con-

tested concept" from W. B. Gallie, who applies it to any term, such as "Art," or "Democracy" whose users, by adhering to competing traditions, contest the right to possession of the honorific appellation. Such contests for a linguistic emblem, settled by the triumph of one sect over its enemies, are characteristically marked by the proclamation of "persuasive definitions": "*True* Christianity is . . . ," "*Genuine* democracy is . . . ," "*Real* freedom consists in . . . ," and the like.

Humanitas, it seems, was Cicero and Varro's Latinization of the Greek *paideia*, and alluded for many centuries to this historical affiliation. For Roman theorists it steadily connoted the syndrome of features, the "human essence," that elevated Man above the condition of mere animality and gave him his proper rank above the beasts, if below the gods. This program has always been controversial. It proved hard to reconcile the "personal" and the "public," the aspirations of an individual with those of his social groups.

Man, in a conception reaching back to Aristotle, and shared by antihumanists no less than by humanists, could become most "fully man" by not being an "idiot"—in short by becoming fully a citizen; and so the "good arts" have always been conceived as "serving ends beyond themselves—ends that involved the moral nature of man or his practical activities as a citizen or public servant."[1] Given the restrictions upon citizenship in all societies in which "humanistic education" has been an effective ideal, it is hardly surprising that, for all its pretensions to universal validity, such education should always have been both elitist and vocational, serving in fact, whether in Greece, Rome, Renaissance Italy, or Victorian England, the special interests of a governing class or their clerks. This is one respectable ground for current suspicion of "humanistic education": it is hard to advocate in good faith a vocational curriculum, designed for gentlemen and their literate aides, when the very concept of a gentleman has become an anachronism.

[1] R. S. Crane, *The Idea of the Humanities* (Chicago, 1967), p. 156.

Tension between the "personal" and the "social" aspects of classical humanism has been exacerbated by background philosophical disputes as to how to define the "human essence," and by endemic wrangles between curriculum-makers. No wonder, then, that no agreement has long prevailed concerning the content of a humanistic curriculum.

The moral to be drawn from this Cook's Tour of the history of humanistic studies is that the concept here proposed for investigation is problematic in the extreme. Our choice is not between relatively well-articulated subtraditions: contrary to popular belief, there never has been a Golden Age of humanistic education. The task is not so much to "save" the Humanities as to *create* them.

3. *The underlying presuppositions of earlier humanistic programs need substantial revision.* The background assumptions of the powerfully persuasive conception that there ought to be a distinctively "humane" education, designed to elicit those powers and virtues that distinguish men from brute beasts, can be captured in the following, deliberately simplified contentions.

(A) *Men are distinct from and potentially superior to other animals.* The "dignity of man" consists in his capacity, through the exercise of deliberation, reason, and choice, to realize this potential superiority.

(B) *There is a human essence or "nature," present in all human beings, the same in all of them, that sharply distinguishes them from mere animals.* Thus the difference between a man and a brute is like that between silver and iron, one of "kind" not of "degree," innate, apt for full realization by suitable education and training, but impossible to alter.

(C) *The human essence is essentially good.* Classical humanisms, to the degree that their aims have been secular, have been guided by an optimistic rejection of original sin. The good for man is to become "fully human," by the full realization of the essential humanity implanted within him; in so doing, he becomes necessarily a *good* man and so, also, a good citizen. Humanistic education, thus conceived, necessarily has moral and social implications.

(D) *There are distinctive "arts" or "disciplines" peculiarly suitable for aiding in the realization of essential "humanity."* It is a noteworthy basis of continuity with present-day conceptions that linguistic studies—"grammar" and "rhetoric"— should always have been recognized to have a central humanizing importance. For if anything prominently distinguishes men from brutes, it is their power to communicate by speech as members of a community possessing a common language.

(E) *The distinctively humanistic disciplines must include some that are nonscientific.* Science is not to be excluded from "the Humanities," as earlier humanistic curricula amply testify. Yet science has only a limited and partial educational value because, in its search for "objectivity," it is committed to "suspending" certain distinctively human interests and preoccupations.

(F) *The overall aim of humanistic education may be summarily described as the development of Reason.* Cf. Erasmus: "What is the proper nature of man? Surely it is to live the life of reason, for reason is the peculiar prerogative of man."[2] If thesis (E) is accepted, the character of "reason" itself becomes problematic: are the same methods and procedures as suitable for literary criticism as for physics? Perhaps no question is more important for advocates of a distinctively humanistic education.

Taking now the position defined by the above six contentions as an "ideal type," and a plausible springboard for a contemporary program, let us consider how much of it remains tenable in the light of present-day knowledge.

Only the fourth and fifth contentions can survive without serious modification. While agreeing that man is strikingly different from other animals, we must acknowledge continuities

---

[2] Quoted from M. H. Abrams, "Humanism," in *A Glossary of Literary Terms* (New York, 1971).

that discredit the oversimplified ancient conception of a unique, innate and sharply defined human "essence." Without adopting the extravagancies of contemporaries who deny any human "essence" as an innate constraint upon development, we have to take more seriously than the ancients did man's extraordinary malleability and adaptability. It is no longer possible to share the romantic and optimistic beliefs of earlier humanisms in the innate goodness and benevolence of uncorrupted "human nature." That increasing knowledge of and sensitivity to humanistic masterpieces should *eo ipso* lead to an access of moral virtue seems too implausible ever to have been seriously maintained. And as much can be said of the simplistic conception of a unitary and sufficient power of Reason, illuminating indifferently all subjects of human concern.

Does this leave the temple of "Humanity" in ruins and as irrelevant to present concerns as the abandoned Acropolis? We may be confident at least that a revived humanism, relevant to our own pressing problems, rather than to those of Athenian gentlemen or Renaissance courtiers, will need to be significantly different from its predecessors.

In what follows, I shall offer some tentative suggestions for the construction of such a humanism. I shall take as a starting point some summary reflections upon the limitations of "scientific method." The power and efficacy of science and its stepsister technology need no further acknowledgment; but if we are to avoid the polar heresies of scientolatry and scientophobia, we need to remind ourselves of what science and technology cannot accomplish. In this way, the opportunities and tasks of a regenerated humanistic education may become somewhat plainer.

4. *Scientific investigation is conducted within special and characteristic "perspectives" whose influence it seeks progressively to neutralize.* The great-great-grandson of Macaulay's schoolboy can be counted upon to "know" that scientific method consists in a resolute suppression of bias and prejudice, for the sake of a resolute confrontation with "neutral facts."

They are the raw material for generalizations and higher-level theories, themselves ultimately judged and evaluated by their power to predict novel "facts." An adherent to this neoempiricist myth, for that is what it is, is unlikely to be unaware of the ways in which the "data" and "principles" of science are necessarily mediated by a man-made apparatus of record and conceptualization. The fruits of scientific investigation are more like a map than like a photograph—and even the most "realistic" photograph is intelligible only in terms of a system of representation.

I propose to use the expression "perspective" in the following technical senses. By a "perspective" I mean a systematic repertoire of devices for recording and formulating data and conclusions relating to them. (The "Mercator Projection" is a paradigm instance of a "perspective" in the intended sense.)

A perspective consists at least of the following: (i) observers and instruments of "observation" or record, together with rules for their use, (ii) a language or other symbolism of representation, (iii) associated, but not necessarily formulated practices (customs, procedures, routines) by means of which the aforementioned observers, instruments, and the language used by them are "applied" or "activated," (iv) a stock of "given," unquestioned deliverances couched in the language of the perspective in question—i.e., the dogmas, axioms, commonplaces, etc., of the system in question.

We might think of a "perspective" as a relatively organized way of grasping (recording, perhaps also interpreting, explaining) some aspects of "experience"—a complex strategic apparatus compounded of material instruments and means of representation, together with relevant beliefs and modes of action, for coming to terms with part of the "world." Maps, chronologies, geometries, scientific theories, myths, *Weltanschauungen*, eschatologies, theodicies, can all be regarded as aspects or features of "perspectives" in the intended sense.

Perspectives are inevitably, to some degree, arbitrary: we can usually distinguish within them what is settled in advance of a

particular report or record, what is *"a priori"* for the user of
that system. Since the features of a report ascribable to the
perspective itself are easily confused with features emanating
from beyond it (the "information," "insight," etc., we seek)
all perspectives are intrinsically error-prone.

Science seeks to mitigate the intrinsic fallibility of each cognitive perspective (a given coordinate system, a given mode of
symbolization, a given methodology) by seeking invariants of
wide classes of perspectives. By seeking what remains true of
each perspective of the preferred class, it overcomes the arbi-
trariness that distinguishes one perspective from another. In
this way, there emerges an etherealized limiting conception of
the goal of "scientific objectivity"—a view of the universe "as
it actually is," no longer transformed or distorted by an arbitrary "perspective," the universe seen from no particular
standpoint, *sub specie aeternitatis,* in a God's eye view.

The conception of "scientific objectivity" I have sketched
has an appealing sublimity: on its own ground it has extraordinary achievements to its credit. But the costs of the splendid
success of "the Scientific Outlook" are substantial, among them
the principled and systematic exclusion of much that might be
said to constitute *human* perspectives—the reference-systems in
terms of which men and women live and cope with their
problems as historically situated and conditioned persons.

5. *The "perspective" in terms of which a human being
makes such sense as he can, at a given time, of his "world"
evades the jurisdiction of any scientific "framework."* A human
being, located at a particular point in space-time, has repeated
occasion to make reports that are excluded from an austerely
scientific perspective. Such remarks as "I am hungry," "I remember his dying words," "That looks horrible," "Help!," "I
am dying of boredom," are, in the first place, essentially *self-
referential,* with the first-person pronoun used or understood.
More generally, the language of ordinary life ("ordinary language" for short) would be paralyzed in the absence of such
"token-reflexive" words as "I," "You," "here," "now," "later."

Our need for such context-dependent words corresponds to the inhomogeneity and anisotropy of the changing "world" in which each of us lives. Unlike the abstract and idealized "world" of physics, in which all spaces and times are intrinsically indistinguishable, "*my* world" has a center, a unique but shifting "origin." This is true, of course, even of a scientific perspective, since science is after all an activity of space-and-time-bound persons. But science, as I have said, drives constantly toward the neutralization of the "personal equation," everything that marks a "report" as emanating from this or that particular human source. In ordinary life, however, the personal reference is of the essence: it is not a matter of indifference to a man that *he* must die, nor is the poignancy of this thought captured by the "impersonal" translation "John Smith will die." Closely related to these points is the reality, in the personal world, of change and hence the indispensability in ordinary language of tenses, which the essentially timeless cosmos of science does not capture. The *t* of physics, whether in its contemporary or its older form, is simply one more variable in a four-dimensional space.

An equally radical point of contrast between "ordinary language" and the "language of science" is the use of the former to express in multifarious ways, feelings, attitudes, intentions, fears, aspirations, the whole gamut of the so-called "noncognitive" uses of language. Here, as in the case of the supposedly "objective" transformation of utterances with essentially personal and "indexical" reference, the step from an expression of some human parameter (attitude, intention, feeling, or whatever) to an assertion about that parameter involves an attenuation of context and a deflection of function.

Try to imagine a "society" whose members, prevented by the poverty of their language from expressing "human parameters," are limited to assertions *about* intentions and the like, and whose only "value" is truth. It is, of course, inconceivable that human beings could be mere reporters and communicators, while never enacting the passions they purported to be observing: in the absence of expressive symbolism, there would be nothing to report.

The "personal language" of a space-and-time-bound person, that part of the common language of the group (s) to which he belongs that is always formulated, whether explicitly or implicitly, in the first-person singular or plural, is incommensurable with the language of science. Scientific talk sometimes applies to persons, for a human body is still a physical body, but to vast numbers of matters of personal concern scientific pronouncements are simply irrelevant.

Yet the "world" of an actual individual, however variable and incoherent, is not a chaos: it, too, may properly be brought under the rubric of "perspective," so that we might speak of "*P* (personal) -perspectives." For here, too, we can discern systematic and relatively stable repertoires of expression (a language, together with paralinguistic "gestures"), resting upon temporarily accepted "commonplaces" and activated by routines of action. It is of decisive importance for the role of humanistic education that such a "world" or "perspective" is unequally illuminated by consciousness and self-awareness: we hardly needed Freud to remind us that much of what we do is masked.

P-perspectives intersect *G* (group) -perspectives. For the language that is a central component of a *P*-perspective, no matter how self-centered, idiosyncratic or solipsistic, is necessarily a social instrument: every utterance is potentially intelligible to another person; every expression might "make sense" to a companion; as integral as the reference to "I" are the correlative references to "We," "You," and "They." From a linguistic standpoint: the first-person singular depends for its use and function upon a contrast (opposition) with the other pronouns.

P-perspectives and the *G*-perspectives that overlap them might be called *H* (human) -perspectives.

6. *A distinctive task of humanistic criticism is the delineation and articulation of "human perspectives."* I use "criticism" here in a broad sense to cover all the second-order activities

of a humanistic scholar, as distinct from those of a humanistic creator. Poets, speculative philosophers, and historians, are *inter alia,* engaged in *presenting* possible worlds, "perspectives," or aspects of them, but not in the relatively detached and "distanced" mode of criticism. Roughly speaking, a creator shows by and in his constructions what *H*-perspectives are and might be; the critical commentator tries to make plainer, within a metalanguage, what the artist is doing in his object-language. The poet presents us with an expressive representation of the human condition; the critic sometimes succeeds in helping us to understand better, to see more clearly, what the poet is doing.

I am using "perspective" here, as before, to stand for a relatively organized constellation of axioms, assumptions, beliefs, expectations, aspirations, attachments, obligations, preferences, evaluations, characteristically crystallized in a distinctive sublanguage, conceptual structures, and set of practices. That is to say, a way of "seeing the world" and acting within it as thus perceived. All such perspectives, I have claimed above, are, to some degree, arbitrary, as embodying some one of many conceivable alternative choices of "modes of representation" that constitute what is *"a priori"* for the committed *user* of the framework in question. Thus any "framework" can in principle be judged as more or less "effective," "adequate," or "valid" by comparison with other frameworks, however difficult this task of comparative evaluation may be for somebody whose very language and modes of perception and thought are determined by a framework that is his own.

The special perspectives that I have distinguished as "human," and particularly those that I have called "personal" (the world-views of individuals) are particularly amenable to criticism, even when possessed by the most dogmatic and authoritarian subjects, for the following reasons: The "ordinary language" that is the central component of a *P*-framework has the important resources of *reflexiveness* (the uses of language to refer to that language itself) and *suspension of assertion* (the expression of possibilities that the language-user can consider prior to commitment or choice). The first of these is crucial for the possibility of the modes of self-criticism manifested in shame, remorse, regret, and, less dramatically, in desire for change and improvement; the second is crucial for the possibility of understanding the standpoint of those other symbol-users with whom the user of a particular *P*-framework necessarily interacts, through his use of a shared language. Each "idiolect" is a variation upon the common dialect of a group.

Another name for what I have rather pompously called "suspension of assertion" is imagination, whether in its humblest or most spectacular exercises. In order to choose anything at all, we have to draw upon our linguistic framework's capacity to represent the possible, delineate in advance of the choice, "what it would be like if we were to choose otherwise." The same is true, more poignantly, of the constant demands of others that we shall "try to understand them." We succeed in this, however imperfectly, to the degree that we make the other's world "our own" by projecting part of his life-space into ours: we understand others' expressions of intention, attitude, feeling, belief by knowing what we might express by those words in their situation; conversely we achieve higher self-awareness of our own intentions, etc., by learning, in speech as well as in nonverbal interaction, how our "public" expressions are interpreted. Such imaginative participation depends strongly upon that temporary "bracketing" or "suspension of disbelief" whose highest elaboration in literature is continuous with its humbler exercises in the market place.

Given that every "private world" (*P*-perspective) is unequally illuminated and that the drive toward illumination of its darker regions ("self-awareness") is as real as the contrary drive to suppress and to conceal by "masking," we can appreciate the centrality for self-education of exercises in imaginative participation. Since every private world, however solipsistic and egoistic, is interested and sustained by a social world, imaginative participation via suspension of disbelief (and hence also suspension of assertion and action) is a potent means for insight into our own worlds. By entering empathically into the expressive utterances of others, and thereby making them our own as possibilities, we deepen our insight into our individual life-space. Through the words and deeds of others we apprehend the grain of our own life-space: we see more clearly what we can and might do. We learn not so much what we *must* do in order to be saved, which implies commitment to an accepted framework, as what we *might* do to be "saved" if we were the kind of person to be "saved" in *that* way. Imaginative participation broadens the range of available, because perceived, choices: that is why all creative literature and art is necessarily innovative, no matter how closely it might seem to adhere to traditional forms.

7. *A basic method for progress toward "perspectival articulation" is "imaginative participation" in works of art.* I have tentatively defined a personal perspective as the system of concepts, axiomatic assumptions and beliefs, modes of expression of feelings and attitudes, strategies for problem-solving, etc., which are, at a certain time, "given" for a particular person: the cognitive, perceptual, expressive, and volitional structure in terms of which, and by reference to which, he "sizes up" *his* "world." Suppose now that we are interested in getting detailed knowledge of such a "perspective"—or, what comes to the same thing, in understanding the other's point of view, his "attitude towards life"; how should we best proceed? I assume that, unless our interest is specifically biographical, we shall focus upon the features of the personal perspective that are shareable, as constituting part of a *group*-perspective.

It is natural, especially for scholars who are professional writers and talkers, to think immediately of verbalizing the perspectival apparatus to which I alluded at the start of the last paragraph. Indispensable as such a verbal formulation of a perspective may be, it has the crucial weakness, all too familiar to any teacher of a humanistic subject, of stereotyping and sloganizing its object. Consider the examinee's task of, say, characterizing Tolstoy's perspective as expressed in *War and Peace:* the best we can hope from even the most sensitive and literate student will be a set of rapid generalities, all-too-true alas, about Tolstoy's commitment to historical determinism, his anxieties about sexual attraction, and so on. The task is, in principle, too difficult to be solved in that way.

The radical untranslatability that we here encounter as an obstacle to the interpreter's charge is present in all art, but also throughout ordinary life: that Pierre's love for Natasha is not the same as Andrei's even though they fall "under the same description" would be a problem for Natasha, too, if she really existed. The difficulty is partly in the higher "multiplicity" of the action vis à vis its verbal description: the near impossibility of capturing in words the difference between the way a child strokes a cat and its mother does. But it is not only that. So far as it goes, the expression "a jealous retort" may be perfectly correct in its application to a particular act and yet, as we say, mean nothing, to somebody who has never been jealous, for whom jealousy is only a name. (There is such a thing as feeling blindness as well as color blindness.) To the extent that actions are the enactments of attitudes, we can fully understand them only by some process of imaginative participation (or empathic communion) in which, by rehearsing the attitude, we come to know it from the inside.

We must avoid the blunder of supposing that because the rhythmic and qualitative aspects of action are not to be captured in verbal description, they are, therefore, inexpressible and somehow ineffable. On the contrary, they are typically expressed, and the attitudes, motives, intentions, etc., that inform them are essentially expressible.

Enough mystifying rubbish has been written about *"Einfühlung"* or "empathy" to make us wary. Nevertheless, I submit that it would be gratuitous reductionist folly to deny it a central place in the enterprise of humanistic criticism.

Suppose, then, that we have the power of imaginative participation or empathic understanding into the actions and works of others; what should we call its outcome? I think knowledge is a plausible answer—the kind of knowledge that we have when we see how a painting looks, or understand, perhaps after reading some fictional depiction of jealous actions, what jealousy is like. Those who would deny this the name of knowledge are, without knowing it, in the grip of an ancient prejudice that insists on restricting knowledge to what can be talked about.

8. *Further Problems.* My positive suggestions might be taken as a preliminary sketch for a philosophy of the Humanities, in whose absence discussion concerning the educational functions of those studies and their bearings upon the pressing social and personal problems created by science and technology is likely to remain confused, incoherent, and ineffective.

Even as a sketch, it has serious deficiencies. I have, for instance, stressed the centrality of literary texts for a revived program of humanistic education, at the expense of historical and philosophical studies, which deserve at least equal prominence. Considered even in its application to literature, my emphasis upon the notion of a "human perspective" runs the risk of treating every work of art as a didactic allegory, which is far from my intention. Indeed, emphasis upon a "perspective" might well be regarded as one-sided, as tending to elide the importance of human projects and predicaments. A professional philosopher may well shy away from my suggestion, toward the end, that knowledge need not be mediated by discursive symbolism. Teachers might well wonder about the bearings of my analysis upon curricula and courses of study. And so on. Some of these problems I hope to discuss eventually, in an ampler context.

Additional Notes
and References

I. REASONABLENESS

Originally published in R. F. Dearden, P. H. Hirst, and R. S. Peters, *Education and the Development of Reason* (London: Routledge & Kegan Paul Ltd, 1972), pp. 194–207. The essays by David Pole, Gilbert Ryle, and Richard Peters, among others in this useful collection, bear upon the topics discussed in my paper.

II. INDUCTION AND EXPERIENCE

This essay continues the discussions on the philosophy of induction in my previous books, *Margins of Precision* (Ithaca, N.Y.: Cornell University Press, 1970), chapters V–IX, and *Models and Metaphors* (Ithaca, N.Y.: Cornell University Press, 1962), chapters XI, XII. Originally published in Lawrence Foster and J. W. Swanson, eds., *Experience and Theory* (Amherst: University of Massachusetts Press, 1970), pp. 135–160.

III. PRACTICAL REASONING

Read at a meeting of the International Institute of Philosophy at Kings College, Cambridge, in September 1972.

IV. THE LOGICAL PARADOXES

Appeared under the title of "Another Logical Paradox" in *L'âge de la science* (Paris), 3 (1970), 91–99. I am indebted to comments by Australian philosophers at Canberra, Melbourne, and Sydney, where this paper was originally read.

V. THE ELUSIVENESS OF SETS

Reprinted from *The Review of Metaphysics*, 24 (June, 1971), 614–636.

It has been discussed in detail by Erick Stenius, in his paper "Sets," in *Synthese*, 27 (1974), 161–188.

VI. MEANING AND INTENTION

Published with the additional subtitle, "An Examination of Grice's Views," in *New Literary History*, 4 (1972–73), 257–279. I am more than usually indebted for comments on an earlier draft by David Armstrong, Lee Cannan, Charles Crittenden, Peter Facione, Carl Ginet, Jack Kaminsky, Robert Matthews, Sidney Siskin, Robert Stalnaker, Kenneth Stern, James Twiggs, and Paul Ziff.

VII. THE NATURE OF REPRESENTATION

Based upon a lecture given at The Johns Hopkins University and published under the title of "How Do Pictures Represent?" in Maurice Mandelbaum, ed., *Art, Perception and Reality* (Baltimore, Md.: The Johns Hopkins University Press, 1972). That book contains a "Postscript" by E. H. Gombrich, in which he makes some urbanely critical remarks on my essay.

VIII. THE STRUCTURE OF SYMBOLS

The original title was "The Structure of Symbol Systems," in *Linguistic Inquiry*, 11 (Fall, 1971), 515–538.

Conversation and correspondence with Professor Nelson Goodman helped me greatly in grasping his sophisticated and complex approach.

IX. PARADIGM CASES AND EVALUATIVE WORDS

Prepared for an international colloquium on philosophical problems of language held in Biel, Switzerland, May 4–7, 1973. The proceedings of this meeting were published in *Dialectica*, vol. 27 (1973).

X. QUESTIONS FOR CHOMSKY

Reprinted, by permission, from Robert Borger and Frank Cioffi, eds., *Explanation in the Behavioral Sciences* (Cambridge: Cambridge University Press, 1970), pp. 452–461. This was a "Comment" on Professor Chomsky's "Problems of Explanation in Linguistics" in the same book (pp. 425–451). His good-humored replies to my questions are also included in the same book (pp. 462–470).

XI. SOME AVERSIVE RESPONSES TO A WOULD-BE REINFORCER

From Harvey Wheeler, ed., *Beyond the Punitive Society: Operant Conditioning, Social and Political Aspects* (San Francisco: W. H. Freeman & Co., 1973), pp. 125–134. It originally appeared in *The Center Magazine,* 5 (1972), 53–58. Reprinted by permission of Fund for the Republic, Inc.

Some reviewers thought me unduly harsh on Skinner. I remain unrepentant, considering the unintended consequences of Skinner's forceful attack on "Freedom" and "Dignity."

XII. SOME TASKS FOR THE HUMANITIES

Originally a "working paper" prepared for a conference on the humanities, sponsored by the American Council of Learned Societies, at Dromoland Castle, Ireland, June 8–12, 1972. It has appeared in W. Roy Niblett, ed., *The Sciences, the Humanities and the Technological Threat* (London: University of London Press, 1975), pp. 79–89.

For reports on this meeting, see "Science, Technology and the Humanities: Reports from an ACLS Colloquium" (Max Black, June Goodfield) in *ACLS Newsletter,* 24 (Spring 1973), 7–29.

Index

Caveats and Critiques

Designed by R. E Rosenbaum.
Composed by Kingsport Press, Inc.,
in 11 point linotype Baskerville, 2 points leaded,
with display lines in monotype Baskerville.
Printed letterpress from type by Kingsport Press
on Warren's Number 66 Text, 60 lb. basis
with the Cornell University Press watermark.
Bound by Kingsport Press
in Joanna Bookcloth
and stamped in All Purpose foil.

88480

160
B
Black, Max, 1909-

88480

Caveats and
critiques

DATE	BORROWER'S NAME		
OCT 11 '83	S. Morris		